OVER THE SEA TO SKYE

Rudh' an Dunain, showing Soay Isle and Canna in the offing.

"Sweet was vengeance to Clan Ranald,
In the nights of long ago . . ."

Frontispiece

Over the Sea to Skye

OR

Ramblings in an Elfin Isle.

BY

ALASDAIR ALPIN MACGREGOR, M.A.

AUTHOR OF "BEHOLD THE HEBRIDES!" ETC., ETC.

FOREWORD
BY
The Rt. Hon. JAMES RAMSAY MACDONALD.

*ILLUSTRATED WITH A SERIES OF
40 BEAUTIFUL PHOTOGRAPHS.*

LONDON: 38 SOHO SQUARE, W.1.
W. & R. CHAMBERS LIMITED.
EDINBURGH: 339 HIGH STREET.

Printed in Great Britain by
W. & R. CHAMBERS LTD., Edinburgh.

TO

KATHLEEN

AND THE

MELLOWING REMEMBRANCE

OF A

FIRST LOVE

" The grey gulls wheeling ever, and the wide arch of the sky."

AGNES MURE MACKENZIE.

FOREWORD

BY

The Right Hon. JAMES RAMSAY MACDONALD

WHOEVER has had the good fortune to fall in with Mr. MacGregor's first book, *Behold the Hebrides!* will take this one up in high expectation ; and he will not be disappointed. I have read the proofs with keen interest. It is long since I set foot on Skye, long since I sat by the hearth of the Sligachan Inn, long since I wandered by Dunvegan and got drenched on the Coolins ; but reading these chapters is like listening to a great tale retold, and the jaunty verse of Sheriff Nicolson comes up in my memory :

> " Jerusalem, Athens and Rome,
>   I would see them before I die !
> But I 'd rather not see any one of the three,
>   Than be exiled for ever from Skye."

The magic of Highland story of ghost or fairy, battle or adventure, chivalry or pillage is not in the tale itself but in the way it is told. Out on the hillside you meet a shepherd, by the ingle of an evening you sit with a family, and they wander with you into fairyland or the dead glowing past. They are the children of seers and of pipers ; they are clansmen. And with them the centuries with their rational scepticism and their political changes roll back, and you join the fellowship of folks whose bodies lie in the churchyards but whose spirits haunt the ruined crofts and live in the misty moors.

Mr. MacGregor has the Highland gift of bringing you back to these old days and making you live with these old people. Often does my hand stretch out to my Alexander Smith's *Summer in Skye*, or to MacCulloch's *Misty Isle of Skye*. Mr. MacGregor's book will now stand beside them, and I shall fill odd half-hours of peace wandering, not only over its pages, but upon the paths it describes and in company with the people whose exploits in belief and action it narrates.

Sad, sad, it is indeed that their children are banished by our neglect from their homes, and have to lie in graves far, far from Kilmuir.

Murray Macdonald

PREFACE

To place within the covers of a book of this nature all that one might wish to say about the Isle of Skye would be impossible. Requirements of space, therefore, have necessitated my omitting certain topics that otherwise would have been included. Nevertheless, I have endeavoured to limit my omissions chiefly to such subject-matter as already is to be found elsewhere. For instance, I have inserted neither a general sketch on Dunvegan Castle, nor a chapter dealing with the wanderings in Skye of Prince Charlie. In the case of the former, I excuse myself on the pretext that such a sketch appears in *Behold the Hebrides!* : in the case of the latter, I feel my omission justified on the grounds that this period of Scottish history has been painfully overdone. Throughout this volume, however, I have referred frequently to Prince Charlie. The intention of including a chapter on the geology of Skye was abandoned on realising that my treatment of its amazing formations was beginning to assume the proportions of a small book in itself.

By the reciting of many old tales and legends, as well as by the introduction of material throwing light on the present-day conditions of the people, I have striven to make this volume as complete,

as comprehensive, and as up-to-date as the knowledge at my disposal would allow.

The parenthetical occurrence throughout the text
of short, Gaelic phrases I have deemed worthy of
inclusion merely for the guidance of those who may
be familiar with original or traditional renderings,
where such exist ; while here and there I have
inserted several ancient quotations on the plea that
their directness and quaintness would have been
impaired, had they appeared in paraphrased form.
I make no apology, however, for my punctuation
and phrasing.

This book innocently may contain a certain
amount of controversial matter ; but, where authorities differ and authoritative opinions are at variance
with one another, I often adopt a *via media* by
recording the incident in the way that to me seems
the most picturesque, probable, and reasonable. No
controversy is intended : I have endeavoured to
treat without bias the sanguine affairs relating to
the MacDonalds and the MacLeods—two clans
whose internecine struggles bulk so largely in this
volume. Deep, deep down I retain a secret love
for both of them ; and I hope that, by reaching
Scotsmen scattered far from the heritage of their
fathers, these somewhat desultory records of the
valour and prowess of their progenitors may quicken
their pulses, and fill their imagination as would a
breath from the peat-scented hills of home.

Since many of the chapters bear slightly upon
one another, most of them have been arranged with

due regard either to historical or to topographical sequence ; but, for all that, I wish my book to be a restful companion for the quiet hour, and a book that may be opened at random and enjoyed.

* * * * * * *

The ten longest papers occur here for the first time. For permission to republish the remaining twenty-six I am again indebted to the Editors of the *Aberdeen Press and Journal*, *British Weekly*, *Chambers's Journal*, *Edinburgh Evening News*, *Glasgow Herald*, *Glasgow Evening Times*, *Glasgow Weekly Herald*, *Scots Magazine*, *Scotsman*, *Scottish Country Life*, and the *Scottish Field*.

For these beautiful illustrations I am beholden to those friends whose names appear under them. To Canon MacLeod of MacLeod I feel more than obliged, not only for his having placed at my disposal such a wonderful collection of photographs, but also for the interesting historical fragments to which he has directed my attention from time to time.

For the success from a literary point of view of my journeyings in Skye I cannot but make mention of the kindnesses of my hostess at Dunvegan Castle, of my host and hostess at Milovaig, of my medical friends and hostesses at Portree and at Broadford, and of my host at Sligachan Inn. To them, as to my dear, seannachie friend, Miss Frances Tolmie, especially am I grateful, because through their hospitality and unqualified generosity I learned much, and saw many parts of Skye that, on account of their remoteness and inaccessibility, otherwise would have remained beyond my reach. To Alasdair MacFarlane, Esq., my thanks are due for the diligence with which he read the proofs. To James Clark, Esq., I am grateful for the assistance he gave me with my map.

And, lastly, I must put on record the tolerance and patience of K. M. T., who, though sorely irritated and provoked during the writing of this book, indexed its pages and never once lost her temper in so doing.

ALASDAIR ALPIN MACGREGOR.

London, *May* 1926.

CONTENTS

LIST OF ILLUSTRATIONS

" Here the birlinns of Clan Ranald
Oft lay splintered and forlorn."

ORAIN NAN EILEAN

(Songs of the Isles)

Sing me a song of the wave-girt Isles,
　　Where the seabirds wheel and cry :
Tell me a tale when the storm beguiles,
　　And the winds go wailing by.

Tell me a tale of a gallant sail,
　　When the " Blue Men " deftly ride :
Sing of the Shiants that are swept by the gale
　　And the fury of the tide.

Sing me a song of a dreamy moor,
　　Where the maids at the shieling spin :
Lull me to sleep by the peat-fire smoor,
　　When the soft night closeth in.

Sing me a song of the morning sun
　　That puts darkness on the star :
Croon me a tune when the day is done,
　　And the pilot-lamps shine far.

Sing me a song of a tiny shell,
　　That the surge on the beach has cast :
Lilt me the muse of its inmost cell
　　When the seas go wailing past.

ALASDAIR ALPIN MACGREGOR.

Photo. by Percy Donald.

Sgurr a' Bhasteir and Glamaig from Bruach na Frithe

A

I

"OVER THE SEA TO SKYE"

AN ISLE OF ENCHANTMENT

"Oh strike the harp in praise of my love, the lonely sun-beam of Dunscaith! Strike the harp in praise of Bragéla; she that I left in the Isle of the Mist, the spouse of Semo's son! Dost thou raise thy fair face from the rock to view the sails of Cuchullin? The sea is rolling distant far: its white foam deceives thee for my sails. Retire, for it is night, my love; the dark winds sing in thy hair. Retire to the halls of my feasts: think of the times that are past. I will not return till the storm of war is ceased."—*Fingal.*

So this is *Eilean a' Cheo*, the Isle of the Mist; and its children are the Children of the Mist. But call it what you will—*Eilean a' Cheo* because of the mists that, rolling over its wild, serrated lines of castellated peaks, portend the coming of a Hebridean storm as the clattering of hoofs and the rattle of limbers signal the irresistible approach of an advancing legion, or *Eilean Sgiathanach* because it rests upon a wind-swept sea like a mighty bird with outstretched pinions.

Skye is a little world all of its own : it is a veritable microcosm where the mystery of Creation is a million fathoms deeper than the deepmost valley, and wherein everything, animate and inanimate, testifies to the omnipotence of the Supreme Architect whose wondrous tectonics no man can comprehend, and whose mercy endureth for ever. Here,

A

in the beginning of time, Vulcan had his forge and employed a score of artificer-blacksmiths : here, trillions of years ago, he marched with his body-guard of tumult and of fire, striking the red-hot earth wheresoever he went. But, since his day, the aeons have reigned with an iron hand ; and the gigantic movements of chaos have so folded and twisted and distorted his rocks that to-day, I fear, he would scarcely recognise his stupendous handiwork.

Here it is that every valley whispers a memory out of the past ; and the deep, mysterious waters of every loch murmur a legend of bygone warriors. Nor are its cliffs without tongues : should you venture to speak with them, they will tell you of the clash and clang of mail and of the wild battle-cry of vanquished chieftains, for here, as elsewhere throughout the Western Isles, the Pict strove hard, but without avail, to stem the onslaught of his Viking foemen when the glory of the battle was for the fearless and for the strong.

The Viking Vision.

There is not a sealoch nor a creek in Skye that does not remember such galleys as the Reindeer of the North and the Rider of the Storm and the Chooser of the Slain and the Elk of the Golden Antlers, and a thousand other triremes of battle that the Kings of Lochlann sent forth upon the high seas in quest of plunder and new lands. Have you never seen the Viking vision in Loch Scavaig or in Loch Dunvegan ? Have you never stood on the shore of Loch Snizort, near Uig, and looked west-ward towards the Ascrib Isles when, clad in all their maritime panoply, the foaming battle-chargers of the Atlantic were laying siege to them as a fleet of white warships storming a cluster of sea-citadels, and imagined that possibly they might have been the spoil-seeking galleys of the intrepid Northmen, who have selected some old Pictish *dun* in Trotternish as the object of their rieving expedition ? If you be vested with any imaginative faculty, I would ask you to steal down to the very edge of a sealoch in Skye when, in the dead of night, the tide is full and sleeping, and the moon is high in the twinkling vault of heaven. There you will be able to picture for yourself a scene such as was enacted during the moonlit nights of long ago, when those tall, fair Norsemen infested every inlet of our western seas.

Can you not imagine that you hear the plashing of oars as their galleys glide into the glistening stillness of the night-encircled loch ? And can you not visualise against the moonlight the silhouetted rowers who bend at their task, and the gleaming spears and helmets of those who, having assembled at the prow, are gathering their accoutrements in readiness for the assault ? Close your eyes for a moment and listen for the stentorian shout of the standard-bearer as he leaps from the bowsprit on to the shingled beach !

An Isle of Enchantment.

There are in Skye gullies and ravines into whose profundity the spilling rays of the morning sun have never pierced ; there are lochs and streams and springs where the inspired wanderer among the Isles may see naiads and kelpies, if he should care ; there are eerie caves wherein once dwelt the monsters that the Fingalian heroes slew. Every *sithean*, or grassy knowe, has its place in elfin lore ; and every clachan has its *genius loci*. Ilka ruin is steeped in Ossianic stories of Cuchullin and Fingal and their valiant retainers ; of Bragéla, Cuchullin's young, white-bosomed bride, whom the hero sent for safety to Dunscaith Castle during his absence at the Ulster Wars ; or of the fleet-footed Caoilte, the hunter of red deer in the highest corries. Caoilte, the swiftest of the Fingalians, was called Thinman : so swift was he, indeed, that when running at full tilt he had the appearance of three individuals. He it was who, at the " Battle of the Sheaves " in the True Hollow of Tiree, returned in triple form from the armoury on the Faery Hill, whither he had gone on learning that the Fingalian harvesters at Kilmoluag (Tiree) were in danger of being molested by the Norsemen, who had disembarked at Besta. When Thinman arrived, every man took his weapon of war and drove the Lochlanners into the sea.

And, then, one cannot think of Skye without recalling such heroic names as Nicolson, Martin, MacLeod, MacDonald, MacCrimmon, and Mac-Kinnon, and remembering the numberless clan feuds this island witnessed in later centuries.

Fortunately, there is so much in Skye that is beyond the reach of the ubiquitous tripper. Here, furthermore, is a safe retreat from the unwholesome, immodest atmosphere of the modern dancing-hall and from the wretched morbidity of imported films.

No island in the world is richer in song and in *sgeulachd* than the Isle of Skye ; and we remember each one of them when there 's a pibroch on the hill and a long, long sigh on the sea, and when the wind is whispering a saga from the heart of the hamleted valley.

O, there is a humility-inducing influence pervading the track that seldom is beaten by the feet of the sons of men !

II

THE DEATH OF DIARMAD

IN PURSUIT OF THE VENOM-BOAR

"And Oscar wept; and Oisin, and Dering, and Mac Luga wept also, for Diarmad was much loved by all."

AMONG the ancient Celtic heroes long ago there was numbered a valiant warrior named Diarmad. Of the Fingalians he was the bravest in war : his mother was the beloved and only sister of Fionn, the Fair One, of whom we hear so much in Gaelic and Erse legend and song. Diarmad was the handsomest knight in all the Isle of Skye ; and, unwittingly, he put the love on every woman who beheld the beauty-spot on his cheek.

Now Graine, the wife of Fionn and, according to the testimony of some reciters, the daughter of the Jarl of Ulster, was reputed to have been the loveliest of all women. One beautiful day, while Graine chanced to be loitering along the seashore, whom did she meet but Diarmad, who was out hunting ; and so full was she of his valour that she hastened to place on him the three spells of love, lest he should remain unaware of her passion for him. No sooner had the spells fallen on Diarmad than his breast was filled with joy, for now before him stood the fairest woman on whom he had ever cast eyes. And, so, Graine and Diarmad resolved to depart together, and to wander by the

mountain track that only the lone deer knew, so
that Fionn and his followers would be unable to
find them.

DIARMAD SLAYS THE VENOM-BOAR.

At night they rested in the dark woods after a
long and weary journeying ; but, ere the dawn of
day, they were startled by the raucous roaring of
stags and the yelling of hounds, for the Feinne, or
Fingalians, long had sought to pursue the poison-
boar that repeatedly had brought them ill-luck in
the hunting-field. Fionn and his men had risen
very early this morning that they might track the
boar to its den in the mountains.

Suddenly they came upon Diarmad, who was
much ashamed and apprehensive lest Fionn should
seek to slay him in revenge for what he had
done.

But Fionn, though deeply wounded, was careful
not to show it, and invited Diarmad to join the
chase. Now Diarmad's bow was never slack ; nor
was he ever loath to accompany any one on an
errand such as this. Well, they tracked the boar
from daylight till sundown without success ; and
the Fingalians were as exhausted as they were disappointed at not having realised the object of their
excursion. But Diarmad followed the boar's track
far up the hill, for he was as brave as he was handsome. At long last he came upon the savage
creature sheltering in a thicket; and straightway he
slew it.

Loud was the rejoicing of Fionn when he learned
that the son of his sister had been so daring, and
had succeeded in slaying the boar of which the
Islesfolks long had lived in terror.

Fionn Hardens his Heart.

And, as the boar lay lifeless on the ground before them, Fionn and Diarmad began to dispute about its length from snout to tail ; and Diarmad determined to prove *his* contention by measuring the creature. While he was thus engaged, *ochoin a righ !* did not one of the poisonous bristles enter his finger ? And soon his hand was *dearg* !—blood-red !

Now Fionn, when he perceived what had happened, hurried off to Tobar nan Eun, the Well of the Birds, and filled the palms of his hands with the healing water of which the little birds were in the habit of sipping. But, on his way back, he tarried long ; and he became so wrathful and revengeful that he spilt the water on the ground, for Diarmad—hereafter called Dearg—had stolen his beautiful wife ; and he decided that he must pay the fullest penalty in consequence. Shortly afterwards, however, he was again filled with compassion, and once more hastened to the well, that he might make the cure to Dearg.

Graine's Death-Watch over Dearg.

But, alas ! Fionn came too late, swift of foot though he was, for death had overtaken Dearg ere he returned a second time. And Graine, so sad and sorrow-laden, wept precious tears over Dearg ; and she kept death-watch beside him all night long, and until the morning sun was putting darkness on the stars.

And, when the Islanders were laying Dearg to his final rest, lo ! Graine leapt in beside him, just as the grave was being closed upon him. Thus do they share the same grave : thus do they take the long, last sleep together.

There are several variants of this legend ; but I have given you the version that, less than a century ago, was widely circulated in Tiree, in Eigg, and in Skye. (As will be admitted by those who have perused Joyce's *Old Celtic Romances*, the Irish rendering of this tale is very much more complete, owing doubtless to the happy accident that Erse became a written language at so comparatively early a date.)

Ere long the Fingalians and, in good sooth, all the folks of Skye had reason to regret the fate that had overtaken the valiant Diarmad, because no one of their number was more adroit at the *clach-neart*, or putting-stone ; and, besides, he outmatched all his contemporaries in the swinging and thrusting of the big sword. After his death, bands of dark, long-haired faeries again sailed over in their hide-bound coracles from Ireland ; but this time they came in such swarms that the native populace was overwhelmed completely, for now Diarmad and his sword were not there to repel them. It was only by the merest accident, they say, that Ossian escaped the vengeance of the Irish faeries, who at this time infested every island of the Hebrides.

And to this day the delver among the Cuchullin peat-mosses often comes upon the great bones of a Fingalian warrior-giant, whose death this little folk encompassed.

III

CAVE OF THE PIPER

A WIDESPREAD HIGHLAND TRADITION

> Pibroch he will play no more:
> Comes he not in peace nor war.

As one might reasonably expect of an island with so wild and martial a history, the Isle of Skye in olden days was renowned for its pipers. There it was that the MacArthurs and the MacCrimmons had their *piobaireachd* or pibroch colleges. And not only did these music-schools compete with one another in the ancient art of piping, but they also vied with the MacKays of Gairloch, the MacGregors of Fortingall and Glen Lyon (" *Clann an Sgeulaich* "), the MacIntyres of Rannoch, and the Rankins of Duart and later of Coll. Moreover, they considered that the certificates of distinction which *they* granted to those of their pupils who attained a certain standard of proficiency were much more to be desired than were the meritorious awards conferred by the rival piping colleges on the mainland.

It was at Peingowen, a free-hold in the parish of Kilmuir, that the MacDonalds of the Isles bestowed upon the MacArthurs a piece of land whereon these illustrious pipers established their music-school, to which the mainland chieftains were wont to send their sons and heirs, that they might acquire a knowledge of the music that before

10

them had carried their fathers into battle and frequently, though not always, to victory. And it was to the grassy hillock in the vicinity of Peingowen known as Cnoc-Phail that the MacArthurs used to conduct their pupils daily, so that they might practise on the *feadan* or chanter, and on the *piob-mhor* or large pipe, without giving annoyance to sensitive ears, and without being molested by inquisitive intruders.

During the residence at Duntulm Castle of the Lords of the Isles the MacArthurs occupied a position of great dignity ; and they were celebrated for their kindness to strangers forby. Pennant would appear to have accepted a substantial repast at the house of Sir Alexander MacDonald's piper, who, he adds, " was quite master of his instrument, and treated us with several tunes."

Many of the MacArthurs were laid to rest in the old churchyard of Kilmuir, which is situated three or four miles to the south-west of Duntulm Castle. I shall have reason to refer again to Kilmuir ; and so in the meantime I need not detain you long with the many interesting things that are to be said about it. On a weather-beaten and lichened gravestone in that churchyard, however, one may read with difficulty the following unfinished inscription :—

HERE LY THE REMAINS OF
CHARLES MACKARTER
WHOSE FAME AS AN HONEST MAN
AND REMARKABLE PIPER
WILL SURVIVE THIS GENERATION
FOR HIS MANNERS WERE EASY & REGULAR
AS HIS MUSIC & THE MELODY OF
HIS FINGERS WILL

The reason given me at Kilmuir some months ago for the fact that this epitaph was never completed was that the executor, a man belonging to the neighbourhood, went on strike as a protest against not receiving adequate remuneration for the work he already had done.

MacCrimmon College at Boreraig.

As one can readily imagine, the tutors at all times were very jealous for their art : nor were they slow to resent the approach of any one who was likely either to disturb their tuition or convey the cherished secrets of their teaching to rival schools.

Not unlike the piping college of the MacArthurs at Peingowen was the still more famous college of the MacCrimmons at Boreraig, on Loch Dunvegan. For unnumbered years the MacCrimmons were the hereditary pipers to the MacLeods of Macleod, who to this day occupy their ancient stronghold at Dunvegan, and who have maintained in unbroken, though sadly diminished, succession their not uneventful suzerainty over this part of the Misty Isle.

It is held that in the elementary stages of their training the MacArthurs were pupils of the Mac-Crimmons at Boreraig before they, themselves, started their first piping-school at Ulva, in Mull. Even the aforementioned Charles MacArthur is recorded to have gone to Boreraig to complete his pibroch studies under the supervision of the Mac-Crimmons. Thither, also, came the MacGregors of Roro (*Ruadh-Shruth*, or Red Stream)—" a famous family of genuine pipers."

I am told that the last of the MacCrimmon pupils

was a MacArthur, who in 1784 was piper to the
Highland Society of Edinburgh.

MacLeod of Dunvegan Offends his Piper.

One of the chiefs of MacLeod endowed the
MacCrimmons with a farm at Boreraig ; but, when
the rental value of land increased, he felt constrained
to recover from them a portion of the territory they
had been granted, rent-free, some years previously.
This was an act of ingratitude that the pipers could
not tolerate ; and so they " left their rock-music-
hall to the seals and cormorants," and deserted
Boreraig. This evacuation took place somewhere
about 1770.

The retention of hereditary clan pipers was a
long recognised practice in the Highlands and
Islands, although the earliest extant documentary
proof does not convey us further back than the
close of the sixteenth century. An entry in the
Stirling Kirk-Session Register, dated May 1604,
concerns a certain Robert MacClure who, four
years earlier, was referred to as " piper to the laird
of Buchanan." But we have no reason to doubt
that hereditary pipers were prevalent in Ireland
many generations prior to the almost unquestionable importation of the bagpipes into Scotland from
that country. It is relevant to note, too, that the
seven years' curriculum once required at the ancient
Irish piping-schools was closely followed by both
the MacCrimmons and the MacArthurs at a later
date.

"MacCrimmon Comes No More."

But, though the MacCrimmons have gone lang
syne, there clings around Boreraig many a tale of

the ancient days when in contest they excelled the pipers of every other part of Scotland ; and to the end of time that cave on Loch Dunvegan will be known as the Piper's Cave. To this day the old folks near Boreraig will tell you blood-curdling stories about Padruig Mor MacCrimmon and his kinsmen pipers.

Concerning the origin of the famous " Mac-Crimmon's Lament " at least two stories are widely circulated. According to one, the MacCrimmon piper, whose tragic death it was designed to commemorate, was the only casualty in a preliminary skirmish in the territory of MacLeod's enemies. According to the other, the piper is supposed to have entered this cave, accompanied by his faithful dog, when gradually—so the story goes—the skirl of his pipes became fainter and fainter, until at length it entirely died away. The islanders, it is said, watched the piper enter the cave ; and they were greatly perturbed when they observed that he did not come back. And long, indeed, did they keep vigil at the mouth of the cave ; but brave MacCrimmon returned no more.

Tradition has it, however, that some time afterwards his poor, woebegone dog hirpled out of the cave in a semi-flayed and exhausted condition ; but no satisfactory account was ever given of the mysterious disappearance of its master. And, so, the Skye folks concluded that MacCrimmon had been " spirited away " by a faery queen, whose ears he had delighted by the rich strains of his pibrochs. This, at any rate, is the story as I received it from the lips of the folks at Dunvegan ; and, except so far as the fate of the dog is concerned, it coincides very closely with the Lewis version that I got from a lance-corporal in the Seaforths named Calum Campbell, who, while we were billeted in a tumble-down barn at the hamlet of Rubrouck, in Flanders, a few days after most of our Gaelic comrades had been killed in a foolish onslaught at Ypres, could only console his troubled spirit by crooning to himself the old Lewisian version of " MacCrimmon's Lament " to the words :—

> " *MacCruimmen's a' phiob cha till iad tuille,*
> *MacCruimmen's a' chu cha till iad tuille.*"

PIPER TRADITION WIDELY DISTRIBUTED.

But the cave at Boreraig is by no means the only cave in Scotland that is associated with the obscure disappearance of a piper, because this story is told with local variations in several other Hebridean islands, and also in different parts of the mainland.

In fact, the cave at Boreraig is not even the only cave in the Isle of Skye into which a piper is said to have gone. In the north-west of the parish of Kilmuir, and not far distant from the promontory known as Bornaskitaig (Borbh na Sgiotaig) Point, there are three caves ; and local legend has it that in one of them—probably in Uamh an Oir, the Cave of Gold, that resembles in miniature Fingal's Cave in Staffa—a piper was lost. This legend must date back at least as far as the seventeenth century, because Martin Martin, who supposed it to be a mile in length, records that the natives around this place told him of an over-curious piper who, having resolved to explore its dark passages and to ascertain its correct dimensions, entered and never came out to give an account of his progress.

It is with the disappearance of a MacArthur piper, however, that the last-mentioned cave is associated. Near Bornaskitaig is the spot where tradition says a MacDonald cut off his hand and flung it ashore, thus having given rise to the mottoes, "The Red Hand of Clan Donald" (*Lamh Dhearg Chloinn Domhnuill*) and "On Land and on Sea" (*Air muir 's air tir*).

In Barra there is a cave into which, the natives aver, a fearless piper went, and out of which he never came ; and the stranger and the unwary are warned not to go too close to Uamh an Oir, the Cave of Gold, lest they also be pounced upon by the sea-dogs that are believed to have devoured the unsuspecting piper.

Of a cave on the western side of the Isle of Colonsay the almost identical story is told ; and the folks of Islay say that long, long ago at the mouth of a cave in *their* island a wretched dog used to sit when the moon was full, and howl a "lament" for his master, who had vanished in a strange manner.

KILLED IN A CAVE.

In the vicinity of Argyll's Bowling Green there is a Piper's Cave ; and there is also a cavern in Mull that is associated with having been the place where a piper, who accompanied a marriage party, met his fate through the fact that, in spite of the protestations of his companions, he would insist on exploring its darkest recesses. And they say that, when his comrades observed he was not returning, they became impatient ; and, having

Photo. by R. C. MacLeod of MacLeod.

Ebb tide at Loch Dunvegan, showing Uiginish and "MacLeod's Tables."

"Where the moonlight meets the Atlantic mists."

entered the cave in search of him, they all were slain by the faery tenant, upon whose private apartments they had trespassed unwittingly in the hope of probing their secret. This Mull piper is said to have been a MacLaine of Loch Buidhe.

Nor is this cave tradition wanting in Lewis, for there is a piper's cavern some miles along the sea-shore from Stornoway. Into this Cave of Gold—for as such it is known to the older inhabitants—an unreturning piper marched with his bagpipes shoulder-high and gaily fingering a well-known Gaelic air.

And was it not somewhere in the Mull of Kintyre that yet another confident piper met a " leddy in a green goon," and lamented that, since he had only two hands, he could not cross swords and play his bagpipes properly at the same time? This is the incident that may have given rise to the Gaelic lines of which a fair translation might be :—

> It 's sad that I am without three hands,
> Two for the pipes and one for the claymore.

But around Loch Aluinn (Lochaline), in Morven, the legend differs slightly : here an aged minstrel vanished, and not a piper, as one might have expected. If this be the case, it seems reasonable to suppose that from this happening originated the not dissimilar tales about pipers, since the harp was widely employed in Scotland long before the intro-duction (some say from France !) of the bagpipes.

AN EDINBURGH PIPER.

I believe that the story of the disappearing piper

also is current in Edinburgh, because I seem to have read somewhere that in the legendary tunnel that, at some time or other, every Auld Reekie schoolboy declares to have linked up Craigmillar and Holyrood Palace with the Castle, a king's piper went amissing.

Generally speaking, these tales of unreturning pipers vary very little in essentials : obviously, therefore, they must have had a common origin. In almost every instance the piper marches in boldly and playing his instrument, the notes of which become fainter and thinner as he passes inwards, until at last they are heard no more. But, then, is there a cave throughout the length and breadth of Scotland that, by those who live in close proximity to it, is not reported to have been occupied as a place of refuge by Wallace or Robert the Bruce or Prince Charles Edward, or by the Red MacGregor ? Perthshire and Argyll are simply teeming with such caves and " sheltering-beds " ; and every one of them has its own particular legend.

PIPES AT A FUNERAL.

Not so very long ago every funeral in the Highlands and Islands was accompanied by a piper, who fingered a melancholy dirge to suit the occasion. And, while writing of funerals, it may not be amiss to mention that till within comparatively recent times the consumption of large potations of whisky by the mourners and friends was not at all uncommon. Funerals, in consequence, often terminated in stand-up fights. References to excessive dramming after burial services frequently occur in the *New Statistical Account*, though the compilers note with a degree of satisfaction that this barbarous survival was steadily on the decline by the middle of last century. But in some of the remoter Hebrides to this day those who attend a death-wake are invariably refreshed with wine and *aquavitae*, when they can be procured. Indeed, often it is considered contrary to long-established custom should the relatives of the deceased fail to supply the death-watchers with something to drink, or with a chunk of tobacco for those of their number who might feel disposed to smoke (or chew !).

PIPERS IN WAR.

The records of Highland Regiments in war are full of allusions to fearless pipers who played their comrades into battle, even when themselves wounded. Was it not at Agra that the piper was politely requested to cease from playing because it was feared that the wild strains of his bagpipes would incite the 78th Highlanders to charge the enemy before the appointed time ? Then, every one who knows anything about the military history of piping has heard of the piper at Vimiera who, though mortally wounded, sat down on a grassy knoll and played such tunes as he felt confident would urge his countrymen to victory. And one cannot but recall the story of MacLauchlain, who at the siege of Ciudad Rodrigo during the Peninsular War marched up and down the ramparts amid a hail of bullets and missiles, playing *The Campbells are Coming*, until a shot pierced his pig-skin and silenced his pipes. But MacLauchlain was not to be dismayed, for, having reclined on the shaft of a gun-limber, he patched up his pipes and commenced to play them again with increasing vigour.

Of the pipes at Waterloo there are many tales that are worthy of being told a score of times. It was here that a piper of the Gordon Highlanders (92nd) was so enraged when a shot carried away his big drone that he flung aside his damaged pipes, and to avenge himself rushed into the thick of the battle.

The music of the pipes is surely the most martial and stirring music in the world ; and for this reason I would venture to say that, in Scotland at any rate, it is a much more persuasive recruiting agent than is the recruiting sergeant. Such it has proved itself north of the Tweed on innumerable occasions.

PIPING IN SCOTLAND.

In Scotland at the present time the art of the pibroch is anything but a dying one—thanks to the unremitting efforts of certain bagpipe enthusiasts, and to the proficiency that is being maintained by the excellent pipe-bands of many of our northern cities and towns. Even old Stornoway, out-of-the-way as it is, has its pipe-band ; and a very distinguished pipe-band it is ! Each session in Stornoway is inaugurated by the playing of *Port-Ceum nan Leodhasach*, the Lewismen's March, a spirited tune in which the writer has an intimate interest.

To the Gael the music of the pipes conveys a fulfilment that he cannot ever hope to explain. And what more pleasing and inspiring music could a Scotsman wish to hear than that of a band of pipers and drummers, whose kilts swing from side to side with the irresistible swagger that the warlike notes produce ?

On the remarkable beauty of pipe-music, however, I need not dilate here ; but I know that the pibroch will survive in Scotland so long as there remains a vestige of the ancient clan spirit and tradition. For my own part, I am convinced that a pipe-band competition is, from every point of view, the most graceful musical performance that can be witnessed. One who has watched the Police Pipe-Band of our Northern Capital, and is at the same time imbued with something of the moorland spirit, will not be slow to realise this.

LAMENT FOR MacLEOD OF RAASAY.

And, while telling you about pipes and chanters, I feel that I must say something of the origin of that beautiful Lament from which I quoted extensively in my last volume, *Behold the Hebrides !* Well, the writer of a letter that is numbered among my very few particular treasures informs me that this Lament was suggested to him by some remarks he heard in France during the late war and from a certain Colonel MacNeill of the Argylls. MacNeill was bemoaning the fact that he had just lost one of his oldest acquaintances, whom he described as having been " about the last of the MacLeods of Raasay." MacLeod had been killed a few weeks previously in an English regiment—

"Brave hearts his English, but they could not fathom
To what old deeps the voice of Alan cried. . . ."

Shortly afterwards MacNeill, himself a redoubtable soldier, also was dead. Sore-stricken with malaria, he lay for days in a shocking farm-steading before Arras, with nothing to console him but a *feadan*, or chanter. This he kept below his pillow,

that he might play on it when he felt weary and
depressed.

And who would gainsay that the author of the
Lament for MacLeod of Raasay has perpetuated in
verse what, doubtless, poor MacNeill would fain
have put on his *feadan* ?

IV

THE ROAD TO DUNVEGAN

AN ISLAND SEPULCHRE

"Some mute inglorious Milton here may rest,
   Some Cromwell guiltless of his country's blood."

BLEAK and wellnigh houseless as is the major part
of the road leading from Portree to the western
seaboard of the Isle of Skye, it has an appeal that
cannot be denied. There are few places in Scotland so comparatively accessible as Portree and at
the same time offering to the lover of the open
highway or of the quiet, secluded byway a more
delightful choice of wanderings. Though, architecturally speaking, the village of Portree in itself
has little to boast of, when viewed from the entrance
to its wide, commodious harbour or from the
summit of an adjacent hill, it certainly has a unique
picturesqueness. What the metropolis of Skye
lacks in interest is amply compensated for by the
charm of its environs.

One feature of Portree, however, cannot fail to
obtrude itself upon the stranger to the Island ;
and that feature is the inordinate number of places
of worship in this tiny village, tacitly competing
for, and offering succour to, the souls of men, and
standing half empty most of the year. If for no
other reason than that of eliminating the wicked
extravagance of maintaining this futile redundancy,

23

the proposed Union will be hailed by every one who has at heart the progressive well-being of the Scottish Churches. How at this stage in the proceedings certain congregations and kirk-sessions of the United Free Church are insisting that the main obstacles to union have *not* been removed, and actually are voting against the proposal that the two great Churches concerned should adopt a tentative or draft basis on which a union might be framed, and on which the somewhat delicate questions arising in connection with the facilitating and consummating of such a union might be adjudicated, is difficult for me to understand. That the outstanding demand of the Disruption has been satisfied seems too patent to justify argument.

Of the United Free Church at least it can be said—" Well done, good and faithful servant." After a protest lasting nearly eighty years, during which time the Free Church principle waxed strong and, incidentally, permeated unconsciously the whole religious life of Scotland with its example of self-denial and its slogan of " spiritual freedom," *that* Church goes forward to arrange a basis of union on terms that are tantamount to disestablishment, and with an untarnished escutcheon. Surely this *coup de maître* over a force that, at any rate in things worldly, was infinitely better entrenched and equipped for the long campaign, constitutes one of the most stupendous fights and one of the most magnificent triumphs in the arduous history of the Christian Church ! In the interval most of the carking, nay, tyrannical, tactics, to which formerly it took exception, have been abandoned ; and we earnestly hope that, through the medium of the Church of Scotland (Property and Endowments)

Photo. by R. C. MacLeod of MacLeod.

The Portals of Dunvegan Castle as seen from the Leffyn Park.

Act of 1925 and by the grace of God, the next few years may witness the disappearance from Scotland of the last vestiges of schism and dissension.

* * * * * * *

Long was I in doubt as to which of the roads leading out of Portree exerted the greatest attraction, until last summer I once again found myself pressing westwards across the Island in the direction of Dunvegan. Perhaps it is because this road leads to such a historic, romantic, poetic place that one is drawn to it.

By the time that you have emerged out of the wooded dells of Sluggans and have ascended the steep mountain road to Drumuie or Borve, you really begin to live as you never have lived before. The moil and toil of the city are forgotten : its grimy unwholesomenesses and its narrow, dingy closes and hovels, where human beings are huddled together in conditions that would ill become the savage tribes of darkest Ethiopia, and into which neither caller air nor daylight—far less the healing rays of sunlight—finds it possible to penetrate, might never exist. " Woe unto them that join house to house, that lay field to field, till there be no place. . . ." What a catalogue of miseries civilisation, so-called, is answerable for ! Are we to take it for granted that slums, inhabited by teeming and seething millions, on the one hand, and palaces and mansions, the select abodes of that fraction of God's people living in languorous luxury, on the other, are the inevitable *sine qua non* of progress ? If they be, then surely competitive civilisation has outlived its usefulness.

But no such eyesores offend the wayfarer on the

road to Dunvegan : nor by such restless thoughts
is the mind distraught.

A Smugglers' Lurking-Place.

Between Borve and Carbost the road serving the
western seaboard of Trotternish strikes off in the
airt of Kensalyre and Kingsburgh. Close to the
shore at Kensalyre are to be seen the huge boulders
on which the Fingalians placed their cauldron and
prepared their venison after the chase ; while on
the farm of Kingsburgh is situated Creag nam
Meann, the Rock of the Kids, that is identified
as having been the sheltering-place of the gray-
faced cow by which the Feinne were supplied with
the milk that they used when cooking the limpets
gathered on the shores of Loch Snizort.

Beyond Carbost is the hamlet of Skeabost, standing at the head of the inmost-reaching arm of
Loch Snizort Beag, and close to where the Snizort
River bickers into that Loch. Long was Loch
Snizort a favourite lurking-place for smugglers.
According to the file of the *Inverness Courier*, as
late as 1829 a large smuggling lugger was captured
in Loch Snizort with a crew of eleven and a valuable
cargo of gin, tea, tobacco, and snuff.

About the same time Loch Dunvegan also became
the retreat of diverse smuggling vessels. On one
occasion a revenue-cutter entered the Loch in pursuit
of a smugglers' lugger, which escaped by rounding
Eilean Garbh and passing out between the north
end of that Island and Fiadhairt. Through fear
of following the lugger into a channel with which
he was entirely unacquainted, the captain of the
revenue-cutter lost his prize. While speaking of
smuggling, it may be of interest to recall in passing

that, at a magistrates' meeting in Skye in the year 1744, the gentlemen present bound themselves not to drink smuggled tea, and to do all that lay in their power, "if it were humanly possible," to prevent their wives and daughters from doing so.

AN ISLAND SEPULCHRE.

On an islet in the centre of the Snizort River, and only a stone-throw from the bridge that bears the west-going road, are the ruins of a Columban chapel. The islet is an ancient burying-ground; and one who is interested in matters antiquarian could spend an enjoyable day pottering among its moss-hidden and nettle-guarded flags and tombstones. When first it came to be used as a sepulchre is unknown, and necessarily must remain so. Perhaps it was resorted to in early centuries, when graves were exposed to the depredations of wolves. But the folks of Skeabost maintain that it was in the days when the Snizort River formed the natural boundary between the ever-warring MacDonalds and MacLeods that this islet first became a graveyard. A fierce dispute, they say, had arisen as to which of the riparian clans possessed the islet; and in a skirmish that took place in the neighbourhood between ten MacDonalds and ten MacLeods to decide the matter, the twenty combatants were slain, whereupon it was mutually agreed that the islet should be considered a fragment of neutral territory in which their corpses might be interred. When last I visited Skeabost, the mortal remains of a native were being committed to this island burying-ground; but, owing to heavy rains, the Snizort River was so high at the time that a horse and cart were employed in conveying the coffin and the funeral party in relays between the islet and a point on the opposite bank where, as a rule, the river is fordable.

The woods of Skeabost, through which, beech-hedged and overshadowed, the road to Dunvegan passes for a considerable distance, are a delightful diversification from the sombre, monotonous moorland of which one finds so many thousands of acres in Skye. Skeabost is the only part of the Hebrides that to my mind has an atmosphere approaching that of Grand Pré where, in the midst of the forest primeval, dwelt Evangeline and the peace-loving Acadian farmers. All one has to do at Skeabost to complete the comparison is to imagine that the pine trees are treble their actual height and girth, that not very far off are the fields golden with grain and merry with the laughter of sun-browned harvesters, and that down by the river can be heard the retarded hum of an overloaded mill. The Skeabost woods are musical with birds, and swarming with conies that hurry and scurry in every direction at the slightest warning of an intruder. Had Edward MacDowell come thither, I am certain that to his *Woodland Sketches* he would have felt himself constrained to add yet another opus.

A Renowned Swordsman.

From Skeabost the Dunvegan road winds circuitously by Bernisdale and Treaslane and Clachamish to Lynedale which, being elevated, commands under suitable conditions a superb view of the Ascrib Isles and of the purple mountains of Harris. At Lynedale, too, one gets a glimpse of " MacLeod's Tables " before descending into the valley at Edinbain, a picturesque, corn-patched township at the head of Loch Greshornish.   Near at hand is Gesto Hospital, the gift of a certain Kenneth MacLeod who, upon a time, tenanted the fine old sheep farm of Greshornish.

A bygone tacksman of Greshornish was an unrivalled swordsman.   On one occasion he accepted for a wager the challenge to combat by an English swordsman, who at the time happened to be the guest of Lady MacLeod at Dunvegan Castle.   On his way across the moors—there were no roads in the days with which we are dealing—to meet his antagonist at Dunvegan, the Greshornish swordsman tried his hand on every object that beset his path, beheading every reed and rush that came within the ambit of his claymore.   Nervous was his servant, however, lest by the time he reached the Castle he should be too weary to stand up to his opponent ;   but all fears were soon dispelled when, to his astonishment, his master clove in two a bumble-bee that chanced to pass before him.

On their arrival at Dunvegan Castle, Lady MacLeod brought out her valiant guest ;   and, without any unnecessary preliminaries, the combat commenced in the presence of many of the Dunvegan people.

But scarcely had the contest begun when Greshornish (in the olden days, as at the present time, it was the custom in the Highlands to style a man by the place to which he belonged, or by the name of the farm he either owned or rented) flicked a button out of the Sassenach's shirt with the point of his sword.   A second or two later he removed the Englishman's collar-stud in a similar manner. " Now look out for the third time ! " said Greshornish, whereupon MacLeod prevailed upon his

Lady to take her friend away while he was yet a living man. This she did ; and thus the fight terminated before any blood was shed. The MacLeods lost their bet on this occasion ; and Greshornish returned to his home in great exultation, and with yet another laurel.

By Faery Bridge to Dunvegan.

Beyond Edinbain the road traverses a moor that is lonely and not a little tedious ; and, except Faery Bridge, the ancient Fording-place of the Three Streams (originally, *atha nan tri allt*, and latterly *drochaid nan tri allt*), there is nothing to detain one until the village of Dunvegan is reached. At Faery Bridge the road divides, one route going due north to Vaternish, and the other leading south to Bracadale and in the south-westerly direction to Dunvegan. Not far from Faery Bridge and now under grass and heather is what one supposes to have been a heathen *anait* or place of worship. At a later date this spot is believed to have become a Christian sanctuary. Situated in a green, secluded coomb, for a time at any rate it escaped the notice of the destructive Norse pirates. The site of this " Temple of Anaitis " is still clearly definable.

You must now imagine that, instead of having trudged round by the village of Dunvegan, you have taken a short-cut across the moors from Faery Bridge to Dunvegan Castle. The actual spot where the beaten track is deserted is defined by the pillars of a gateway, unfinished and forlorn, indicating the presence of a path that one might think led to a far-off city such as long since might have been ravished and laid waste at the terrible hands of the destroying Moguls, or, perchance, overwhelmed

by the drifting sands of an Arabian desert. To
me there is something strangely eastern, strangely
mysterious, strangely uncanny about this spot. It
has an eothen weirdness : it conveys the suggestion
of a vanquished and buried civilisation in the heart
of a desolate plain.

THE QUINTESSENCE OF CELTIC POETRY.

To all intents and purposes you are now standing
at the entrance to the world-famous stronghold on
Loch Follart that the daughter of MacCrailt
Armuinn, a Scandinavian knight, brought as her
dowry many hundreds of years ago to Leod, the
progenitor of the great MacLeods of Skye and
Harris and of Lewis. It was a splendid marriage
from Leod's point of view because, in addition to
his having become the possessor of Dunvegan
Castle, he succeeded to the extensive lands of
Bracadale, Minginish, Duirinish, and Lynedale. I
believe that to this day there are a few MacCrailts
living in " MacLeod's Country."

Meantime, I must needs leave you outwith the
portals of Dunvegan Castle. Fain would I invite
you to cross its elysian threshold ; but the hour
is late. Should you care to saunter round in the
morning, however, it would give me great delight
to introduce you to the tame seagulls that seldom
fly far from our battlements. We feed them on
such dainty titbits that they seem to have lost all
taste for their natural food and all desire to return
to their wave-girt surroundings, though sometimes,
at the incoming of the tide, they do betake themselves to the Loch, a few yards away. But you
should hear them screaming for scraps as they wheel
impatiently around your bedroom window half an

hour before breakfast-time. Their avarice only increases when our piper strikes up *Hey, Johnnie Cope, are ye waukin' yet ?*

To-night I am too drowsy to tell you more ; and inadvertently I have allowed the fire to get a little lower than is compatible with comfort. But, perhaps, another time I may be able to conduct you, at least in spirit, round the treasures that are enshrined within these hallowed walls.

Cogitating on the wealth of romance and poetry that permeate this very room where I sit, listening to the wind that blows in from the Atlantic, hearing the crooning of the Hebridean tide that creeps under our windows, in my vain moments I wish that I had been born a MacLeod, or even half a MacLeod, because at Dunvegan Castle is to be found the quintessence of Celtic poetry.

But, then, I intend going over to the Outer Isles in a few weeks' time ; and I am certain that I shall feel myself related to the MacDonalds (as in reality I am !) long before the boat is in sight of Arnish Lighthouse, at the entrance to Stornoway harbour—Good-night !

Room in the Faery Tower—where the romance of the ninth
century vies with the luxury of the twentieth.

C

FROM MY WINDOW

V

FROM MY WINDOW

NIGHT AT DUNVEGAN CASTLE

The waters lull me, and the breeze
That bloweth from the scented seas . . .

LATE, late is the hour ; and I have been awakened
by the deep, mysterious silence that pervades everything. Have you never found yourself unable to
sleep when your environment has been too peaceful ?
Indeed, it is about the witching hour ; and, just
as Sir Walter Scott did more than a century ago, I
am constrained to "take possession." Long have
I waited to behold the Ghost of Dunvegan, that is
said to haunt the Faery Chamber ; but he has
failed to make his appearance since I arrived. My
friends aver that this evanescent creature, who in
past generations visited their ancestors in the small
hours, has neither been seen nor heard for years.
And, so, we are forced to the conclusion that, in
the meantime at any rate, he has betaken himself
to one of the many ruined castles that are to be
found throughout the length and breadth of the
Misty Isle. Perhaps, he has gone to the eerie
ruins of Duntulm to fraternise with the ghost that
has frequented Trotternish since Donald Gorm Mor
MacDonald of the Isles resided there !

At all events, I can assure you that he has forsaken us at Dunvegan these days.

THE "NURSE" OF RORY MOR.

Would that you might see from, and listen at, my castellated window this moonlit night ! Moveless and full in Loch Follart is the tide, whose glittering waters creep immediately beneath my bedroom window. And at odd intervals I can hear the ducks that quack and croak quietly and almost inaudibly among the dulse-fringed rocks by the shore ; and my ears are in tune with the crooning that issues from the timber-sheltered dene a hundred yards or so away, where the "Nurse" of Rory Mor has whispered her night-lullaby ever since the warlike MacLeods took up their abode within these historic walls—and that was not yesterday!

Rory Mor is accredited with having had a profound affection for this waterfall ; and he declared that he never enjoyed a complete night's rest when far removed from its lullaby.

It is surely Scott who writes of this cascade in the lines—

> "I would old Torquil were to show
> His maidens with their breasts of snow,
> Or that my noble liege were nigh
> To hear his Nurse sing lullaby.
> (The Maids—tall cliffs with breakers white,
> The Nurse—a torrent's roaring might.)"

WHERE JOHNSON AND BOSWELL SLEPT.

I wonder whether Johnson and his Scottish biographer realised the magic of their surroundings when they tarried here, and tasted lotus, and discovered withal that they had entered the Island at the wrong end. Boswell tells us that, after he and his fellow-traveller had been regaled to excess at this ancient Castle, having "found the lady of the house a very polite and sensible woman," they repaired to the drawing-room which, he urges, was formerly the bed-chamber of Rory Mor, Big Roderic of Dunvegan, who selected it because the sound of the cascade, that ever since has been referred to as his " Nurse," disposed him to sleep.

And " Sir Rory M'Leod of Dunvegan, Knight. God send good rest!" was the inscription that once upon a time might have been read above Rory's bed.

The actual room is in the celebrated tower, that was added to Dunvegan Castle by Alasdair Crotach. It is called the Faery Room, for it is thought to be the apartment in which the baby chieftain was lying when his mother saw a tiny, sprightly woman rocking his cradle, and lilting the *Dunvegan Lullaby*. This strange, little woman is said to have wrapped the child in the Faery Flag and, according to one version of the legend, to have thus presented the family of MacLeod with one of its most unique heirlooms. It was when the mother entered and addressed the little woman with the words, " *I* am the mother of this child," that the latter quickly vanished, having left behind her the Faery Flag and the Croon of which I mean to tell you something directly. Then it was, too, that the astounded lady took the Flag down the winding staircase and along to the banqueting-hall, and revealed it for the first time to the assembled clan. In Boswell's day the room, wherein this incident is recorded to have taken place, was the drawing-room.

In a room immediately below the Faery Chamber are the famous MacCrimmon pipes which, they say, were last used by Iain Dubh who was born in 1731. Perhaps it was he who disappeared into

Uamh an Oir, the Cave of Gold. But, then, tradition insists that the MacCrimmon piper who mysteriously vanished had his pipes with him, and actually entered the cave playing them!

THE NIGHT HARVESTER.

Too far have I digressed from what may be seen this moonlit night from my window in Dunvegan. Gleaming and pale is the harvest moon ; and the slowly moving tide is sparkling as gems that glisten in the sunshine of a summer's noon. In the autumned fields on the further side of Loch Dunvegan the harvester of yesterday is gone : tonight's harvester is in his boat well out in the bay, for I hear the creaking of his rowlocks, and in the moonlight see the glittering wetness of his rhythmic oar blades.

SEA-SILENCE.

But away out toward the western sea, where the night-waves speak with a voice like thunder and the irresistible ocean rolls in a phosphorescent splendour that is synonymous with Infinitude, the grey mists are drifting eastward and southward in the direction of Boreraig and Glendale ; and ere long " MacLeod's Tables "—those plateau-like summits away in the west of Duirinish, from which it is believed a chief of long ago was in the habit of administering the law to his gathered clansfolk —will be hidden completely from human eyes by nature's napery.

What a wonderful silence there is just at the line where the moonlight meets the Atlantic mists!

And the whaup that speeds over the face of the Loch, and sometimes hurries past my bedroom window, crying eerily, eerily in its flight, reminds me of the night-bird whose hollow call breaks the stillness that encircles my stepping-stones in the heart of the Forest of Harris. You will remember that some time ago I told you of my elfin stepping-stones in Harris.

> " Bird of the lone, red moor,
>   Red moor and dreary,
> What brings thee questing here
>   With cry so eerie ? "
>
> ELAINE H. BLAKE.

window, crying eerily, eerily in its flight, reminds
me of the night-bird whose hollow call breaks the
stillness that encircles my stepping-stones in the
heart of the Forest of Harris. You will remember

VI

CAVE LORE OF SKYE

A SEA-ROBBER'S RETREAT

DR. JOHNSON AND BOSWELL IN BRACADALE

THE other day I was telling you something of the
" Caves of Gold " ; but my survey did not exhaust
even the caves in the Isle of Skye associated with
the mysterious disappearance of a piper. At Harlosh Point on Loch Bracadale, for example, there
is an Uamh an Oir or Cave of Gold, the other end
of which the natives aver is at Greshornish on Loch
Snizort, a distance of over ten miles away. Of
the Harlosh cave the least one can say is that in
size as well as in structure it is remarkable. Here,
too, local tradition affirms that a piper entered and
never came out. This cave is only accessible by
land and when the tide is low ; and even then no
little risk is entailed in reaching it. But it is easily
located because it is situated within a few feet of
a huge, columnar stack that rises abruptly out of
the sea, not very far from the face of the cliffs on
the southern side of Harlosh Point. It was with
great interest and suppressed excitement that I
explored this cave one bright summer's day ; and
my first impression was that, although I could
scarcely have imagined a piper playing his instrument and at the same time scrambling over the
rocks and dulse-covered boulders that are strewn

38

about its lofty entrance, possibly a piper may have lost himself within, and been devoured by some cave-monster ere he rediscovered the exit.

This Cave of Gold is a huge one : its inmost recesses are far removed from the light of day because of a gentle bend that begins about the centre of the passage ; and, unless you are suitably equipped with a candle and a box of reliable matches, you will grope in the darkness with the uncomfortable sensation that every moment you are likely to plunge into a deep, water-filled cavity.

My somewhat sudden arrival at the mouth of this cave was a signal to the great flocks of rock-pigeons that inhabit it all the year round, and in due season nest on the broad fern and moss-hidden ledges and crannies that occur near the seaward end of it. Indeed, I have always maintained that a more fitting designation for this cave would be Uamh nan Columan, the Cave of the (Blue) Pigeons. But I would advise no one lacking the spirit of adventure to enter this eerie cavern without some means of creating artificial light. When last I visited it, the noonday sun stood right in front of the entrance ; but, as you will understand from what I have just told you of its form, the sun's radiance cannot penetrate further than the curve that commences about half-way in. Beyond this point the grotto is blacker than the blackest night.

Almost undeniable is the temptation when at Harlosh to loiter along the shore and under the shadow of the crimsoned cliffs in search of partans and kindred strange creatures that by the tide are stranded high, but not necessarily dry, in the tiny creeks and pot-holes here and there among the wrack and shell-strewn rocks ; and, were it not that, owing to the huge perpendicular crags rising so closely to the margin of the sea and rendering one liable to be isolated except at low water, you might saunter contentedly about these rocks until sundown. The joy of lingering alone along the shore and of singing to the ceaseless tide, whether it be calm or rapturous, cannot be excelled : every boulder has its story, and every cavern its surprise. Harlosh Island was one of the three lesser isles on which, according to a seventeenth-century description of the Hebrides, red currants grew wild and abundantly.

Dr. Johnson and Boswell in Bracadale.

By the shore of Loch Bracadale there is any number of caves. Looking across the water on a sunlit day from Harlosh and in the direction of " MacLeod's Tables " you will notice that the cliffs on the further side are simply honeycombed with caves of all shapes and sizes. It was to a cave on an island in Loch Bracadale that Dr. Johnson and James Boswell were escorted by the Laird of Ullinish. Johnson here remarked that he thought this cave more deserving of the title of *antrum immane* than that of the Sibyl sung by Virgil. It was supposed to have had an unusual echo ; but to their disappointment *MacTalla*, the Son of the Hall, was absent on the day that the English snippet-gatherer and his *persona grata* visited it. However, their guide made the plausible excuse that the echo had been silenced temporarily by the recent rains that had penetrated the roof of the cave, and thus had rendered it exceptionally damp—" Such are the excuses by which the exaggerations of Highland narratives is palliated,"

Photo. by A. D. Young.

Entrance to Portree Harbour from Scorribreac.

40

concludes Boswell. But it was near this cave that for the first time in his life Johnson saw limpets and mussels in their natural state ; and, no doubt, the fish Boswell caught with a rod, that he borrowed from a little boy close at hand, was the first live cuddy *he* had ever seen.

It may have been to one of the caves on Wiay— an island in Loch Bracadale, a couple of miles south-west of Ullinish and opposite Idrigil, where " MacLeod's Tables " are—that the then laird of that property conducted his touring visitors. In addition to its wonderful arches, Wiay can boast at least two respectable caves. In one of the many caves near Idrigil the unfortunate Lady Grange is said to have been confined for some time.

That the cave near Duntulm Castle known as the Cave of Gold once may have been the cache wherein the MacDonalds of the Isles used to conceal their treasure-trove when in danger of siege is a feasible explanation for the name (*Uamh an Oir*) of one of the several caves in that part of Trotternish. An old woman, with whom I had a conversation lately near that ancient justice-seat still referred to as the Hill of Pleas, actually gave me a detailed account of the MacDonald pot of gold that gave to this cave its name.

CAVE OF THE *SCOTSMAN*.

Close to Idrigil Point is the Cave of the Candlestick (*Uamh a' Choinnleir*), so-called from the indispensability of candles when exploring it. But the still more famous Spar Cave on the eastern shore of Strathaird also is referred to as the Cave of the Candlestick. In the case of Spar Cave the probability is, however, that this name was given to describe the stalactites and stalagmites that since souvenir-hunters have destroyed.

When we come to Dun Osdail, an ancient watch-tower not far from Dunvegan, we discover a cavern that became historical only within living memory. It is known as the cave or grave of the *Scotsman* (*Uamh* or *Uaigh an t-Albannaich*). Herein, during the acute agrarian troubles of the 'eighties of last century, the *Scotsman*, in the form of an effigy, was solemnly " interred " as an ostensible protest against the attitude it had taken up on the land question.

PRINCE CHARLIE'S CAVES.

Neither the time nor yet the space at my disposal will allow of my dilating here on the caves in Skye in which Prince Charlie is reported to have hidden himself. In the Misty Isle there are at least four caves with the appellation of the Prince's Cave. Was it not to a cave south of Elgol, in Strathaird, that the Lady MacKinnon brought a sumptuous supply of meat and wine for the royal refugee ? While journeying along the bleak road between Sligachan and Elgol the Prince is said to have remarked to those who accompanied him that even the devil would think twice of following him into such a wild, forsaken region.

In the direction of Holm, and about five miles from the entrance to Portree Harbour, there is another Prince Charlie's Cave. Holm, you will recall, is the rocky, dromedary-shaped islet close to the shore and not very far from the Old Man of Storr : it possesses the unique reputation of being able to rear one sheep to obesity (if the animal could be induced to remain there !), to feed two to leanness, and to starve three.

Then, near the south-eastern end of Loch Coruisg is a third cave connected with Prince Charlie. From this cave he is said to have sailed for the mainland under the guidance of a couple of MacKinnon's retainers.

Coruisg is an eerie, creepy place ; and assuredly I would advise any one visiting this mysterious loch, who is afraid of spooks and spirits, not to venture too close to the Cave of the Ghost that is haunted by the spectre of a shepherd, who in untold circumstances perished there long ago.

At Dunvegan Head is a fourth cave wherein, according to local lore, the Prince hid : already I have hinted that Prince Charlie and Rob Roy and Robert the Bruce must have spent the best part of their time on earth either living in, or looking for, caves!

A Sea-Robber's Retreat.

Between the Sgeir Mhor and the Beal (Creag Mhor), two frowning headlands on the northern side of the entrance to Portree Harbour, is Mac-Coiter's Cave. MacCoiter was a sea-riever of no feeble account. A wee, rocky inlet along the shore of the Speckled Rock (Scorribreac) and not far removed from the cave is the spot where the old folks of Portree declared James v. landed, thus having given to the metropolis of Skye its present name. In meet season this part of the shore is besieged by children gathering hazel-nuts. A little inland, and not far from Old Scorribreac House, is the site of the ancient fort of Dun Torvaig ; and at a point nearer the sea may be seen the ruins of an old chapel. The neighbourhood of Scorribreac is associated with having been one of the places where the *crodh-sith*, or faery cows, came ashore. These mythical creatures were said to feed on bladderwort. Forbes, in his *Gaelic Names of Beasts*, gives us an interesting account of the manner in which such faery cattle were prevented from returning to the sea by the simple process of sprinkling the ground between them and the sea with a little soil, that, as a rule, was conveyed from a churchyard.

MacCoiter's Cave is certainly four hundred feet above sea-level; and its mouth looks right on to the Cuchullins and the Red Hills, that are more than a dozen miles away. From the sea the cave's entrance, which is just a perpendicular slit some fifteen feet or more in height, resembles for all the world a dash of tar on the face of the cliff.

On the opposite side of the loch and under Ben Tianavaig are the renowned Scart or Scarf Caves, thus named because they are the residence of innumerable shags and scarfs. Seldom have I sailed out of Portree without having observed a group of inquisitive cormorants sitting on the rocks nearby and stretching their long necks in eagerness to notice everything around them. Martin mentions a few of the caves in the locality of Portree; and among them he speaks of the Scarf Caves in which cormorants used to nest in such great numbers that at night-time the natives frequently burnt straw at their entrances and so scared the fowls that they flew out in panic and were trapped in nets and baskets set for the purpose. Dr. Johnson, in his *Journey to the Western Isles of Scotland*, speaks of having passed by these caves while he was being conveyed from Raasay to Portree in a stout boat built in Norway, and manned by six oars. But in his day this bird-trapping had ceased, as the cormorants had selected more congenial quarters.

Though the interior of MacCoiter's Cave is lofty and capacious, its atmosphere is damp and muggy, with the result that a box of matches is of no earthly use as a means of illumination. I found that even a well-oiled torch burns in it with difficulty. To most people this cave is extremely inaccessible ; and it is getting more and more so every year because the constant rains are steadily washing away any reliable foothold. But, apart from this, the ascent from the shore track is positively dangerous in places, and certainly should not be undertaken by any one who is inclined to feel squeamish when looking down from a precipitous height. From the shelving pasture-topped crags twenty feet above the entrance to MacCoiter's Cave one might be lowered by a rope, though such tactics would be attended with a considerable element of risk.

Within this cave there is a sudden drop to a lower level. Eager was I to scrutinise this level, and would have done so, had my illuminants been more serviceable. By the echo in it, as well as by the plop of a stone accidentally found when feeling my way in the darkness, I surmised that the rest of the cave was half filled with water and, therefore, had better remain unexplored.

Immediately below MacCoiter's Cave and on the seashore there is a huge boulder that, with a twinkle in his eye, the Portree fisherman will tell you was thrown by a Raasay man, who in a fit of temper pitched it at his wife. The boulder missed her, however ; but so herculean was the thrower that it spun across the Inner Sound and fell where it now lies—a spent force!

In olden days this cave must have been an ideal retreat for a sea-robber. Never a vessel sailed between the Beal and the tall, basaltic cliffs below Ben Tianavaig that the wily MacCoiter did not espy from his almost impregnable outpost; and I have no doubt he and his rieving confederates had more than their legitimate share of the sea-borne cargoes that were destined for Portree.

The Wolf Tradition.

And, in conclusion, the name, Sloc a' Mhadaidh, denoting the cave or den of the wolf, is evidence that even in Skye traces of the wolf tradition survive. One of the peaks of the Coolins is known as Sgurr a' Mhadaidh; and there is also a Stac a' Mhadaidh on the Minginish coast, north of Loch Eynort. Between Sgurr a' Mhadaidh and Bruach na Frithe is Coir' a' Mhadaidh, a name to which Sheriff Nicolson prefers to affix the adjective, *ruadh* (red), thus identifying this hollow as the Corrie of the Fox. Then, in Strath Mor and close to Luib there is a small loch called Loch nam Madadh Uisge, or Loch of the Water-Dogs. Some authorities declare, however, that this name refers, neither to water-dogs nor to " water-wolves," but to mussels and cockles. The most patent objection to this theory is that the latter mollusc, at any rate, thrives only in salt water. At Trumpan may still be defined the traps into which, in olden times, wolves were enticed by living bait such as a tethered fowl.

VII

LEGENDS OF THE FAERY FLAG

THE SPOILING OF THE DYKE

DIVERSE and manifold are the relics that may be seen in the oldest inhabited castle in Scotland ; and by no means the least interesting of them is the Faery Flag whose mysterious charm has engaged the pens of writers, many of whom cannot claim to have seen it. But there it is in what presently is the drawing-room of Dunvegan Castle ; and beside it are the drinking-horn of Ruairaidh Mor and the celebrated Dunvegan cup.

Innumerable litterateurs (myself at one time not excepted!) have insisted that the Faery Flag is green. Even the great Sir Walter Scott fell into this error, despite the fact that he, himself, must have examined it, and heard first-hand during his sojourn at Dunvegan the stories connected with it. Possibly subsequent writers, who likewise have maintained that the Faery Flag is green, not having seen it for themselves, were led into this error by reading Scott's account of his tour in the Hebrides. In point of fact the Flag is biscuit-coloured. It is reasonable to suggest, however, that poetic licence and association of ideas may have led many to assume that it is green, because that colour is so closely identified with faeries and faerylore. Is it not the case that certain classes of Highland faeries are dressed almost entirely in green raiment ?

The Burning of Royalist Banners.

In the Highlands and Islands in olden times the banner was an essential part of a clan's equipage ; and, although few are now extant, many a *bratach* has gone down to history.   In the annals of Fingal we read of the raising of Deo-Greine, the mighty banner of the King of Spears which, when unfurled to the wind, filled with emotion the soul of every Celtic knight and henchman.   Again, Iain Lom sings of the battle-flag of MacDonald of Clan Ranald with—

> "The tower, the galley, and the tree,
> The blood-red hand and lion free,
> And the bright salmon of the sea,
> While bound upon the standard's head,
> The blooming heath victorious spread."

John MacKay, the celebrated Blind Piper (*Am Piobaire Dall*), has described in equally eloquent terms the banner of MacDonald of Sleat ; while bards have sung of the MacGregor banner held firm and erect in the hand of MacVurich, the hereditary standard-bearer.

In the National Museum at Edinburgh one has access to the now tattered White Banner of the MacKays.   Concerning it the following passage, written in 1792 by the minister of Tongue, occurs in the *Old Statistical Account* : "There is a cave in a rock upon which the Castle (Bharaich, near Tongue) is built, called Leabuidh Eoin Abaruich, *i.e.* John of Lochaber's bed, whither he is said to have retired in time of danger.   A family of MacKay is descended from him and are reported still to have in their possession his banner, with the motto wrought in golden letters, *Biodh treun, Biodh treun,* Be valiant."

Photo. by Farquhar MacKenzie Matheson.

Luib and Loch Ainort with Lord MacDonald's Forest behind.

John's mother was a Lochaber woman : hence her son was nicknamed Iain Abrach—John of Lochaber.

No less noteworthy is the green banner (*Bratach Uaine*) of the MacPhersons. It dates back to the seventeenth century, and still is preserved at Cluny Castle. Owing to the fact that the MacPhersons were absent from Culloden, their pennon on that fateful day did not suffer the summary destruction that befell the banners of so many routed clans. You will recall that Cumberland offered a handsome reward to whomsoever would carry off the banner of a royalist clan, with the result that "fourteen of these melancholy emblems of departed glory" were captured and contemptuously burned at the Mercat Cross of Edinburgh by the common hangman.

THE FAERY WOMAN'S CROON.

Without doubt the Faery Flag at Dunvegan is one of the most interesting historical relics of its kind in the country. According to one version of its origin, we are told that late on an autumn evening a faery, clad in green apparel, entered the Castle and found her way to what since has been termed the Faery Chamber. There she discovered the baby heir of MacLeod, asleep in his cradle. You can imagine how surprised MacLeod's nurse was when she looked up to find a strange, little woman seated beside the cradle, and rocking it gently. The faery visitor raised the child in her arms and wrapped him up in the Faery Flag, crooning the while *Taladh na Mna Sithe*, the Lullaby of the Faery Woman—"Behold my child, limbed like the kid or fawn, smiting horses, grasping the accoutrements of the shod horses, the spirited steeds, *mo leanabh beag*, my little child. . . . Oh that I could behold thy team of horses ; men following them, serving women returning home, and the Catanaich sowing the corn. . . . Oh ! not of Clan Kenneth (Mac-Kenzie) art thou ! Oh ! not of Clan Conn. Descendant of a race more esteemed ; that of Clan Leod of the swords and armour, whose fathers' native land was Lochlainn."

Thus runs an extract from a free translation of the faery woman's *taladh* or croon by my venerated friend, Frances Tolmie. Spellbound and motionless during the singing of it sat the nurse of the infant heir ; and so impressed upon her memory was the croon that she forgot neither its words nor its melody. When the faery woman disappeared, the nurse lifted the child from his cot wherein he had been replaced ; and, having hurried with him down the stair that still winds in the Faery Tower, carried him into the banqueting-hall, where in splendour and elegance were assembled many members of the Clan. And great, to be sure, was their consternation when they cast eyes upon the magic banner, and listened to the strange story that the nurse had to tell.

And for a long, long time the MacLeods of Dunvegan insisted that every nurse should be able to sing *Taladh na Mna Sithe*, the Lullaby of the Faery Woman, because they firmly believed it acted as a *seun* or charm that would protect the infant chieftains from all manner of ill.

In those times the Faery Flag was committed to the charge of a family whose paterfamilias acted as hereditary custodian of it, and bore it into battle whenever the occasion demanded. MacLeod maintained his *duin'-bratach* or standard-bearer in a free-hold near Bracadale in return for his services in this connection.

A RELIC OF THE CRUSADES.

But the more generally accepted theory of the Faery Flag is that it came into the possession of a young MacLeod warrior during his absence in the Land of the Infidel. This crusader was none other than Mac a' Phearsan ; to wit, the Son of the Parson. During his wanderings in the Holy Land this knight-errant came to a broad river where he met the *maighdean-shith*—the faery maiden—who would not permit him to cross until he had wrestled with her as Jacob wrestled with the angel at Penuel. In the legendary struggle that ensued the MacLeod warrior overcame his elfin adversary ; and, while departing from her, he was presented with the Faery Flag that she assured him, when unfurled, would give the appearance of a great multitude of armed men. Be it said, moreover, that the faery maid forewarned the crusader only to use the banner on three specific occasions, and told him that, among other calamities, the misuse of it would result in there being no young cattle nor sheep in the territory of the MacLeods : no cow would have a calf ; and likewise every mare and ewe would become sterile. Furthermore, there would be plenteousness neither of crops nor of fish for a whole year : nor would any children be born unto MacLeod.

BRIDGE OF THE THREE BROOKS.

A third version states that one of the chiefs of MacLeod was betrothed to a faery who dwelt on earth with him only for a short space of time, and that, when she was bidding him farewell before her return to faeryland, she presented him with the Faery Flag as a keepsake. The actual spot where the chief and the faery finally took leave of one another is about three miles from Dunvegan. It is still known as Faery Bridge (*Drochaid nan tri Allt*, the Bridge of the Three Brooks), and is situated just at the point where the Portree, Dunvegan, and Vaternish roads converge.

THE BATTLE OF THE SPOILING OF THE DYKE.

Island folklorists tell us that on two occasions the unfurling of the Faery Flag was the means of averting catastrophe. To commence with, it was waved during the cattle plague that threatened to destroy the vast herds belonging to MacLeod. On this point some enthusiasts differ, and religiously or capriciously maintain that the first unfurling resulted from the over-curiosity of MacLeod's lady, who long had been impatient to unfold it. Consequently, the dreadful afflictions predicted by the faery maid in the event of misuse followed.

But the second occasion on which it was unfurled was unquestionably the more memorable. Clan Ranald's fleet, glittering in all its maritime armoury, arrived off the coast of Vaternish one holy day. Great were the numbers of Clan Ranald's men ; and truly bent were they on vengeance. And, having disembarked in Ardmore Bay, they hastened to the now ruined church at Trumpan, wherein the MacLeods were congregated and at worship. The MacDonalds fired the church and put to the sword every occupant with the exception of one terror-stricken woman, who escaped and fled with the doleful tidings towards Dunvegan. To this day *Clach Mairearaid*, Margaret's Stone, is applied locally to the spot where the woman who escaped died of her injuries. Without delay MacLeod mustered as many clansmen as the time at his disposal would permit ; and with meet haste he set out for Vaternish, accompanied by the Faery Flag, which he knew would be indispensable, as the invading army was several times larger than the small body of men he had been able to collect at a moment's notice.

On the arrival of the MacLeods at Trumpan the flag was appropriately unfurled ; and the Mac-Donalds, having beheld what they thought was an enormous and irresistible host, made a dash for their boats that they had drawn up on the beach of Ardmore Bay. But the MacLeods, eager to carry fire into the enemy's camp, pursued the invaders with unabating zeal and unrelenting fury ; and, having overtaken them ere they gained the seashore, cut them in pieces. And, when the strife was ended and all those who had offered resistance to the incensed MacLeods had been vanquished *ad unum*, the corpses of the slain MacDonalds were collected and placed in a row along the base of an old dyke that was finally cast down upon them. So concealed were they beneath its stones that neither the eagle nor the carrion-crow could get at them.

This incident is still referred to as *Blar Milleadh Garaidh*, the Battle of the Spoiling of the Dyke. And there's a song called *Latha Milleadh Garaidh*, the Day of the Spoiling of the Dyke—men were there that day in sad, sad plight, their heads down and the soles of their feet uppermost, relates an old Gaelic chronicler. And it is recorded that from Vaternish not a man of Clan Ranald escaped with impunity that day. The few stragglers, who succeeded in retracing their steps as far as the shore, were pursued by the MacLeods, who, like good strategists, had broken and burnt the boats of the invaders, lest any one of them should go without his desert.

FAERY FLAG EXHIBITED FOR THE THIRD TIME.

Pennant expresses an opinion on the tattered condition of the Faery Flag ; and in his *Misty Isle of Skye* MacCulloch tells us that he feared it would not bear the strain of being unfurled a third time because " the material is threadbare . . . and even a faery might scarcely touch it without tearing it." But, as a matter of fact, it *was* actually brought to light again ; and not only is this third and last occasion the most interesting, but it also partakes " rather of the nature of history than of tradition."

The circumstances are revealed in a letter written by Dr. Norman MacLeod, the eminent father of an even more eminent son. In the summer of 1799 Dr. MacLeod set sail from Morven in a wherry on a visit to Dunvegan, where he relates he was put to sleep in a small closet off MacLeod's own bedroom. It was during this visit to the Castle that Dr. MacLeod (as he, himself, records) became rather friendly with an English blacksmith, who told him in solemn secrecy that on the following morning the iron chest containing the Faery Flag was to be forced open, and that he might witness this operation if he promised not to tell the Chief what was about to take place. Dr. MacLeod describes at length the great violence employed by the smith in tearing off the lid of the chest, and how, on removing the metal top, a key was discovered that would have performed the task with less manual labour, had it been found earlier.

Within the chest lay a box of strongly scented wood ; and in it was enclosed the Faery Flag. The Flag was duly examined ; and, after it was observed to have " several elf spots stitched on it with great care," it was once more consigned to its old box.

A Prophecy Fulfilled.

Legion are the prophecies regarding the fate of many ancient Highland families : in our own day we have witnessed the almost complete fulfilment of the curse pronounced on the Breadalbanes. It was on the occasion referred to by Dr. Norman MacLeod that an extraordinary prophecy concerning the Dunvegan MacLeods was fulfilled, and in a very remarkable way. Years before the English smith had made his tools felt on the lid of the iron chest, it had been said that, when the third Norman (*Tormoid nan tri Tormoidean*), the son of an English mother (*mac na maighdean caol Sassanaich*), met an untimely death, when "MacLeod's Maidens" became the property of the Campbells, when a fox deposited her whelps in one of the bartizans of Dunvegan Castle, and, finally, when the magic banner was waved for the last time, the ancient power and prestige of the MacLeods would vanish so completely that a *curach* (coracle) could bear across the Loch all the surviving male representatives of their race. But it was predicted further that in distant days to come there would arise another Iain MacLeod whose prowess would raise his family to a position of greatness such as it never before had enjoyed. Well, not long after the exhibiting of the Faery Flag on this occasion, Norman MacLeod (" the third Norman " and heir to the chief), who was an officer on the *Queen Charlotte*, perished at sea when that ship was blown up with all hands. A few weeks later " MacLeod's Maidens " found a purchaser in the person of Campbell of Ensay ; and I believe they still are in the possession of his grandson.

A Fox and her Whelps.

One condition was required to complete the literal fulfilment of the prophecy—that a fox should have her young in Dunvegan Castle. And, strangely enough, some time afterwards a fox, the property of a Lieutenant MacLean, did lay her young in the western turret. These whelps Dr. Norman MacLeod depones to having seen and handled.

To-day only one item of the prophecy remains unfulfilled—the MacLeods are still waiting expectantly for the kinsman who is to exalt his ancient heritage. To the chieftainship of MacLeod there is no direct male heir : Iain Breac MacLeod, nephew of Norman, the present and twenty-third Chief, was killed in action in 1915. Herein lies a tragedy : Iain Breac was the last male heir of his line.

Sir Walter Scott and the Faery Flag.

Sir Walter Scott, who stayed here while on a tour of inspection in his capacity as a lighthouse commissioner, tells us that the Faery Flag possessed three definite properties—that of multiplying the numbers of the MacLeods in battle ; that of guaranteeing fertility when spread on a nuptial bed ;

Photo. by R. C. MacLeod of MacLeod.

Ruins of the Church at Trumpan.

and, lastly, that of bringing abundant shoals of herring into Loch Dunvegan.

Historical accounts of the displaying of this magic banner at Vaternish, when the Battle of the Spoiling of the Wall was fought, are to be found with minor variations in many books dealing with troublous times in the Highlands and Islands. But the version I have given you of the burning of the church at Trumpan and of the rout of Clan Ranald I received in Dunvegan, and at a *ceilidh* round the cosy hearth of my dear seannachie friend, Frances Tolmie.

And it was from the lips of an old native of Vaternish—Oighrig Ross by name—that Miss Tolmie learnt this rendering many winters ago. Oighrig it was who could not tell you the date of her birth : when asked her age her reply was that she was born in the year in which a poor woman, while herding cattle, fell over the rocks at Vaternish and was drowned.

But, though she knew not the year of her birth, Oighrig was conversant with the augury of the birds in their flight ; and she could tell you of the sun's journeyings, of the stars in their courses, of the winds, of the tides, of the changes of the moon.

VIII

DUNVEGAN'S RELICS

ITS LITERARY CORRESPONDENCE

ORIGINAL LETTERS FROM SCOTT AND JOHNSON

THE Faery Flag is by no means the only outstanding heirloom preserved at Dunvegan Castle. There is, forby, a remarkable cup or chalice made out of a solid piece of oak, delicately embossed with silver, and once studded with jewels. This cup stands on four little silver feet, and is 10¼ inches in height. On the four panels of the rim is engraved in magnificent style an inscription that has been the subject of many readings, perhaps the most accurate and reliable of which is the following :—

> "Katherina ingen ui Neill (O'Neill's daughter) uxor Johannis Meguighir principis de Firmanach me fieri fecit. Anno Domini 1493. Oculi omnium in te spectant Domine et tu das escam illorum in tempore opportuno." (Katherine, the daughter of Neil, wife of John MacGuire, chief of Fermanagh, caused me to make this. In the year of our Lord 1493. The eyes of all wait upon Thee, O Lord ; and Thou givest them their meat in due season.)

It is singular that, though Pennant, Johnson, and Boswell visited Dunvegan Castle during the eighteenth century, not one of them makes mention of this celebrated cup. I believe the earliest extant literary reference to it occurs in *The Lord of the*

Isles, where Sir Walter Scott speaks of the " mighty cup . . . erst owned by royal Somerled." In his explanatory note, however, Scott committed (innocently, no doubt) a number of serious errors that prove his having misinterpreted entirely the inscription on this cup, which, he says, was at one time the property of Neil Ghlune-dhubh, or Black-knee. The cup, in fact, is usually referred to as the cup of Neil Glun-dubh, who was King of Ulster during part of the tenth century, and who is regarded as having been the progenitor of the Irish family of O'Neill. That the cup was once the property of the O'Neills is clearly borne out by at least two fairly reliable authorities. In the first place, Gregory relates that in 1595 Rory Mor and Hugh MacDonald of Sleat went over to Ireland to assist some rebels against Queen Bess, and that while there the former made friends with Shane O'Neill, who afterwards visited Dunvegan Castle and brought the cup with him. In support of Gregory's statement is a tradition in the O'Neill family—a tradition that only the other day was communicated to Canon MacLeod of MacLeod by Lady O'Neill.

The actual date on the cup is 1493. Here, also, Scott is in error, for he gives us the date as 993. In his favour it may be said, however, that experts have declared the cup to be a remarkably fine specimen of early Irish workmanship, probably belonging to the ninth or tenth century. It has been suggested that the rim may have been added in 1493, and that the inscription, therefore, refers to that date. How the cup found its way into the possession of the MacLeods of Dunvegan is uncertain, though it has been conjectured that during the military operations in northern Ireland in the

sixteenth century, in which the Dunvegan Mac-
Leods took a prominent part, it may have been a
reward for services rendered, or a trophy of war.
Into the legend and remaining details of the
Dunvegan chalice we need not enter herein ; but
I would refer those interested to the *Proceedings of
the Society of Antiquaries* (1912-13), where will be
found a delightfully illustrated account of the cup
and the traditions associated with it.

A TEST OF PROWESS.

With the drinking-horn of Sir Rory Mor many
traditional tales are connected, one being that it
was taken from the head of a wild bull slain in the
woods of Glenelg by Malcolm, the third Chief of
MacLeod. From this incident is said to have
originated both the bull's head cabossed between
two flags, which is the crest of the MacLeods, and
their device " Hold Fast." According to another
tradition anent the origin of the horn, MacLeod
had gone to Inveraray, where he found within a
fenced arena a young man whom Argyll had con-
demned to be gored to death by a bull. MacLeod
remarked to Argyll that his victim was far too fine
a fellow to be killed ; but to his pleadings that his
life should be spared Argyll replied that it was now
too late.

" Will you give him to me if I save him ? "
asked MacLeod.

" Yes, but you go to your death," retorted Argyll.
MacLeod thereupon sprang into the arena and
seized the enraged bull by the horns. " Hold
Fast ! " shrieked the auditorium, as MacLeod
buried his dirk in the bull's heart and lopped off
one of its horns. I am told that to this day there is

in Dunvegan a family of Campbells claiming descent from the young man whom MacLeod so valiantly rescued.

The horn is a large ox horn rimmed with a deep silver band, on which is engraved a familiar Celtic interlacing design. In ancient days every young heir, on succeeding to the chieftainship, was required to prove his worth by draining to the lees, and in a single breath, the brimful horn ; but in more temperate times this ordeal was considerably mitigated by the insertion within the horn of a wooden lining. To-day the bumpering of Rory Mor's horn is entirely discontinued.

The corridors of Dunvegan Castle have the unmistakable air of an armoury, for their walls are tastefully hung with diverse weapons of many ages and countries, and their niches are occupied by the chain mail of several warriors. Among the former may be seen the great broadsword that was wielded by the hand of Rory Mor, and that Dr. Johnson bumptiously declared he would challenge with a dirk. Then, there is also the claymore used by Sir Norman MacLeod of Bernera at the Battle of Worcester (1651), where, as an ardent supporter of the Royalist cause, he commanded a battalion of MacLeods that was decimated by Cromwell's reserves.

While mentioning armoury it should be remembered that MacLeod maintained a hereditary blacksmith or armourer, who, I believe, resided either at Suardal or at Claigean, neither of which places are very far from the Castle. From MacLeod's armourer are descended the illustrious MacLeods of Morven. The old road leading from Dunvegan and through fragrant moors of bog-myrtle and long, shaggy heather to the farm at Claigean is, I think, one of the sweetest and most poetic in all the Isle of Skye.

Another relic associated with Rory Mor is the ancient gourd, mounted in silver and fitted with silver hasps, and bearing the armorial devices of a lion rampant, a stag's head, a castle, and a birlinn, together with the initials, " S. R. M.," signifying Sir Rory Mor. Rory, you will remember, was knighted in 1613.

LINKS WITH LADY GRANGE.

In the dining-room at Dunvegan is a magnificent, ornate sideboard, bearing the date 1603. It is thought to have been brought home by Rory Mor from Edinburgh, whither he journeyed on several occasions. It must have been a considerable undertaking in those days bringing such a massive piece of furniture all the way from Edinburgh without damaging it. Probably it came by boat direct to Loch Follart from Leith.

A small case in the same apartment contains many treasures, including a lock of Prince Charlie's hair, his drinking-glass, and a waistcoat of his, presented to MacLeod by the family of Flora MacDonald. Flora's own pin-cushion, her stays, and a fragment of black lace once worn by her are also in this case. On the pin-cushion are sewn the names of many who suffered in the '45. Under this case is a cable-patterned stone that of a time formed part of the historic walls of Duntulm Castle.

Links with the unfortunate Lady Grange, who on St. Kilda was held in captivity by MacLeod, are preserved in a detailed account of her board for a year and her funeral expenses ; while the cruisie she used during her unhappy banishment now hangs in the hall. As is shown by the bill referred to, she died in 1745 at Trumpan, in Vaternish, where she lies buried. Her interment cost thirty pounds and a few odd shillings—undertakers in Skye during the eighteenth century were immoderate in their charges! The tragic story of Lady Grange has attracted the attention of many pens : herein we need only record our regret that MacLeod was tempted to participate so whole-heartedly in such a shady affair.

ISABELLA'S EFFIGY IN STONE.

In the courtyard of the Castle and facing my bedroom window is an effigy in stone, popularly believed to represent Rory Mor's wife, Isabella. This, doubtless, is one of the effigies referred to by MacIan in his *Custumes of the Clans*, and in the passage—" Sir Roderick MacLeod built that portion of Dunvegan which is called Ruarie Mor's Tower, on which were placed curious effigies of himself and his lady, the last of which still exists, but is thrown from its original position." Isabella was a daughter of MacDonald of Glengarry. There is also in the courtyard a stone, the inscription whereon is now difficult to decipher. It purports chiefly to the restoration of the tower in 1686 by the then chief. Boswell in 1773 was able to read the inscription, however ; and he records it accurately with the exception of one word (*lafactatam* should read *labefactatam*).

Dunvegan Castle can boast a tolerable collection of pictures, which includes two Zoffani full-length portraits, and two exquisite Raeburns. Not the least interesting of the pictures is one of " The

Wicked Man," as Norman, the nineteenth Chief, was called, partly owing to his having contracted great debts that necessitated the disposal of the properties of Glenelg and Harris, and partly owing to his share in the abduction and banishment of Lady Grange. Numbered among " The Wicked Man's " other shortcomings was his duplicity in at first encouraging the Prince to come over, and afterwards withdrawing his support. Then, " he took a fancy to a pretty girl " ; and, in order to expedite his marriage to her, he invited his real wife to return to the Castle, whereupon he seized her, and cast her into the bottle-dungeon in which, tradition says, she died of starvation. His portrait by Allan Ramsay shows him attired in Rob Roy tartan : we have evidence that he was on intimate terms with the honourable freebooter whose tartan he wore.

Dunvegan's Correspondence.

Indeed, it is unfortunate that, though copies have been preserved, the original latters addressed to various chiefs by King James VI. of Scotland and by James II. of the United Kingdom have been lost with one exception. The exception is an original letter bearing the signature, " James R.," and addressed to " Our Trustie and well-beloved McLoud." It is dated from " Our Courte at Dublin Castle the 29th day of May 1690." I believe that at present it is in the possession of the MacDonalds. But the comparative paucity of sixteenth and seventeenth-century correspondence is certainly compensated for by the wealth of letters received in later times from such celebrities as Sir Walter Scott, Dr. Johnson, James Boswell, Pennant,

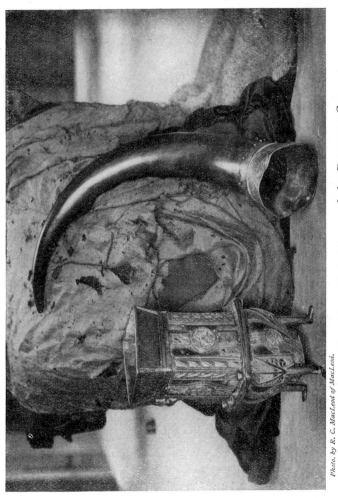

Photo. by R. C. MacLeod of MacLeod.

The Faery Flag, Rory Mor's Horn, and the Dunvegan Cup.

E

the Ettrick Shepherd, Tippoo Sahib, President Forbes, and Warren Hastings. In addition to these, the Dunvegan charter chest is chock-full of documents shedding an accurate light on the social and economic conditions of the periods to which they belong.

The most recent acquisition to the Dunvegan treasures is a labradorite pendant that was sent to Sir Reginald MacLeod of MacLeod in January of 1914, accompanied by an anonymous letter bearing the postmark, Whitby. I am going to quote in full the letter here, in the hope that some imaginative or psychic person may be able to throw light upon it.

" Mrs. —— thinks this has belonged to a very old lady. It brings to her mind some ancestral history and a very old building, somewhat dilapidated but rebuilt. In the family there seem to have been many vicissitudes— attachments, changes of circumstances, political inter- ference, and persecutions.

The family is Scotch—a distinguished line of aristo- crats—their position and power are not now what it was, but there will be an ascent again. A child will be born more dark than fair and very intelligent, who will be the means of lifting up this family—the father thin and intelligent, the mother dark and *psychic*. The child will grow into a God-fearing man and will be enterprising and psychic. This pendant should *not be worn* but put in a case, and it should be sent back to the family it came from.

Mrs. —— felt a very proud tall lady had once worn it who had carried on some clandestine correspondence, and who had been no good in some political crisis and had pushed someone out of some place, and believed to have caused the beheading of this person.

Let the thing lie in a case : don't wear it.

The above was what a lady said to be psychic said

of the enclosed old pendant, which was given many years ago to the present sender and was said to have come from the family of MacLeod of MacLeod of Dunvegan."

"On the Margin of the Sea."

In conclusion, I have deemed the two following letters, one from the pen of Sir Walter Scott and the other from that of Dr. Johnson, of sufficient interest to justify my reproducing them here :—

"Dear Madam,

I have been postponing from day to day requesting your kind acceptance of my best thanks for the beautiful purse of your workmanship with which I was sometime since honoured. The hospitality of Dunvegan will long live in my recollection and I am not a little flattered by a token which infers that my visit was not forgotten by the Lady of the Castle. I venture to send (what has long delayed this letter) a copy of a poem which owes its best passages to MacLeod's kindness and taste in directing me to visit the extraordinary scenery between his country and Strathard which rivals in grandeur and desolate sublimity any thing that the Highlands can produce. The volume should have reached you in a quarto shape but while I sought an opportunity of sending it behold the quartos disappeared and I was obliged to wait for the second impression of which I now send a copy. I shall be proud and happy if it serves to amuse a leisure hour at Dunvegan. It has had one good consequence to the author that it has served to replenish the purse with which the Lady MacLeod presented him. Yet he has so much the spirit of the old Bard, that he values the purse more than the contents.

Should MacLeod and you ever come to Edinburgh I will scarce forgive you unless you let such a hermit as I am know of your being in the neighbourhood of his recess and I would have particular pleasure in endeavouring to show you any thing that might interest you. I do not despair of (what would give me the most sincere pleasure) again being a guest at Dunvegan. My eldest girl sings Cathail Gu la—excuse Saxen spelling—and I hope to send you in a few weeks a very curious treatise on the second sight published (not for sale) from a manuscript in 1691 which fell into my hands. Hector Macdonald has promised me the means to send it.

I beg my respectful compliments to Miss MacLeod my kindest remembrances to the chieftain and my best wishes to the little tartan chief and nursery.

Believe me with much respect

Dear Madam (for I will not say Mrs. MacLeod and Lad^y M—— is out of fashion)

Your honoured & obliged & truly grateful

WALTER SCOTT."

"EDIN. 3 *March* 1815."

Now comes this delightful epistle written by Dr. Johnson at Ostaig on September 28th, 1773:—

" DEAR SIR,

We are now on the margin of the sea, waiting for a boat and a wind. Boswel grows impatient, but the kind treatment which I find everywhere I go makes me leave with some heaviness of heart an Island which I am not very likely to see again. Having now gone as far as horses can carry us, we thankfully return them. My steed will, I hope, be received with kindness : he has born me, heavy as I am, over ground both rough and stony with great fidelity, and for the use of him, as for your other favours, I hope you will believe me thankful, and willing at whatever distance we may be placed, to show my sense of your kindness by any office of friendship that may fall within my power.

Lady MacLeod and the young ladies have by their hospitality and politeness made an impression on my mind which will not easily be effaced. Be pleased to tell them that I remember them with great tenderness and great respect.

I am,
Sir,
Your most obliged
and
most humble servant
SAM. JOHNSON."

To this letter is appended the following post-script—"We passed two days at Talisker very happily, both by the pleasantness of the place, and the elegance of our reception."

There is at Dunvegan a painting of Dr. Johnson by Joshua Reynolds. It may have been sent to MacLeod by Johnson, after he returned to London.

I think the last quoted letter has a literary charm all of its own. You can just picture Dr. Johnson at Ostaig, in Sleat, and "on the margin of the sea, waiting for a boat and a wind" to take him away from an Isle that, to his regret, he was never likely to revisit.

And could his sojourn among this kindly people have terminated in a more delightful atmosphere than that of waiting on the margin of a windless sea at Ostaig, on the shadowy Sound of Sleat?

IX

AT A HIGHLAND PIER

AN EARLY MORNING SCENE

The blue peat smoke is curling up anew,
And Mairi's cheeks are wet with morning dew.

To a rickety dwelling-place over at Talisker, and during the night-time nigh out of bounds to those who are unacquainted with the twists and turns of the mountain road, we had been called out at an unearthly hour of the morning to give our counsel and to lend our assistance in the performance of a somewhat delicate operation. But, apart from the patient and his condition, I can remember little of the habitat wherein we found him, except that ingress thereto was gained by an outer stone staircase, slippery, decaying, and lichen-green, from a large aperture in which grew a hip-laden briar whose prickly offshoots were not slow to entangle those who passed by it unwarily.

(From the foregoing remark you will have gathered that our visit was made in the autumn.)

A WARLOCK'S ROOM.

Assembled round the foot of this staircase when we arrived was a considerable number of the villagers, who murmured among themselves as to the real nature of our nocturnal visit, and hopefully expected a verdict to show that, haply, things weren't quite so serious after all.

In an instant we were ushered into a warlock's room. There a neatly improvised lampshade threw a reflection upon the ruddy countenance of one who reclined on a couch, and nervously awaited our arrival.

Bandages and chloroform were the order of the hour ; and everything was in readiness for us : we could not have been called into the operating-theatre of the most up-to-date city infirmary and found the necessary appliances more carefully and diligently laid out for us—and only one pair of hands to do the whole thing in this out-of-the-way place ! It said a great deal for Dr. M. that, despite incessant enquiries from anxious relatives and friends as to the patient's latest condition, he had carried through the preparatory treatment of the case without a hitch, and had even made time to don a skull-cap that gave to the proceedings a decided suggestion of warlockry.

Long may Dr. M. be spared to carry on with such good work at Talisker.

* * * * * * *

Thus it was that at a morning hour far too early to be abroad in normal circumstances, and too late to think seriously of going back to bed, I found myself in Portree before the cocks had begun to crow.

Often had I been awakened in the small, dark hours by the unceasing barking of sheep dogs in the neighbourhood of Portree House : often, too, had I desired to witness these lithe creatures working sheep and cattle in the darkness ; and here I was afforded an opportunity with a minimum of personal inconvenience.

A Rendezvous for Drovers.

From the metropolis of Skye our house is approached by a fairly steep brae that is flanked on either side by a stately line of trees, most of which are deciduous. So dense in season is the foliage of this avenue that the old drove road running past the gable of Portree House, and for most purposes terminating with the sheep buchts at the farm, a few hundred yards further up the brae, is completely embowered and protected from the glare of the sun in the noonday of summer.

It is in the extensive pens and fanks at the top of this road that overnight the Island herdsmen and drovers usually leave the cattle and sheep that have been driven into Portree the previous evening. There they remain till about 4 A.M., at which hour they are herded down to the pier for trans-shipment to the mainland marts.

October and November, however, are the months during which many hundreds of sheep are conveyed across the Inner Sound to more congenial wintering quarters, because in most parts of Skye the pasture is insufficient to maintain satisfactorily large flocks.

Under My Bedroom Window.

If the late autumn nights should happen to be mild enough to justify your bedroom window being left open, you are almost certain to be awakened from your slumbers by the conversation of a couple of shepherds who in the dark slowly dawdle up to the sheep fanks, stopping every few minutes to argue some trivial point, or to re-light the seldom neglected pipe. The first time I heard these shepherds, I thought they were thieves in conclave, disputing as to which window or door would yield most readily to their unlawful admittance. I since have discovered that they halt habitually for a moment or two at our gable in order to strike a match. But the striking of a match, though an operation occupying, as a rule, only a few seconds, very often provides the opportunity for finding a topic of common interest—so smokers have told me ! Some shepherds seem to linger there long enough to permit of your dozing off again, and forgetting that they are within miles of you.

ON THE WAY TO THE PIER.

And, then, maybe an hour or so later, you are re-awakened with a vengeance ; and your heart goes pit-a-pat; and you stretch your hand out of bed to make certain that you are still on earth. Have you never experienced a rude awakening such as this?

Our avenue is now the scene of the most perfect pandemonium conceivable : the patter of hundreds of trotters, the squelching of a sodden embankment under the hoofs of a bullock that, owing chiefly to innate stubbornness, pretends to have defective eyesight, the bleating of sheep, the bellowing of oxen, the agitated barking of half a dozen collie dogs, and the shouting and yelling of as many frenzied drovers, who wisely rebuke their four-footed assistants in Gaelic and compliment them in the best English, all go to create a miniature scene such as might have been taken from Dante's *Inferno*.

Then something really serious goes wrong : a pickle of sheep has managed to find its way through a gap in the straggling fence, and is lost among the still blacker copse of beeches. For the time

Photo. by R. C. MacLeod of MacLeod.

On the Claigean Road.

"The most poetic road in all the Isle of Skye."

being at any rate, progress towards the pier is interrupted.

One who could sleep through the babel that now ensues would never be disturbed by the noise of a box-barrage !

But, regardless of its tumult, this simple scene has an old-world picturesqueness.

THROUGH THE SLEEPING VILLAGE.

And, if the morning be calm and the labour be done, a wondrous silence follows. The sheep and cattle are aboard, and are quiet : the lanterns and flaming torches, that have guided them through the narrow streets of a sleeping village, are now extinguished : the collies—those grand little workers—are lying at rest on the pier, and are weary of their barking : thankful are their masters that the intricate task of shipping their flocks is ended.

All is silent ; so silent, indeed, that you can hear the inky-black tide as it licks the barnacled under-stagings of the quay and laps against the timbers of the boat, for man and beast are now enjoying a brief respite.

And at a scheduled hour the stillness of the morning air again is disturbed ; but this time by the clanging of a bell. It is now 6 A.M. (Parliamentary Time !). The last belated passenger scoots up the gangway ; and the gangway is removed. You hear the creaking of ropes as the engines take the reversed strain, and the boat swings out into the darkened harbour.

In a moment three distinct ting-a-lings are heard in swift succession, as the skipper signals to the engine-room : Stand By ! Stop ! Full Steam Ahead !

And the steamer glides out of the black, glittering bay ; and the throb of her engines and the plash of her paddles become fainter and fainter, as she bears over against the first of the dawn that is breaking behind Raasay.

When her lights have vanished from view beyond the Caves of the Cormorants, you retrace your steps through the village that now is beginning to show signs of life. And, again, but with muddy boots that you feel too lazy to remove, you find yourself lying on the top of your bed, having another forty winks at half-past six !

Here is a morning picture, a memory, and a poem.

X

SPAR CAVE

SCOTLAND'S MOST WONDERFUL CAVERN AND ITS LEGEND

"Deep in Strathaird's enchanted cell."

THERE is at least a score of caves throughout Sleat and Strath, each of which has its own particular legend ; but by far the most remarkable cave in all the Isle of Skye is Sloc an Altrumain, the Cave of the Nursling—better known as Spar Cave.

It was only rediscovered early last century ; and it is situated a little over a mile to the north of the Point of the Eels (*Rudha na h-Easgainne*), and is almost immediately opposite the ruins of the storied Castle of Dunscaith, in Sleat. You will remember it was to Dunscaith that Cuchullin sent his young bride, Bragéla, for safety while he was absent at the Ulster Wars.

In this cave was weaned the heir of the Chief of Colonsay. And you may rightly enquire how *he* found a cradle so strangely remote from the Isle of his forbears.

THE KING OF ULSTER INVADES THE WESTERN ISLES.

Well, in an early century (probably the ninth) the King of Ulster, MacCairbe to name, having taken advantage of the fact that at the time most

75

of the Hebridean chieftains and their retinues were assisting their kinsfolk, the Lochlannaich, in northern seas, raised anchor and set sail for the Western Isles in quest of plunder. On his way north MacCairbe was forced to seek shelter in a bay in Colonsay, whose Chief, by the way, could scarcely refuse the Ulstermen hospitality, as their King was sib to him. During the remainder of this Erse expedition young Colonsay accompanied the King of Ulster ; and so enraged by their ravagings and plunderings was the people of Skye that it gathered together a mighty force with the object of paying a similar visit to the territory of its aggressors. Off this contingent sailed for Ulster, where it not only routed MacCairbe, but into the bargain carried off his fair daughter and young Colonsay, who was there on furlough, so to speak.

A Great Storm.

Now, the return voyage to Skye was the occasion of a terrific storm—the almost indispensable feature of a successful Hebridean sea story ; and so overwhelming was the tempest that all the Skye galleys were lost with the exception of one. This solitary remnant of the island-fleet managed to reach Loch Slapin : there, in a heavy ground-swell, it capsized.

Anxious all this time for the safety of her kinsfolk had Dounhuila been ; and patiently did she watch from the outlook tower of Dun Glas for the return of her father's birlinn. And it was while glancing round the loch, as if in despair, that her eyes fell upon the overturned boat.

FOUND ON THE SHORE.

On hastening to the shore, whom did she find but young Colonsay : he had been washed up on the beach by the fury of the waves.

Though Dounhuila knew him to be one of her father's bitterest enemies, she brought him to Dun Glas, and concealed him there for many months. But it was during her father's absence on yet another campaign, and before the long-standing quarrel between him and the Chief of Colonsay had been patched up, that the daughter of Dun Glas bore a child to Colonsay. This child was nursed by a faithful handmaiden in the cave that ever since has been known as the Cave of the Nursling. And the infant was named Dounhuila (*donn-shuil*) because its eyes were brown like the eyes of its mother.

THE RETREAT OF AN EPISCOPAL MINISTER.

Spar Cave also is associated with having been the hiding-place of Neil MacKinnon, an Episcopal minister and the first Protestant clergyman of Strath. It was he who at his ordination in 1627 took a " grite and solemne oathe that he sal treulie, according to his knowledge, gif up to the Clerk of Counsell the names of all the Papists he knew within the Ilis." Lamont in his book on Strath reminds us that the said Neil used to preach in the now-ruined church of Kilchrist (*Cill Chriosd*), near Suardal, dressed in a kilt and clad in a complete set of armour.

Without a doubt, Spar Cave is by far the most extraordinary cavern in the country. Except at low tide, it is inaccessible, unless approached by a boat, when a landing is usually effected with a considerable amount of risk. In many ways it reminds one of the famous Jenolan Caves in the Blue Mountains, though years ago its stalagmites and stalactites were sorely damaged by souvenir-hunting tourists. Across its entrance may still be seen the doorless wall that a past proprietor erected, in order to exclude from the cave those who were unwilling to pay a small, nominal fee to inspect it. But one fine day a gunboat sauntered along, looking for a suitable target on which to practise ; and a shot was fired from it that shattered the door, so that to-day you may examine this unique cave without fear of being accosted by any one. When Dr. MacCulloch arrived at Spar Cave, he was not a little disconcerted at finding that the philosophy of those who thought a stalactite a specimen of a cave had necessitated the construction of a scarlet door that could only be opened by a vulgar, terrestrial key—a precautionary measure that swiftly disillusioned any one who came to this grotto in the hope of fraternising with tritons and naiads.

SUBMERGED ROCKS.

At times it is no easy matter getting to the entrance of Spar Cave. From the sea it is practically impossible when there is the slightest swell, because the sunken rocks that lie in the canyon-like channel leading to it are extremely difficult to negotiate. The chances are that, unless you are very alert with your oars and navigate this maritime vestibule of approach successfully on the crest of an ingoing wave, your frail craft will be holed or possibly smashed to atoms. The old Glasnacille seaman who conveyed me in his boat to Spar Cave manipulated his oars in a manner that certainly excited admiration : to this day I do not know how he kept his oars in open rowlocks, and prevented his boat from drifting on the reefs with the strength of the undertow.

Within the actual cave there are two steep climbs and two equally steep descents over rounded surfaces of marble-like rocks that might be likened unto sheets of foaming water, whose flow suddenly had been interrupted by the wave of a magician's wand. Then, you pass glittering pools which are skirted with comparative ease, except when excessive percolation has raised their levels. When last I visited Spar Cave, the plank that used to serve as a means of access across the last miniature lake to the inmost recess had disappeared. In any case, however, the water in this pool seemed to have risen so considerably that I doubted very much whether the longest single plank procurable could have spanned it, and at the same time borne the weight of the average person.

Elfin Pools.

Sir Archibald Geikie tells us that, when he visited Spar Cave, its interior was defaced beyond belief, for its white, crystalline pillars had been smoke-blackened and broken by ruthless iconoclasts.

This is the cave that Dr. Johnson described as the greatest natural curiosity he had ever seen ; and readers of Scott will recall that in *The Lord of the Isles* the poet sings of—

> " The mermaid's alabaster grot,
>   Who bathes her limbs in sunless well
>   Deep in Strathaird's enchanted cell."

Even in Scott's time this cave, with its smooth, sloping slabs and its rough frost-work and its still

more entrancing galleries of dazzling crystallisa-
tions, had attracted tourists of the undesirable order;
and, no doubt, it was with a certain sense of propriety that Alexander MacAllister, Esq., a past
laird of Strathaird, constructed the exterior wall
and door already alluded to. Before the damage
was committed, one annotator informs us that not
only were the pools exquisitely elegant and fanciful,
but that there was scarcely a form or group on which
an active imagination might not trace figures or
grotesque ornaments.

No plank led across the last pool in Scott's time,
for in a footnote to his description he remarks that
one of the sailors who rowed him to Spar Cave
was obliged to swim across it with a torch in one
hand, in order to ascertain exactly where the cavern
terminated.

So clear and silvery and cool are the shimmering
waters of these elfin pools, I am certain that they
are the bathing-ponds of those " nymphs call'd
naiads of the wand'ring brooks " !

Photo. by A. D. Young.

"Sandy Ross's" at Inveralavaig, near the Fiddler's Pennyland. (Peina Filer.)

XI

VAGRANT THOUGHTS OF A NIGHT WANDERER

AN ECHO OF THE LAND CLEARANCES

> The scent of the soft breeze
> Where night's shadows creep;
> And doves in the pine-trees
> To coo me to sleep.

It is the hour of midnight; and once again I find myself seated comfortably in our cottage by the sea with a soft, soothing light that diffuses a welcome for a mile and more along the Bracadale road. Before me the fire is red and redolent with sweet-scented pine logs that sizzle and crackle in a wide, open hearth, for our estovers and common of turbary supply us plenteously with fuel. Nothing is more cheerful at the fall of the year than a wood-fire: it irresistibly reminds me of the nineteenth century writer who, on gazing into a glowing fire of wood in the late autumn, was convinced that the little noises he heard were the twitters and chirps of the robins and blue-birds that all spring and summer had been singing on the boughs of the tree, of which the logs once formed a part. Thus it was that, even when the trees were leafless and bird-less in winter, he had singing all the year round.

By the side of this hearth many a winter's tale

F

has been recited, when the sleet-laden gales have
been beleaguering Duirinish like a barrage that
creeps upon a walled city.

And I have only returned from one of my
nocturnal wanderings along the darkened wood-
road leading up from the sea, and terminating
within a stone-throw of Dunvegan Castle. Black,
ominous, eerie was the ancient keep to-night, as it
stood out against the last vestige of the twilight.
The gay concourse of summer is gone : the mirth
and festive laughter, that so recently rang through
its venerable halls, are over for another year.

Until the Roses Bloom Again.

But for the spirit rehearsals of its hoary past, the
corridors of the Castle of the Hospitality of the
Winecups will be almost silent and echoless, until
the roses bloom again, and until the summer-loving
bees once more are a-humming in the fuchsia bower
that in the heat of noon leans lazily against the
eastern wall of the old castle garden.   Fuchsias
seem to thrive particularly well in Skye. The
fuchsias at Armadale attracted Pennant's attention ;
and I have seldom seen more wonderful fuchsias
than are to be found in the policies of Raasay
House.

To-night the giant conifers, bearded " like Druids
of eld, indistinct in the twilight," stood stark against
the darkness as blackened ghosts ; and leafless and
lifeless seemed those tall oaks and beeches, whose
boughs only a few weeks ago were melodious with
the trilling and the twittering of countless finches
and sparrows. Swiftly has autumn tripped by in
her slippers of gold and scarlet ; and the flower-
bordered lawns, where so lately hosts of antirrhinums

and velvety-faced begonias and night-scented stocks strove zealously for the place of honour amid the floral display foretelling that the fall of the year is imminent, are seared and weathered.

To-night, too, Dunvegan Castle looked as though it had neither been inhabited nor heard the voice of even the most casual passer-by for a thousand years.

A Sleeping Village.

Silent is the shore road that meanders past the deserted pier and through the now sleeping village—nothing to break its midnight solemnity but the heavy footfall, perhaps half a mile distant, of another night wanderer who wends his way along the hard, uneven road, and the barking of a collie that follows a lantern away in the direction of Glendale, over which an ebon sky lowers mysteriously and fore-bodingly. Certain am I that at this moment my kindly friends near Loch Pooltiel are senseless in the lap of sleep after another day's toiling on their croft. It is with felicity that I reflect on a sunny, autumn morning recently spent there with a scythe in an earnest endeavour to make a beginning with a harvest that each year, I feel, is getting rather heavy for the old folks, who have sown and reaped on the hillside of Milovaig for more than half a century.

An Echo of the Clearances.

By this time, too, rest will have fallen upon the Rev. Donald MacCallum, a bard of no mean account who, having returned to his native heath in Glendale after many persecutions, has just completed and published his admirable series of Gaelic poems known to us as *Leaves in the Wind* (*Duilleagan 'sa Ghaoith*).

Was it not round his own fireside in Glendale one stormy day that Donald told me of the notorious land clearances, and of the agitation that began in 1883 to crush the power and tyranny of the landlords, who were driving forth the Highland people like cattle that are driven to the slaughter? Here, in this isolated glen, more than forty years ago John MacPherson, the " Glendale Martyr," and his companions kindled the first of the fire that ultimately brought freedom to the crofter : to-day the crofter in Glendale is his own landlord.

But you ought to hear MacCallum, himself, tell how in the end he became so persistently aggressive that at length the government of the day thought the time had arrived when he ought to be clapped in gaol. So it despatched the man-o'-war called the *Sea Horse* to Vaternish on Hallowe'en in 1884, in order to intimidate and overawe the rioting crofters, and, incidentally, to arrest Donald MacCallum. But the officers learnt that the rebel whom they sought was in Stencholl ; and on the following evening the vessel sailed round to that part of the Trotternish coast. Great was the storm that during these restless days raged around the reefy shores of north-western Skye ; and, tempest-worthy as was the *Sea Horse*, it could not effect a landing without incurring the risk of being dashed to atoms upon the treacherous rocks that fringe this wild and barren coast-line.

At this time MacCallum was residing with a friend ; and it was while he happened to be at a *ceilidh* in the school-house, in close proximity, that

a little girl came running in to inform the company
that the police had arrived from Portree in a horse-
drawn vehicle. There and then the charge was
read aloud—" inciting the lieges to violence."
Instantly MacCallum was removed to Portree, and
lodged in the gaol there, until he was liberated on
bail for a hundred pounds, which was found by
two merchants in dear old Stornoway. Meantime
his manse in Vaternish had been raided by law-
officers, who ransacked it from top to bottom in
the hope of discovering seditious literature. Having
been entirely ignorant of the Gaelic, they laid their
hands on a number of his Gaelic MSS., in the
belief that they were seditious. These MSS.
poor MacCallum never saw again. Nor did his
misfortunes come singly : the clerk of presbytery
had called a meeting in Portree at which he was
asked to answer for having made false returns—a
charge that came to naught, because it could not
be substantiated. When MacCallum returned to
Glendale after his incarceration, he found that in
his absence lawyers and other crown officials had
been sent round the crofting communities to question the people, and to enquire into the causes of
its disaffection.

But the outcome of the whole agitation was the
report in 1886 of the Royal Commission, whose
findings ultimately produced the Crofters' Act.
And, although subsequent modifications have limited
to some extent the recommendations of that Commission, the measure of freedom gained from arbi-
trary and unscrupulous landlordism far exceeded
the expectations of even the most sanguine land
reformers in Glendale at the time.

The Bards of Glendale.

While mentioning this picturesque and eventful part of Skye, it ought to be remembered that in Glendale was born Neil MacLeod, son of Donald MacLeod, who had a holding at the Pass of the Cairn (*Bealach nan Carn*), and who was widely known throughout the north as the Skye Bard. On Neil fell the mantle of Gaelic poesy by which his father had become distinguished in 1811 by the publication, at the age of twenty, of a volume of original poems in Gaelic. Though during his early manhood evictions had been rife throughout the Highlands and Islands generally, the high-handed policy of the depopulator had not spread to Neil's native strath in the days when Glendale was "*An Gleann 's an robh mi og*"—the Glen in which I was young. But the bard also sings mournfully of "the change twixt now and then."

It was when a young man that, according to *Modern Gaelic Bards*, Neil MacLeod became the proud possessor of MacKenzie's *Beauties of Gaelic Poetry*, a volume from which he was inseparable, and a volume that inspired in him the tradition of his race, and aroused within him that same desire as had prompted Burns "to sing a sang at least."

Then, among other scholars, Glendale is also the birthplace of the Rev. Neil Ross (presently of Laggan) who, besides being a piper of some standing, is one of our foremost living authorities on matters relating to Celtic literature in general, and to the Gaelic language in particular.

A Sentinel Star.

But we must return for a moment to our Hebridean night, from which we have strayed a little. The tide, that was flowing into the loch when I sat down an hour or two ago to record these somewhat desultory and vagrant remarks, is now ebbing and murmurous : the log fire, to which I introduced you earlier in the evening, is sinking low ; and its cinders are creaking in this shadowy room. Soon the chirpings and the twitterings of those little robins and blue-birds will be heard no more.

The door of our snug island-home opens before " MacLeod's Tables " ; and to it there comes a scented whisper from the loch, where everything is still and quiet save for the wailing of the sea-birds that lose themselves among the marshy places, just where the bell-heathered moors incline to touch the yonter side of the starry loch. There is no moon to-night ; but a segment of the firmament is brilliantly illumined by the twinkling of numberless stars, for *this* " night has a thousand eyes."

And through our open doorway streams the gladsome glimmer of one star, whose effulgence puts all the other stars to shame. Such was the brightness of the star that, with exceeding great joy, was beheld more than nineteen contentious centuries ago by those who journeyed toward Bethlehem with their gold and frankincense and myrrh.

XII

AN ISLAND SUNSET

OLD-WORLD STONES IN THE HEBRIDES

The day is done; and far beneath the hill
The sun sifts down, and all the world is still :

IT was while spending a few days at the house of
Ruairaidh MacPharlain and his canty *cailleach* at
Milovaig, in Glendale, that I took to the hill early
one evening, accompanied by a lithe collie that I
felt confident would be able to lead me home, were
I to lose my bearings in the darkness that directly
would be upon us. My real object in setting out
so late was to inspect about the bewitching hour
what is known locally as Clach na Banachaig, or
the Dairymaids' Stone. Hereon in bygone days
the dairymaids were in the habit of sprinkling a
drop or two of warm milk when milking their
cows on the moor, in order to scare away evil
spirits and those who were regarded as having been
dexterous in the " Black Art." You will recall
that during his visit to Trodday Dr. Johnson was
acquainted with a very similar custom : there he
was informed by the minister, who actually abolished
the practice, of the ancient rule of reserving every
Saturday a quantity of milk for " Greogach," who
was described to him as being the Old Man with
the Long Beard. Pennant also came in contact
with this custom because he speaks of gruagach-

88

Photo. by R. C. MacLeod of MacLeod.

Corridor in Rory Mor's Wing.

stones, on which were poured libations of milk on Sunday for the preservation of the cattle during the ensuing week—a custom from which, according to him, Apollo may have derived the epithet, Galaxius. At Skeabost is a typical gruagach-stone that within living memory was used to protect cows against witchcraft.

Duntulm also could boast a mischievous *gruagach* of whom I hope to tell you something at another time.

On this particular evening, however, I failed to discover Clach na Banachaig ; and for two reasons. Firstly, my arrival at Milovaig had been unavoidably delayed, since a passenger on our boat from Dunvegan Castle was anxious to see the celebrated Manners Stone near Galtrigil and the MacCrimmons' piping-ground at Boreraig, both in close proximity to Loch Dunvegan. The result was that I was borne too far down the loch, and had to retrace my steps through the township of Husabost and almost as far south as Colbost to regain the road that, climbing into a narrow saddle in the hills, meanders past Fasach and eventually conveys you across an old wooden *drochaid* to Glendale proper.

MacLeod's Offer to Dr. Johnson.

At first sight the name of the Manners Stone is a little misleading. On it, the old folks of Glendale will tell you, the sheriff or judge sat and administered the law ; and on approaching this seat of jurisdiction all suitors and accused persons were required to pay their respects by making a bow or curtsy.

From Galtrigil on a clear day one gets a

magnificent prospect of Isay, an island situated in
Loch Dunvegan and midway between Duirinish and
Vaternish. This is the Isle MacLeod of MacLeod
offered to Dr. Johnson on the explicit understanding
that the latter resided on it for three months of
the year, nay, for one month. Johnson spoke at
length on how he would erect a house on Isay,
plant round it, defend it with artillery, and sally
forth to capture the Isle of Muck. But journalism
in Fleet Street held for him greater attractions than
the honour of becoming a Highland laird ; and so
this island-dream never materialised.

Was it not on Isay, by the way, that in 1596
Ruairaidh MacAilein MacLeod despatched his
kinsman, Raasay, together with a band of the
latter's followers ?

How a Dispute Was Settled.

And, as I write, there comes to my mind one
other historical reminiscence connected with Galtrigil that is illustrative of the somewhat rude and
ready legal system of the period to which it belongs.
A cow had fallen over a cliff, and into a boat : the
boat was destroyed, and the cow was killed. The
owner of the cow sued the owner of the boat for
damages on the grounds that, had his boat not
been where it was, the cow would have been
uninjured : the owner of the boat made a counter-
claim in respect of his boat. Now MacLeod of
Dunvegan was asked to adjudicate the dispute ;
but the poor Chief found it no easy matter to
determine on whom the responsibility should have
been placed. Finally, it was agreed that they would
seek the advice of a wise man in the neighbourhood. This they did ; and the wise man found a

simple way out of the quandary by deciding that MacLeod was responsible to both litigants, since the cow could not have fallen into the boat had his cliff not been there. And the chronicler records : " MacLeod good-humouredly assented ; and so the dispute was settled."

THE GLORY OF THE SUNSET.

My other excuse for having failed to discover the Dairymaids' Stone was that the inexplicable tendency to move westward at eventide came creeping over me. To explain this impulse I have tried aforetime, but without success. Sure enough, I reached the sheep-fanks that lay sheltered in a purple corrie among the hills, and at which I was advised by my friend, Ruairaidh, to re-adjust my bearings ; but in the glory of the sunset I completely forgot my instructions for the latter part of this journey, and found myself an hour or two later ascending the grassy surface of Vaterstein Head, a wild and precipitous promontory that rises wellnigh a thousand feet above the sea. Within half a mile of this headland, and on the opposite side of Moonen Bay, is Neist Point, the westernmost part of the Isle of Skye. There a lighthouse sends forth its message at the hour of sundown.

In my eagerness to gain the summit of this huge, shelving promontory I observed myself to be rising just a little faster than the sun was setting ; and never in all my life have I witnessed a more mystical and magical scene than that which I viewed from Vaterstein on this occasion.

It was with a sense of fear and awe that I crawled to the very edge of this " nightmare of nature," and looked down a thousand feet to the narrow margin of detritus that lay between the base of the rocks and the line to which the tide had ebbed. What a wondrous silence was there !—nothing but the occasional bleating of a solitary sheep that, un-numbered fathoms below me, had lost its way, and that at this stupendous height was barely visible to the naked eye.

The Gleaming Fords of Uist.

Well repaid was I for the energy expended in reaching the seamost finger of this dizzy precipice ; and, since mere words can never adequately portray the Hebridean sunset I beheld therefrom, you must endeavour as best you can to visualise it for yourself. The Outer Isles, from Barra Head to the north of Harris, were delineated against a sun-gold back-ground in the deepest purples and blues. How Titian would have enjoyed this colouring ! Facing me lay North Uist, as I afterwards ascertained when the lighthouse on the Weaver's Point at the northern entrance to Loch Maddy commenced to flash. A little further south lay Benbecula ; and the sands of the great Fords, between four and five leagues away, were sparkling and gleaming in the glow of the evening. I am almost certain that, as I lay watching them, many wayfarers among the Outer Hebrides were journeying hither and thither before the incoming of the tide, because these Fords are the established routes of communication between North Uist and South Uist when the tides are suitable.

Toward the south, Hecla's peak towered proudly above all the other mountains ; and, down in the direction of Loch Bracadale, whose harbour is deep "and unspeakably secure," Canna and Rum stood in a motionless sea, and against a windless sky. In the south-south-east lay Duthaich na Mogan— the Country of the Footless Stocking, as the territory of the MacLeods is sometimes called ; and far behind Healaval Mor and Healaval Beag (" Mac-Leod's Tables ") the jagged spires of the Coolian, in their anxiety to partake of the last of the sunset, stood erect in purple robes before the onset of night, and with a solemnity that bespoke Eternity.

In the Airt of Tir-nan-Og.

Long did I linger at Vaterstein to watch the solan geese that flew restlessly around Dunvegan Head and sought in the pink, sea-wracked waters of Loch Pooltiel their evening feast of saithe. But too soon the northern mists were beginning to hide from mortal eyes the gigantic mountains of Harris. And in the afterglow naught remained of that magic sunset but the thinnest strip of red and orange which tinged the Atlantic far, far beyond the geese-haunted plains of the Uists and the low-lying islands that stud the Fords on either side of Benbecula, and are dotted haphazardly about the treacherous Sound of Harris like jewels of gold and emerald.

No wind ruffled the face of the Hebridean sea that moved imperceptibly before me and hundreds of feet below me ; and ere long the tiny puffer, that an hour or two previously had been steaming southward through the Little Minch and towards Barra, was completely lost in the haze that so frequently accompanies our Hebridean twilights. Loath, indeed, was I to depart when a little later on I found myself engirdled on three sides by the flashes from the innumerable lighthouses that whispered a word of warning and cheer to the mariners and fishermen who must needs traverse our wild and dangerous seas in the night-time ; and profoundly did I regret that my ignorance of the characters of these lights precluded me from fixing their geographical positions with any degree of accuracy.

However, I was able to recognise the flash of Huisinish, because earlier in the evening I had noticed the exact location of Hecla. And I know that the light which thrust itself through the darkness that stretched beyond the line of the Outer Isles came from lonely Monach—one of the group of rocky islets away out in the Atlantic, and in the airt of *Tir-nan-Og*, the land where the youthful never grow old and where, they say, there is no dark !

But, for all I knew, those flashes might have been the faery night-lights lit each evening at the setting of the sun, that our Hebrides may be guarded through the magic hours of darkness !

XIII

AN ISLAND FAERYLAND

MEMORIES OF THE LITTLE FOLKS

" Up the airy mountains, down the rushy glen,
　We dare not go a-hunting for fear of little men : "

SHOULD you traverse the part of Skye that stretches
between the Dairymaids' Stone and the point at
which the overflow of Loch Mor Vaterstein spills
in a waterfall upon the shingling shore of Moonen
Bay, you pass through a veritable faeryland. I
would never have become acquainted with this elfin
region had it not been for the aforesaid Ruairaidh
MacPharlain who recently accompanied me on an
expedition there, and who, among other things,
told me of the great flocks of wild swans that
haunt the reedy fringes of Loch Vaterstein in
winter-time.

Near the edge of this loch, and on what is known
locally as Bruthach an Fhiona, the Wine-Brae, is the
once-celebrated Tobar an Fhiona, the Well of Wine ;
but to-day brackens and rabbits are more plentiful
on this hillside than wine.

The water of Tobar an Fhiona was recom-
mended (as was the water of Tobar Iaruinn, the
Iron Well, at Sgaladal in Glendale) by Fearchar
Lighiche, Farquhar the Physician, who was a renowned herbalist of the Beaton family. Of Farquhar
and of the Beatons of Skye—those much misunder-

stood practitioners of the Northern Hebrides—I would like to tell you something later on.

THE FAERIES' BYRE.

Beyond the Well of Wine is another brae called Bruach na Sithean—the Brae of the Faeries ; and at the base of this brae is an old, ruined byre called Bathach na Sithean, the Faeries' Byre. At one time this byre must have been a place of considerable size. It is reached by following toward the Atlantic the Fisherman's Path that passes along the south side of Loch Mor Vaterstein. Close at hand are the divot-hidden ruins of what probably was at one time the dwelling-place of the tacksman of Vaterstein.

Once there lived in the vicinity of the Faeries' Brae an aged woman whose only daughter had been ailing for some time. At length the daughter died ; and all alone with the corpse in this dark, eerie place was the old woman left. If you should visit this uncanny spot on a dark night, you will be able to judge for yourself how lonely and solitary the old mother must have felt during the long nights when lamps were certainly unknown, and when only the meagrest artificial light could be produced. Well, one night as she sat mourning her loss—so the story goes—who should enter her sorrowful home but a man whom she knew not. And he seated himself beside her ; and whenever the fire would be getting low, he would strike it with his magic stick and say, " *O chaorain, dean solus !* O little peat, make a light ! " As you will understand, these were the times when the folks of Skye, and, indeed, of the Hebrides generally, believed in the existence of the *each-uisge*, or

Photo. by M. A. MacFarlane.

Where the "Skye Bard" was born—Glendale.

G

water-horse, a strange creature that had the power of assuming human form whenever the occasion required. And the people of Vaterstein was convinced it was the *each-uisge* that all night long had sat with the lonely and bereaved widow, and vanished with the first flush of day.

Later on I hope to tell you one or two more stories about the mysterious behaviour of the water-horse.

Perhaps, in their day the old woman and her daughter were the *ban-bhuachaillean* or herdswomen of the tacksman of Vaterstein—who knows ?

THE PASS OF THE DEER.

Although the sun was bright when last I visited this part of Vaterstein, the wind was high and howling ; and before it the waves on the loch rolled with a fury that befitted a storm on the open sea : it was an ideal drying day for the stooks and uncut corn that had been laid low by the torrential rains of the previous night. Down the steep slopes of the Bioda Mor the fragments of withered bracken fronds were being carried like clouds of russet-brown feathers. Still, I did notice a weasel poke his head out of a hole among the confused mass of tumbled stones that marks the site of the long-since deserted Faeries' Byre, to have a squint at the passer-by. The visibility was extraordinarily good ; and in the offing one could easily discern Cadha nam Fiadh, The Deers' Pass, and Cadha nam Ba, the Cows' Pass. The former pass, as one might imagine, is particularly steep and dangerous, and is seldom, if ever, scaled by the feet of men. The Cows' Pass, on the other hand, presents no obstacle to the hill-wanderer who is moderately energetic. It leads over in the direction of *Clach na Banachaig*, the Milkmaids' Stone, an object of old-world interest to which I have had occasion to allude once or twice already.

In this neighbourhood there is another celebrated stone which in Gaelic is designated *Clach na Gruagach*, meaning the Brownie's Stone.

CAVE OF THE FAERIES.

Now we come to Uamh na Sithean, the Faeries' Cave. It is to be sought immediately under the waterfall that tumbles into the part of Moonen Bay known to the Islesfolk as Camus nan Sithean, the Faeries' Bay. At high tide it is almost impossible to gain access to this cave ; and, on the other hand, should the level of the water in Loch Mor Vaterstein be raised owing to heavy rains, the waterfall concealing the entrance to the cave makes ingoing rather unpleasant. Often, however, when the wind is blowing in from the sea, an occasional gust drives the water past in spindrift, thus giving an opportunity of entering in comfort. The only disadvantage arises when sometimes you are imprisoned within until another gust permits of your getting out with equal convenience.

Within twenty yards of the Faeries' Cave there is another fine cave whose legend, I fear, has been lost. The kindly folks with whom I came in contact while residing at Milovaig refer to the former cave as *Uamh an Oir* ; and they solemnly declare that it was into *this* " Cave of Gold," and not into the cave of the same name at Harlosh, that the unreturning piper went. But the cave in Camus nan Sithean appears to be better adapted for elves than for pipers !

There was once a mill at the outlet of Loch Mor Vaterstein ; but it has disappeared long since. Hither, I have no doubt, the faeries were accustomed to convey their grain, when they were the rulers of this part of Skye. To-day scarcely a trace of this mill is to be found : even its old-time grindstones have been removed, or perchance buried among the spreading mosses and grasses of the centuries.

FAERY LORE IN SKYE.

We need not herein enter into the vexed question of faery-lore except so far as to mention that Skye is remarkably rich in allusions to these little folks. Many are the hillocks (usually called *Sithein* too) throughout the Isle of the Mist that the inhabitants associate with the faeries. Not far from Portree such a hillock is called *Sithean a' Bhealaich Chumhaig*, the Hillock of the Narrow Pass. There the female faeries are dressed in livid green ; while the *daoine beaga ruadh*, the little red men, are clad in crotal-dyed raiment and wear little blue bonnets. Near Tarskavaig there is a knoll known as *Sithean Beag agus Mor*, the Little and the Big Faery Hillock ; and, then, every one who knows Skye is more or less familiar with the *sithean* not far from Broadford.

At one time the faeries are supposed to have taken possession of an old fort on the way to Carbost called Dun Borve. Long had the rightful owner endeavoured to get rid of them, but little success attended his efforts. At last he raised the false alarm that the Dun was ablaze, whereupon the faeries skedaddled with all speed, and never troubled him again. But this story is told also of a *dun* near the head of Loch Beag, in Bracadale : in the latter case, however, the wee folks sallied forth in the moonlight and celebrated their eviction by dancing themselves dry.

There is an abundance of faery-lore in Sleat. One has merely to glance at some of the place-names on a large map of that region to be assured of this.

And, then, elsewhere in this volume I have commented on the faeries at Duntulm, who, if we are to believe the story that the Trotternish witch gave to the factor, drove away his horse to a secret hollow in the hills. In Lord Archibald Campbell's *Waifs and Strays of Celtic Tradition* we read that on this occasion the host of the Little Folks of the Hill (*muinntir nan cnoc*) numbered five thousand, and that not one of them was larger than a bottle. I never go to Duntulm without glancing around me on the chance of seeing this faery army reconnoitring among the hills.

STRAINS OF FAERY MUSIC.

In spite of the fact that the sithean-dwellers are not likely to venture out on such a cold, wet night as this, I fear that with Forbes I ought to refrain from dilating further on the perplexing subject of faeries and elves. But I must tell you that, when at Oskaig, in Raasay, the other day, I was chatting with an old woman who declared that in her childhood she saw hundreds of faeries and gruagachs and brownies ; and " they all had white shirts, just like the gentry."

And only last summer a man and his wife, living in Strath, threeped to me that on several occasions they had noticed faeries scurrying around a mound near Glasnacille, and actually had listened to the strains of faery music to which these sprightly creatures danced. Such music is also said to issue on moonlit nights from a turf-concealed heap of stones at Flodigarry.

near Glenachulie, and actually had listened to the
strains of faery music to which these sprightly
creatures danced. Such music is also said to issue
on moonlit nights from a turf-concealed heap of
stones at Flodigarry.

XIV

BRACADALE AND ITS FOLKLORE

AN OLD-TIME KIDNAPPING STORY

WEIRD TALES OF GRUAGACHS AND WATER-HORSES

An intensely interesting and romantic district is
Bracadale. I always think that in some ways it is
richer in legend and in folklore than almost any
other parish in the Highlands. Exactly why this
should be the case I have no conception, because,
after all, it was no more intimately connected with
the general trend of historical events than any other
part of the Isle of Skye. Some of the tales I am
about to tell you have been told and retold round
the glimmer of the peat-fire ; and, doubtless, they
have been added to from time to time by the
happy worthies in the whisky-houses, of which last
century there were five in Bracadale " to the mani-
fest injury of the temporal interests of the people,
and the progressive and sure destruction of their
morals." Carbost with its far-famed Talisker distillery is in Bracadale, by the way ; and the same
annotator as is quoted above makes the observation
that the erection of this distillery was " one of the
greatest curses which, in the ordinary course of
Providence, could befall it (Bracadale) or any other
place."

KIDNAPPED BY SPANISH PIRATES.

There was a time when the mossy slopes impinging upon the shore near Ullinish and opposite Wiay were richly garlanded with scented flowers in spring. (I have no doubt that spring flowers still bloom there.) Now, in the days when Spanish pirates used to frequent the coasts of the Hebrides, they sometimes moored their galleons in Loch Bracadale in misty weather, and replenished their water-supply from a never-failing well in this locality. And it was when in Ullinish on such an errand that some heartless Spaniards resolved to seize a young and beautiful Bracadale girl named Gormul, whom they found gathering primroses one hazy spring morning. So mirky was the morning, indeed, that no one had observed the pirates entering the Loch. Well, they kidnapped Gormul and conveyed her to their vessel, where she found many other children in a plight similar to her own. To the grief and distress of her kindred she never returned to her home, though for several days and nights in succession the whole of Bracadale was traversed in quest of her. And it was only after an exhaustive search a shepherd suddenly recollected that one day, while he happened to be gazing seaward from an eminence in the Cuchullins, his eyes had lit upon a strange, foreign sailing-vessel moving in a northerly direction. This vessel, he conjectured, might have abducted Gormul.

Be it noted that during the seventeenth and eighteenth centuries the Islanders lived in holy dread of Spanish pirates, who systematically reduced many Hebridean creeks and kyles and fiords to the status of a veritable despoiling ground for lawless sea-rievers.

But the Spaniards were no more to be feared than were the resolute and redoubtable pirates who lived in state and by their wits on other Hebridean islands, and who, at the same time, were of their very own stock. It was only natural, however, that the people would resent in a more marked degree the encroachments of piratical bands consisting of men who neither knew their customs nor spoke their language. Furthermore, these foreign sea-robbers were in a position to commit outrages against, and inflict penalties upon, a helpless and defenceless people with ease and composure, because they realised that the latter had no effectual means of retaliation. Apropos of this, it is well recognised that in the veins of many a Western Islander there flows a decided admixture of Spanish blood—an admixture rendered possible through trading, through persistent piracy, and through the wreck on the western coast of Scotland of the Armada.

GORMUL'S WHEREABOUTS REVEALED.

Years and years and more years passed ; but never a word was heard of the *caileag* who so mysteriously had disappeared from her home in Bracadale : along with the other unfortunate victims, whom she found on the vessel to which she had been led captive, she was conveyed to a Spanish island in the West Indies. And you may rightly be wondering how even this piece of intelligence was ascertained.

It was not until after many years' absence at sea, when a sailor, Alan MacAskill to name (there are many MacAskills in this part of Skye to this day), came home to his native hamlet in Bracadale brimful of strange and thrilling stories of his ad-

Photo. by A. MacFarlane.

His Morning Sip—at Milovaig.

ventures in diverse parts of the world, that the whereabouts of Gormul were revealed. One wintry evening, and at a gathering round the peat-fire in the house of his father, Alan surprised his listeners by informing them that the girl who, it was thought, had been kidnapped at Ullinish while plucking primroses, was not dead but on the contrary was very much alive, and that she was the happy and contented wife of a potentate on one of the western, island possessions of Spain.

SHIPWRECKED ON THE WEST INDIES.

How did the sailor, Alan MacAskill, discover this? you may enquire. He happened to be sailing on an English vessel that in a cyclone was totally wrecked on one of the islands of the Antilles. On this island the shipless and luckless crew was treated with unqualified kindness by the native population. One day Alan and his seafaring companions were invited to the chateau of the Spanish nobleman who ruled the island : so hospitably received were they, and so greatly impressed by the munificence and splendour of his habitation, that their eyes thirsted to behold the lady of the house, of whose delightful and generous character they had oft-times heard tell from other Scottish mariners who in former times had risked a call at this sea-plunderers' haven. They had even heard it said that she was a native of Scotland, and had been bought by the nobleman of this Spanish settlement from the captain of a pirate galleon.

Much did Alan MacAskill wish to see her. Though she did not appear during the night that the shipwrecked sailors were entertained, he actually heard in an adjoining apartment that was open to the southern skies the low voice of a woman, who almost inaudibly murmured entreaties in a language certainly not understood by the West Indians. So, one evening, about vesper-time, he stole into the darkness of the castle grounds and concealed himself within listening distance of a mournful monologue that whispered among the lambent palm groves when the short-lived summer night was calm and starlit, and when the vociferous birds were silent in the lemoned bowers. And what did he hear but a Gaelic prayer with an unforgotten burden—a remembrance for MacLeod's shieling on Ben Duagraich in Bracadale, a sigh for unseen faces, and a secret sob for a breath of the hills of home.

GORMUL MEETS HER PLAYMATE.

Eventually, it came to the ears of the pray-er that among the shipwrecked crew there was a sailor who hailed from somewhere in Scotland, and who spoke a tongue unintelligible to his seafaring companions. So she sent for him one day ; and on seeing him she burst into ecstasies of joy, for who was he but Alan MacAskill, her playmate in tender years. And Gormul told Alan of how she and other young girls from the Outer Isles had been taken aboard a pirate vessel, and how she had been sold to the Spanish chief who was now her husband, and who ruled this West Indian island. And Alan was able to tell Gormul of her folks who, in expectation, still lived by the shores of Bracadale.

As the wife of a Spanish nobleman Gormul was a person of some standing in the West Indies : she was what we would term a *bean-tighearna*—a lady of rank ; and, although having lived in an

environment that at one time she must have felt
unpleasantly strange, she filled her place admirably.
Withal, Gormul was satisfied with her foreign surroundings and felt that, much as she longed to
visit her native Isle again, she could not forsake
her duties. In any case, of course, a voyage from
the Indies to Skye was a very formidable one in
those times. Nevertheless, she did not forget her
Bracadale associations ; and hereafter she often
sent home gifts that were precious in the sight of
poor folks dwelling in a lonely Highland hamlet
in the wind-swept Isle of Skye.

You can imagine how thrilled Bracadale was
when, in process of time, Alan MacAskill returned to the place of his childhood and told of
his strange discovery on the other side of the
Atlantic.

And in the West Indies Gormul died a Spanish
subject.

THE EVIL GRUAGACH.

While mentioning the name of MacAskill I am
reminded that in Bracadale there is a valley called
Glen MacAskill (so named, it is thought, after
Ketil, who is alleged to have been a Norse prince,
and to have become King of the Hebrides about
the beginning of the tenth century), with which is
connected a story of the *gruagach*, or long-haired
one. On a time there lived at a shieling in this
glen a gentle mother and a harsh daughter. But
the glen was also the abode of a *gruagach* who
appeared in the form of a beautiful young man,
whose bosom was as snow, whose long, fair tresses
fell over his shoulders, and who carried in his hand
a magic rod. Now, the *gruagach* loved the cattle of

Glen MacAskill ; and, if any one should chance to be unkind to a cow, he was not slow to demonstrate his resentment merely by touching the offender with his rod. One evening, while the cattle were being impounded in the fold at the shieling about milking-time, a particular cow could not be induced to enter the byre. The young daughter of the shieling became so impatient at length that she used " rough words " to the animal, thereby confusing it more than ever. The cow was seeing what the maiden had not the power to see, namely, the benign *gruagach* who loved all cattle. In the end the *gruagach* touched the maiden with his rod ; and instantly she dropped dead.

That night the old and gentle woman at the shieling in Glen MacAskill was lamenting the loss of her daughter ; but she was not alone in her sorrow, for the *gruagach* thoughtfully had remained beside her until dawn.

It was the avowed belief in the power of the *gruagach* that made the Islanders careful not to assault nor utter imprecations against their cows, from whom they derived one of their chiefest means of sustenance. And it is through the widely diffused belief that the cattle are charmed and blessed, and are occasionally visited by the invisible being known in Celtic lore as the *gruagach*, that to this day many Hebridean dairymaids are meticulously particular about their cows.

Not so long ago an old Skye maid, on learning that a Mull lady was requiring a dairymaid to look after her cows on that Island, exclaimed : " If I were young, nothing would please me more than to tend the blessed cattle ! "

Away in the Isle of Vallay, in North Uist, a spot is still pointed out to the stranger where centuries ago a woman, who was found guilty of having been in the habit of stealing milk from cows that grazed on the machar at night-time, was buried alive—so heinous a crime was it deemed in olden days to interfere with cows and their milk. In *Behold the Hebrides !* I noted one or two similar cases where witches were accused of taking the substance out of the milk of a neighbour's cow, and of doing the cows injury in other ways.

THE DREADED WATER-HORSE.

In common with other parts of the Highlands, Bracadale boasted at least one *each-uisge*, or water-horse. On one occasion the maidens who were in attendance at an old-time shieling up on the slopes of Beinn a' Sgath, the Shadowy Hill situated not far from Loch Snizort Beag, and in Trotternish, had rather an uncomfortable experience. At night-fall they had lain down to rest on their big bed of heather and bracken (*leaba mhor na h-airidh* is the name given to the shieling bed) ; and, just as they were falling asleep in their innocence, they heard a voice without saying—" *Leigibh an stigh mi, a chloinn gaolach !* Let me in, you beloved children !" And the maid who arose to answer the stranger at the door was asked by a feeble and worn cratur—" *C'aite an cadail cailleachag an nochd ?* Where will sleep a little old woman to-night ?"

" She will rest at the feet of the maidens," replied the shieling lassie who had let her in.

" Oh, but the beast of the feet will take hold of me !" answered the frail woman. And, when she was offered a place behind the maidens, she replied that she was equally terrified of the beast that haunted the back of the bed.

As there remained no alternative, the old cratur was given a place in the centre of the *leaba mhor* (big bed) ; and before long the heavy sleep was on all its weary occupants.

But the maid nearest the door of the shieling bothy was conscious that the frail stranger-woman was suspiciously restless and slept very spasmodically. Soon she felt the old woman crawling towards her ; and on turning round she observed that she had her teeth in the arm of the maiden who lay next to her.

What was the old woman but an *each-uisge* or water-horse in disguise !

Up the observant maid arose and fled as quickly as her legs could carry her. But she was pursued by this ugly creature, who with a terrific shriek had resumed his own form again. Eventually, they came to a little stream that to this day runs between Totarder and Balgowan, and in the locality of Bracadale church. Over the stream leapt the terror-stricken maiden just as the cock began to crow in Balgowan, the Smith's Hamlet.

Now, the cock's crowing meant the saving of the girl's life, since it acted as a spell on the enraged water-horse, who thus was hindered from crossing the little brook. In this way the maiden escaped to her home ; but the chagrined *each-uisge* cried after her—" *Duilich e, duilich e, alltan !* Sad it is, sad it is, streamlet !"

And to this day the little stream that flows by the church of Bracadale goes by the name of the *Alltan Duilich*, or Difficult Streamlet.

Betrayed by Strands of Seaweed.

A not altogether dissimilar tale is told about a Lewis shieling, to the *bothan* or hut of which hirpled a beautiful young woman who complained of ennui. But the shieling maids became suspicious of her when it was noticed that the hair of the alms-seeker was full of sand and gravel and dried strands of seaweed. They concluded, therefore, that in reality she was an *each-uisge*.

Traces of seaweed in the hair frequently led to the identification of the water-horse. John Bellenden, the esteemed Archbishop of Moray, had more than a mere nodding acquaintance with the water-horse ; and from Barry's *History of the Orkney Islands* (1805) we learn that, besides having the likeness of a young horse, this weird creature is often " covered all over with seaweed."

The Hebridean water-horse commonly came to unsuspecting doors far away on the heath, and gained admittance by feigning weariness and fatigue. Under such pretence did a water-horse in Eigg commit a number of dastardly outrages.

Corrie of the Hobgoblins.

The Isle of Skye harbours many water-horses and kindred supernatural monsters. Loch Fada, a blue lochan on the way to the Old Man of Storr, is regarded as being the abode both of a water-horse and of a water-bull. Again, in the Cuchullins there is a deep hollow known as Coire nan Uruisg because it is believed to be haunted by satyrical monsters and hobgoblins called *uruisgs* and *glaisrigs*. Incidentally, there is another Coire nan Uruisg in the region of Loch Katrine.

Elsewhere in this volume I have recited how,

according to Boswell, a native of Raasay ensnared the water-horse that terrorised those who passed by Dun Caan. Then, near Castle Maol is Loch na Beiste, the Loch of the Beast, where once upon a time such a fierce monster was captured and slain. This locality, by the by, is regarded by some as having been the actual spot where, in the Fingalian chase, Diarmad slew the poison-boar. The last-mentioned loch is in Strath, as is also Loch Sgubaidh, which possesses yet another water-horse tradition.

And, finally, within a few yards of the road that runs between Knock and Isle Oronsay, in Sleat, and not far from where the road to Ord branches off at right angles, there is a sheet of water called Loch nan Dubhrachan. As recently as 1870 this Loch was searched systematically to lay the monstrous water-ghost concerning which rumours had been so persistent. But the " beast " evaded capture. When the Loch was being dragged, however, the net became entangled with an obstacle. So terrified were the onlookers by this temporary interruption in the operations that they beat a hasty retreat to their homes, fearing that the obstacle might turn out to be the dreaded water-horse.

The district round Knock Castle (*Caisteal Chamuis*) is saturated with superstitions about a green-attired *glaisrig* or hobgoblin, and about a *gruagach* or long-haired damsel with daemonic propensities.

The Bleeding Bone.

Not unlike the shieling tale that concluded so fortuitously at the Alltan Duilich, or Difficult Streamlet, is a story connected with Meadale, a hirsel just above the sinuous fiord of Harport, in

Photo. by M. A. MacFarlane.

Loch Pooltiel with Dunvegan Head towering a thousand feet, on the right.
(Note the "cairidh" in the foreground.)

Loch Bracadale. One autumn night, when the shepherd and his wife were about to be falling asleep, there was heard a tirling at the pin of their cot on the hillside of Meadale. Who could it be at the door at such an hour of the night, they wondered. The goodman immediately went to the door to find at it an old, bent, decrepit *bodachan*—a little, old man—who requested nothing but to be permitted to lie by the warmth of the peat-fire, that in those times smouldered away in the middle of the floor and was ventilated by a hole in the roof directly above it. Readily did the shepherd and his wife give their consent ; and, having provided the nightfarer with warm wrappage and satisfied an aching void from the bounteousness of their larder (if at any time you are cold and hungry and storm-distressed on a Highland moor, you need have no qualms about accepting hospitality at the nearest shepherd's house), they again retired for the night. Off they dozed ; but the *bodachan* was not shutting an eye. Several times during the night he disturbed his host to complain not of cold or of physical pain of any kind, as one might have expected, but of the *snigh-dubh*, or black raindrops that, he declared, were oozing through the turfen roof of the dwelling.

" It 's a beautiful, starry night that 's in it, and it cannot be the *snigh-dubh* that 's dropping on you," observed the shepherd.

When daylight came, and it was discovered that instead of the *snigh-dubh* it was blood that had been falling on him, the unfortunate old man deponed to having been under punishment for an evil deed that long ago he had committed : he confessed to having killed in his adolescence a man whom he buried in a hollow close to where the shepherd's hirsel at Meadale stood. And it was conjectured that among the rafters there was a dripping bone of the murdered man, it accidentally having found its way there in a divot that, when the shepherd's house at Meadale was being erected, had been taken from the very spot where the dead man's body lay concealed.

* * * * * *

From a general collation of the tales that are told of the water-horse, he would seem to be a creature with a decided dualism in his nature : his disposition is either amatory and benign or overwhelmingly dictatorial and aggressive.

Many folklorists are prone to the belief that from the very rare appearance of the walrus along our coasts may have originated the conception of the *each-uisge* or water-horse. But, then, how are we to explain the fact that several fresh-water lochs, in many cases considerably removed from the sea, also have a water-horse tradition ?

XV

TIL : THE WARRIOR-PRINCE FROM LOCHLANN

HIS STRANGE FORETELLINGS

THAT the famous Brahan Seer named Coinneach Odhar had a traditional prototype is more than mere fancy, for in Uist and in Skye there is current a legend that tells of the birth of an earlier Coinneach Odhar, a personality who possessed in an extraordinarily marked degree the gift of prophecy. It is quite feasible to predicate that Kenneth Mac-Kenzie, the Brahan Seer, was called after a traditional character whom he resembled in appearance, and in common with whom he possessed certain well-defined soothsaying faculties. Of course, the Coinneach Odhar with whom we are more familiar was a Lewisman : the traditional Coinneach Odhar, on the other hand, was a native of South Uist, although, as in the case of many personages illustrious in ancient history, several localities claim to have been his birthplace.

Interestingly enough, however, the story I am about to relate was collected originally from an Uist sailor, who heard it in his childhood.

THE SPIRIT HOSTS.

It was toward the evening of an autumn day in the years unmeasured by dates that some women were gathered together to discuss the joyous festival, which on the morrow was to be observed by all the countryside. And sad, sad were two young women that it was their lot to tend the cattle while their neighbours were to be rejoicing. But there came to their solace a kind, elderly woman who, in order that they might partake of the latter part of the festivities, willingly offered to take their place during the following night.

Gratefully did the maidens accept her thoughtful proposal ; and at falling light they hied away to adorn themselves for the feast, while the old woman repaired to the moor, where the cattle in the meantime had been left to roam about at will. As was the usual custom in those far-off times, she kindled in a hollow on the moor a large fire that, at varying intervals throughout the night, was enfuelled in order to scare away evil spirits and the monstrous creatures that long were dreaded by those endowed with supernatural insight. And with her distaff and spindle she seated herself on the outskirts of a cemetery that we may surmise was a pagan and not a Christian one. (Let us assume, at any rate, that at the moment we are dealing with pre-Christian times.)

About midnight the earth about the old woman began to heave heavily ; and the graves in the pagan burying-ground were opened ; and groups of weird, spirit-like creatures hurried hither and thither in a state of noiseless confusion, and then vanished in a northerly direction. From a huge grave immediately in front of her there arose a tall, warrior figure that paused for a brief moment, and then did likewise.

TIL RETURNS TO HIS GRAVE.

Hours later the warrior returned ; but in the interval the old woman had cast her distaff across the grave in the hope that it would prevent his re-entering it, until he had given an account of himself.

" And wilt thou not remove thy distaff that I may return to earth ? " asked the warrior figure of the old woman, whom he found by his grave when he came back from his mysterious journey.

" If thou wilt answer me three questions, I will do so," replied the old woman, who by this time had forgotten all about her wandering cattle.

And the first question she put to him was— " Where hast thou been ? " To this he answered that on each Hallowe'en he and all his countrymen, wheresoever buried, had the privilege of returning for an hour or two to Lochlann, as Norway is called in our ancient language.

" Who art thou, and what is thy name ? " she then asked him.

" My name was Til. I was a son of the King of Norway ; but off the coast of Skye my warriors and I were drowned in a storm. My body was washed ashore here ; and I was interred in the grave to which I now seek to return."

And to this day the place is called Pooltiel.

THE ELDER TREE AT POOLTIEL.

Now, the folks of Glendale believe that the body of Til, *Mac Righ Lochlainn* (Til, Son of the King of Norway), came ashore at a point near the head of Loch Pooltiel, and that ultimately his remains were committed to earth in their burying-ground of Cille Chomgain, the Cell of Saint Comgan (*cf.* Colvin). Indeed, Til, *Mac Righ Lochlainn*, is regarded as having been the very first person buried in the churchyard of Saint Comgan.

And there's an elder-tree of unknown antiquity in that burying-ground, under which Til is supposed to lie ; and it is still taboo for any one to injure that tree in any way.

Some years ago it was accidentally damaged while a grave was being dug ; and greatly perturbed thereby were the folks of Glendale. Then, a crofter living nearby, whose patience was sorely tried by sheep nibbling continually at his stack of corn, cut a few branches off the elder-tree, and arranged them round the lower part of his stack. And a brother of the famous Gaelic bard, Neil MacLeod, who was a native of Glendale, heard of this incident in Boston, where at the time he was living ; and so he composed some humorous verses to com-memorate the occasion on which the sacred elder-tree was damaged.

It is supposed that before the drowning of Til, the Norse warrior-prince, Loch Pooltiel was termed simply *Loch a' Chuain*, the Loch of the Ocean. The name, "Lochlannach," that to this day is applied to a crag in the vicinity of Loch Pooltiel, also is reminiscent of this traditional connection between Glendale and Norway.

Til Foretells the Birth of a Son.

And the third and last question that the old woman asked the warrior vision was what would be her fate in days to come. And Til replied : "Thou shalt yet have a son ; and thou shalt call his name Coinneach (Kenneth). And thy son shall possess the gift of the *taibhsear* (seer)."

Thereupon she removed her distaff ; and permitted him once more to return to his lair.

Now, within a year or so of these strange happenings the old woman, to the great astonishment of her acquaintances, was as Sarah, for she bare a child in her old age. And she called her son Coinneach, or Kenneth. And this Coinneach, on account of his sallow complexion, was named *odhar*.

Soon Coinneach Odhar manifested signs of divination ; and in his manhood he became revered throughout the length and breadth of the Hebrides. Naught was there in oneiromancy and capnomancy that he could not explain.

COINNEACH IS DROWNED.

In eldage Coinneach lost his sight ; and either he, himself, had a premonition, or another seer had told him, that one day he would be drowned, though the place where this fatality was likely to occur was not specified. On account of his blindness, therefore, it was loath that Coinneach was to venture near the sea or rivers or pools. But, while he lived in a now desolate castle in South Uist, whose dilapidated stones are sorely stained by the unheeding storms of the centuries, he wandered out upon the moorland, in order to escape the ravages of the flames that consumed the castle. On the moor he fell into a peat-hag, and was drowned.

In this curious manner was fulfilled the prophecy concerning his death.

* * * * * * *

Such is the story of the traditional Coinneach Odhar as I got it lately at Kilchoan (*Cille Chomgain*), in Dunvegan, and from the lips of a much respected native, whose snug cottage nestles beside the loch and in the shadow of the recently dis-timbered slope known as Creag a' Chlachain, where the rooks used to call at eventide.

You should hear Sisera when, of a wild winter's night, he and his nine hundred chariots of iron are abroad on Creag a' Chlachain. Like the blast of the desert that " cried aloud in a voice so wild and free," or like the giant Nigerian forests, that in the death-dream of the worn-out slave shouted tumultuously for liberty, the winds that blow in from the western sea speak to Creag a' Chlachain with a myriad tongues !

Photo. by R. C. MacLeod of MacLeod.

Arch made by the Sea in Loch Bracadale.

XVI

"THE WAR IS AGAINST CLAN RANALD"

A TALE OF SOUTH UIST AND SKYE

THE spiritual pilgrimage to Lochlann of Til and his fellow-countrymen brings to mind the curious manner in which a dispute on a matter now forgotten was settled between MacLeod and Clan Ranald, after the death of the Chiefs actually concerned. During their lives these Chiefs agreed that the question at issue would be decided by strength of arms ; and, so as to give both contestants ample opportunity of equipping and mustering their forces, they specified a day on which their warfare was to have commenced. Howbeit, both Chiefs died unexpectedly, with the result that this arrangement fell through. But from the strange story I am about to relate it would appear as though the dispute had not terminated with their passing hence.

A Skyeman in his own house at Fearann na Leatha (sometimes called Fearann na Chatha, the Land of Battle) was one day in the act of flaying a sheep when, suddenly, there came upon him a strong impulse to go to the door in order to look out. In an instant he was carried off his feet and borne away to the churchyard at Eynort, where a great concourse of the dead awaited his arrival. From Eynort he and his ghostly company floated in the air until they came to the churchyard at

Loch Harport. There they were joined by another batch of spectres. Thence they all visited Loch Bracadale, Kilmuir in Dunvegan, and finally Trumpan, in Vaternish, having had their numbers considerably augmented by spectral contingents from each of these localities. From Vaternish this vast multitude, led by a short, dark man, sped across the Minch to South Uist, where it encountered an identical " rising " assembled from all the burying-grounds throughout the extensive territories of the MacDonalds. It, likewise, was commanded by a living man who, on the contrary, was ruddy in complexion and tall in stature.

CLAN RANALD'S CAPTAIN IS KILLED.

Now, the captains agreed that they would wrestle out the dispute between them, while their spirit armies would see that no foul tactics were resorted to by either of the corrivals. This they did ; and very nearly was the short, dark captain overpowered by his tall, red adversary when he remembered that in his hose was the *sgian-dubh* with which he had been flaying the sheep. Thereupon he drew it and stabbed to the brisket the tall, red man, who dropped dead at his feet.

Then there arose from the spectral forces of the MacLeods a tremendous shout ; and thrice they called out—" The war is against Clan Ranald (*An cogadh an aghaidh Chlann Raonuill*)." When all the wraiths had returned to their own lairs, the MacLeod was suddenly deposited at the door of his house at Fearann na Leatha. He had gone out for a moment to look at the sky, as it were ; and his wife was wondering why he was so long in returning to the flaying of the sheep.

How the Black Knife was Recovered.

When he *did* come in to complete his task, he discovered that his *sgian-dubh* was missing. But a few days after the spectral gathering it was recovered in South Uist in rather a remarkable way, when some Uistmen were horrified at finding one of their own clansmen dead on the machar, with the *sgian-dubh* piercing his side. So it looked as though the captain of the MacLeod host had overcome his Clan Ranald victim by unfair means, since they had agreed to wrestle honourably.

Perhaps some of you may read into what I have said the meaning of this obscure, unfinished story. It does not do to tell the whole of everything: *something* at times must be left to the imagination!

XVII

SEA SPOIL

THE TOLL OF THE FOG AND TEMPEST

There 's music in the cavern where the Viking rievers dwelled
'Mong the rich sea spoil that lay strewn upon its floor ;

Go to the Eist when the firmament is cloudless
and a sunlit blue, and when there blows a gale so
strong that you are compelled to creep cautiously
on your hands and knees across the wildest and
most exposed places, lest you be carried bodily into
the sea that booms and thunders at the base of the
aeon-rent cliffs, hundreds of feet below you.   Often
have I set out for the lighthouse at the Eist (Neist
Point), that westernmost promontory of the Isle of
Skye, when, but for the discontinuous stretches of
railing flanking the seaward and precipitous side of
the sledge-track by which all land communication
of necessity must be made, the tempest has assaulted
with such vigour and determination that even the
sturdiest wayfarer would be swept literally off the
face of the earth, and plunged into a seething
cauldron of spindrift and foam and storm-torn
seawrack.

Foothold in places there is none ; and after a
hot summer the parched and sheep-nibbled grass
is so short and slippery and brittle that, were a
hurricane to catch you unawares, there is nothing
whatever to seize hold of—not even an odd tuft of

heather. If, perchance, in gusty weather you should be constrained to wander far from those crimsoned railings that are erected just where they are most required, and a squall suddenly breaks, the safest thing to do is to lie prostrate on the sward, and thus give the wind as little purchase as possible.

After having experienced one or two gales at an exposed altitude such as this, the prone position becomes a second nature : you learn to dodge the wind as you would the stray splinters of a shell.

On a boisterous night a false step on the way to the Eist may precipitate you without any warning into a seething sea : were you to deviate a little to the left where, owing to the encroachments of Annat Bay, the neck of the Eist peninsula is particularly narrow, down like a plummet you would drop upon a shingled beach that ofttimes has harboured the richest spoil of an angry sea. From the edge of the steep declivity overhanging this bay you may number some of the exposed fragments of many a wreck. And, should you bear even a yard to the right of the sledge-track at this point, you would tumble into a deep, sea-filled canyon, and in a moment and for ever be unconscious of the world around you.

Often I wonder how the light-keepers manage to reach their destination in the darkness, especially when it is blowing a blizzard, and the rains of the Atlantic are beating like mechanically driven hail-stones.

THE WRECKS OF MANY SHIPS.

What a nightmare to shipping was the Eist before the construction of that lighthouse about eighteen years ago as part of a scheme for improving the lighting of the West Coast ! You have only to visit it in a storm to be assured of this. Take an old seafarer with you to the Eist, and he will recount many a tragedy that has occurred there during his own lifetime. And, if you should have a desire to experience the ferocity of the tide that is being hurled against the Eist by a south-west wind, I would urge you to scramble into a cave nearby, and seek shelter on the great stone bench that has been scooped out at the back of it by the continual erosion of the water-worn boulders and ovoid stones and pebbles that are scattered in banks and ridges along the storm-beach. On the floor of that very cave, and among the tide-laved sea-wrack, you will find driftwood that has been left by exceptionally heavy seas ; and there is no gain-saying that the chips and splinters one eagerly picks up to examine once formed part of a vessel that foundered off the Eist in a storm. What epics of the sea these bits of wood withhold from us ! Maybe they are portions of the flotsam of ships that met their doom hundreds or even thousands of miles away ; or, perhaps, they are odd fragments of jettisoned cargoes. Here, too, the wanderer by the sea may come upon beans and other seeds, that have been borne across the ocean from the tropical shores of another hemisphere.

At the Eist there is a wondrous wealth of international poesy : here the spoil of Boreal and Austral seas is inseparably commingled with the spoil of the Occident and the Orient. At times the seeker by the shore may find tree trunks and logs and boughs that have drifted over from the great Canadian or Mexican or Brazilian forests ; or, perchance, a bamboo or an odd bale of cotton or even a sack of coffee beans from the West Indies. Thus were discovered most of the charms and amulets in which the Hebrideans placed so much faith in bygone days.

The very straws that float upon the tide have been wafted from a foreign strand. Like autumned leaves that, willy-nilly, are carried and strewn by the winds of winter, they know not whither next they may be transported. They are powerless and impotent in the extreme : like so many of us humans, who are as the backwash and have been cast ashore by the swirling currents of life and its unrealised dreams, they can offer no resistance to the whimsicalities of winds and the fluctuating temperaments of tides. Already have they travelled unleagued distances ; and weary, weary must they be of voyaging. There is a stupendous microcosm of thought embraced in the simple term, " sea-level " : at the Eist, as everywhere else on the globe where the ocean sweeps, all things, animate and inanimate, are reduced to an elementary, common denominator—a denominator that man cannot influence in the slightest degree.

And it occurred to me lately, while Auld Reekie was enveloped by a fog so thick that for days (November 1925) you could not see a yard ahead and the entire traffic of the city was dislocated, that, for the time being at any rate, the fog had reduced all its citizens to a somewhat similar denominator, above or below which most of us in our everyday lives find ourselves, owing to the absurdities that render our existence more artificial than human and social.

Every one alike was affected by the fog : the

rich and the poor, the man of high degree and of low, the owner of the gorgeous limousine and the mother wheeling her rickety perambulator, the motorman of the electric tram and the message-boy hurling a barrow of groceries, the driver of the rattling taxicab with its glaring headlights and the coachman of the horse-drawn vehicle with its dim, flickering candle lamps, the express train to King's Cross and the ships whose syrens hooted their warning night and day in the Firth of Forth were, one and all, compelled to creep along at a snail's pace.   Would that such fogs might visit us occasionally if merely to remind us that we are all Jock Tamson's bairns.   Though the fog had its unpleasantnesses and inconveniences and made the shortest distances seem almost interminable, one could not help reflecting on its object-lesson.

Then, there is another aspect which we are prone to overlook, namely, that when no physical fog impedes us, we frequently impede ourselves and others by creating artificial fog.   Are we not continually wrapping ourselves up in mist ?   Are we not constantly befogging our own or some one else's pilgrimage by selfishness and supercilious airs ?

And from the newspapers I learn with gratification that, owing to fog and snow, the number of hunts that last season had to be cancelled constituted a record.   Thus some poor, hunted creatures were granted longer respite than ordinary climatic circumstances would have permitted.   The more humane of us would welcome fogs and snowstorms oftener, if only as a means of bringing home to the British pseudo-sportsman that there are more manly recreations than chasing little foxes with

Photo. by M. A. MacFarlane.

Sheep-dipping in Glendale.

1

organised squadrons of horses and packs of blood-thirsty hounds, or digging out exhausted badgers that have run to earth. Lest there should be any misunderstanding, however, let me make it clear that the above observation refers *not* to the killing of vermin as such.

A Ship's Deck Cast Ashore.

Perhaps the bits of wood, of which I have been speaking, are all that now remain of the Norwegian steamer which sixteen or eighteen years ago ran aground at the Eist, while the lighthouse was being built. This vessel was bound for the Baltic from Liverpool with a general cargo ; and there she was stranded for four or five days until at last a gale from the west turned her round, and smashed her to smithereens against the reefs.

O, how cruel and merciless is the sea that is hungry for the lives of men !

In a tiny bay near the Eist chersonese, where in olden days, when fishing-boats in the Hebrides were more abundant than they are to-day, the local fishermen used to draw up their craft, one might discover much of the spoil of the sea, if inclined to delve beneath the sand and rubble.

About thirty years ago a Danish brigantine, bound for Copenhagen with a cargo of Indian corn, went aground in a fog at the Eist, and became a total wreck in no time. These were the days before fog-horns were used so extensively as they are now. While dawdling along the shore close at hand the other day, I chanced to find among the seaweed part of a windlass that might have belonged to this vessel.

And yet another Scandinavian boat met her fate

I

in this locality, when a large, wooden vessel struck that sunken rock in Oisgill Bay, known as the " Gruagach," and was irreparably fractured amidships. Apart from its deck that was cast upon the beach of Camus na h-Annait, not far from the lighthouse, little else was found of this wreck, though the captain's desk containing the ship's papers came ashore in a small boat belonging to the vessel. The remnant of this small boat still may be seen at Pooltiel Pier. Thither it was conveyed by a man in the neighbourhood of Glendale, who, I am told, purchased it from Lloyd's Agent and Receiver of Wrecks at Dunvegan.

You may be certain that more than once the Lutine Bell has sounded through the corridors of the Royal Exchange the death-knell of a ship in peril at the Eist. Picture the tense faces of the underwriters who awaited such an announcement, and whose undivided attention, on having heard the fateful news, was focussed for the moment on this wild, Hebridean promontory.

And, by the bye, the Lutine Bell itself is reminiscent of the spoil of the sea, because it belonged to the *Lutine*, a frigate of thirty-two guns that in 1799 sank off the Dutch coast. Its sole survivor was a man who lived long enough to tell of the disaster. The loss of the *Lutine* was a tremendous blow to Lloyd's, for at the time the vessel was carrying bullion valued at a million pounds, only the merest fraction of which has been salved.

Wizard Curses Clan Ranald.

Scarcely a boat sailed past the Eist when last I visited its lighthouse ; and not a bird ventured to stretch its pinions into the gale with its cold, flying sleet—so wild, so forbidding was this Hebridean sea! But long will I remember the handsome, three-masted schooner that half-way between Skye and Uist was fleeing helplessly with shortened sail before a sou'wester, for she was, indeed, a bonnie boat. The clouds seemed lowered as if to touch her mast-tops; and away behind her a splash of sunshine followed closely in the wake of the passing storm. Untrimmed as was her rigging, she filled me with a great content.

It was at the Eist that the noted Wizard, Mac-Vurich of the Talents, was accredited with having raised a sou'west wind that drove to destruction an enemy galley with all hands.

Here, also, on this tempestuous shore, an old woman in Glendale, whose son had been killed by the Clan Ranalds, wished a sou'west wind to the Eist; with fog and rain; with a cargo of empty barrels; with water to the thofts; with each member of the crew at his fellow's throat; and Clan Ranald's birlinns broken in splinters.

No cargo is more jeopardising than a cargo of empty barrels; and water is more than plentiful when there's water to the thofts.

Unwritten are the epics of the sea that, with nonchalance, have been enacted within earshot of this tumultuous coast; and unwritten will they remain: here, unrecorded except traditionally and fragmentarily, are the wildest themes for a sea-anthology.

How ravenous is the tempest at the Eist when the fog is drizzling and low, when the wind is from the sou'west, and when on the foam-flecked tide there's a hunger for the lives of men!

And how precious is the spoil of the sea!

XVIII

SHIANT ISLES

THE BLUE MEN OF THE MINCH

Tell me a tale of a gallant sail
When the " Blue Men " deftly ride :
Sing of the Shiants that are swept by the gale
And the fury of the tide.

MR. COMPTON MACKENZIE'S recent purchase of the
Shiant or "Charmed Isles" at the sale of the
Leverhulme Lewis and Harris estates was appropriate in respect that the new novelist-laird has a
long-standing connection with the Outer Hebrides.
You will remember that in 1844 the whole of the
Island of Lewis (of which the Shiants form a part)
belonged to the once-powerful MacKenzies of Seaforth, who, when in the zenith of their suzerainty,
"played Rex," and were even in a position to
circulate their own private currency.   In the aforesaid year the late Sir James Matheson bought
Lewis and the appurtenant islands from the Trustees
of the MacKenzies of Seaforth for the sum of
£190,000. The MacKenzies had remained in
possession of Lewis for more than two centuries.
The passing of that Island into their hands was
confirmed by Charter in July of 1610, in which
year Roderic MacKenzie, the intrepid and redoubtable Tutor of Kintail, undertook by hook or
by crook to subdue the bellicose MacLeods of

Lewis, and to dislodge from Berisay, a rocky and almost impregnable islet in Loch Roag, the crafty Neil and his garrison of sea-rievers.

Lewis gained much by this change in ownership, for the MacKenzies, who were hardly strangers to the Hebrides, introduced into the Long Island with beneficial results a certain measure of law and order, of which heretofore the people had prided itself in having lived in complete ignorance.

Through his ancestor, the Rev. Bernard Mac-Kenzie, who was the last Episcopal minister at Cromarty, Mr. Compton MacKenzie is descended from the Seaforth MacKenzies. The son of this minister was, in pre-railway days, a shipowner of no inconsiderable standing. His vessels plied chiefly between London and the north of Scotland. The novelist's grandfather, having gone on the stage, took the name of Compton, as did also his father ; and it may be fitting to mention here that Mr. Compton MacKenzie is the brother of Miss Fay Compton, the actress, whose moving perform-ances in Barrie's *Mary Rose*, it is perhaps not delusive to imagine, were inspired by that sense of atmosphere and sympathetic understanding which only an innate tradition could have produced.

A Hermit's Retreat.

The Shiant Isles are not without their interest : their ecclesiastical history conveys us back to very early times. One of the three largest islands of the group is actually called *Eilean na Cille*, the Isle of the Cell or Church ; and a small pond in another is named *Loch Seunta*, the Sacred Loch, thus called from the Gaelic word, *seun*, denoting a charm or spell. The word, Shiant, or more correctly Siant, is derived from the adjective, *seunta*, meaning enchanted or charmed ; and, since in Gaelic the Shiants are known as *Na h-Eileanan Sianta*, they are commonly alluded to as the " Charmed Isles." The name, *Eileanan Mora*, is also applied to them. They are among the few islands in the Hebrides possessing a name of real Celtic origin : though the Viking invaders did not supplant the ancient language of the Gael, they gave to almost every mountain and stream, creek and hamlet, in the Western Isles a Scandinavian name.

That on Eilean na Cille—the Island from whose sanctity the group appears to have taken its name—there existed a small devotional chapel dedicated to St. Columba, and under the aegis and protection of Iona, one has every reason to believe. An island such as this was peculiarly adapted to the hermitical seclusion that was desired by the old Celtic Church, and distinguished it from the Benedictine with its enormous common-rooms and dormitories and refectories. One still may examine on Eilean na Cille the hermitage-like ruins of an ancient place of worship.

This Island, which is the southernmost of the group, is more frequently referred to as *Eilean an Tighe*, the Isle of the House. It is about a mile in length, and is separated from *Garbh-Eilean* (Rough Island) by a ridge of sea-rolled pebbles, over which it is feasible to pass dryshod except at the concurrence of the spring tides, or during very boisterous weather. Garbh-Eilean is the loftiest and most conspicuous of the Shiant Isles.

The third island is designated *Eilean Mhuire* ; to wit, Mary's Isle. It is called Island-More by Martin ; but in many old MSS. this name appears in the more corrupted form of Wirrey. Doubtless, at one time or other it was sanctified to the Virgin Mary, and possessed a shrine.

There is at present no house on the Shiant Isles, though the ruins of the dwelling-place occupied by the shepherd, who lived there during the tenancy of the late Rory Martin, are still to be traced. Mr. Compton MacKenzie has expressed the desire to erect a house on one of the Islands; but he will find the climate of Lewis very different from that of the Isle of Jethou, where meantime he resides.

SHIANTS RENOWNED FOR SHEEP.

Now, you may be wondering where exactly these mysterious Islands are situated. They lie in the fickle Minch not far distant from Uisinish in Lewis, and are about fifteen miles out from Trotternish, the most northerly part of the Isle of Skye. In appearance they closely resemble Staffa, for in places their great, columnar structures rise perpendicularly above the waves to a height of at least five hundred feet. Many of these basaltic columns measure nine and ten feet in diameter. Along the shore fringing the Shiants may be seen much of the accumulated debris that has been cast down by the denuding hand of Time; but with the geological eye and a moderate degree of imagination one easily might visualise these broken masses of rock in their original positions. Huge as they are, they represent mere fragments of the stupendous faces from which they have fallen.

For information regarding the somewhat complicated geological structure of the Shiant Isles one could not do better than peruse MacCulloch's account of them. Be it stated in passing that it is only the relative inaccessibility of the Shiants that has denied their magnificent columns the popularity enjoyed by the very similar formations at Fingal's Cave and at the Giant's Causeway. In the nooks and crannies that aeons of epigene and chemical weathering have produced on these tremendous basaltic faces, puffins and guillemots and diverse other seabirds, in undisturbed succession and for unnumbered centuries, have maintained their prescriptive title. As well you may imagine, the cliffs of the Shiants are not to be approached from above without incurring an element of risk : many lives have been lost here either through carelessness or through unwarranted boldness. In the *Old Statistical Account* we read, for instance, that, of the family residing there for the purpose of attending the sheep and black cattle pastured on these Islands, no fewer than three members were killed by falling over the cliffs. The mother and son perished at different times while herding sheep ; and a daughter tumbled over a precipice when in quest of seafowls' eggs.

It ought to be mentioned that the pasture-clad declivities of the Shiant Isles are still famous for the sheep that are reared on them. At present the grazing rights there are let to a Harrisman at an annual rental of £60. I cannot say what stock of sheep they carry in the meantime ; but during a recent tenancy the number was not below five hundred. When we remember that the total area of the Shiants is only about four hundred and seventy acres, this figure testifies to the succulence of their grass. It is held that sheep pastured on the Shiant Isles thrive so well that, be they ever so lean when placed there in the springtime, they fetch extraordinarily good prices a month or two later.

"PROFITABLE IN CORNE, STORE, AND FISHEING."

During his tour of inspection towards the close of the sixteenth century, and in his capacity as High Dean of the Isles, Dean Monro observed that, in common with most of the islands he visited (which, by the way, were church-lands, and therefore the most productive of the barren Hebrides !), the Shiant Isles were " profitable in corne, store, and fisheing." Here it was that his attention was drawn to a " bore, maid like a vylt (vault), mair nore an arrowshot of any man under the eirde, through the quilk vylt we use to row ore saill with our bottis, for fear of the horrible breake of the seas that is on the outwar side thereof, bot na grate shipes can saill ther." MacCulloch was particularly anxious to examine this great, arched passage that had been perforated by the action of the sea ; but the tide was so turbulent when he arrived there, that his boat was carried through with a rapidity which denied him an opportunity of recording accurately either its picturesqueness or its dimensions.

Martin Martin (*circa* 1695), in what is one of the most fascinating contemporary accounts of the Western Isles we possess, also refers to the fertility of the Shiants, because he speaks of Island-More (Mary's Isle) as being unusually fruitful in corn and pasturage, inasmuch as the cows he saw there were fatter than any he had seen in Lewis. He tells us, too, of a couple of strange eagles that dwelt on the Shiants. The natives told him that these carrion-eaters would not suffer any of their kind to live on these Islands, and drove away even their own young whenever the latter could fly. He informs us further that the parent birds had a great respect for the place of their abode, and were never known to have killed a sheep or lamb on their own particular island. Ossific remains of many a feast were littered around and below their nest ; but the inhabitants always urged that these were the bones of lambs and fawns and birds which the eagles had purloined from adjacent islands.

THE BLUE MEN OF THE MINCH.

But it is in folklore and legend that the Shiant Isles have figured most conspicuously, because in the Straits between them and the Isle of Lewis live those restless creatures who are known to us as the Blue Men (*Na Fir Gorma*). They are, in fact, our Hebridean storm-kelpies ; and they really work their mischief in the Sound of Shiant, which in the ancient Lewisian legend is called the Stream of the Blue Men (*Sruth nam Fear Gorma*).

Many a storm the Blue Men are blamed for having raised : many an unsuspecting fishing crew have they harassed : many a galley's keel have they stranded on the wrack-spent reefs and sgeirs : many an innocent ship have they beguiled and sent to her doom !

The Minch can be very rough at times, especially if the winds be uncertain ; but, even when it is at rest, the skeeliest skipper is often obliged to exercise the greatest care and diligence in the Stream of the Blue Men. And I can vouch for this from personal experience, for I have seen these deft and wily horsemen riding on their snowy steeds in wild furore before a loudly wailing gale.

Although to-day the Blue Men are almost forgotten in Lewis, they are remembered in Skye and
in other Hebridean islands as the " Sea-Gods " who
are akin to the Nimble Men (*Fir Chlis*) associated
with the Aurora Borealis—those energetic, little
gentlemen better known to us northerners as the
" Merry Dancers " or " Northern Lights."

So, Mr. Compton MacKenzie has acquired a
fragment of Hebridean faeryland.

" Oh ! weary on the Blue Men, their anger and their wiles !
    The whole day long, the whole night long, they 're splash-
        ing round the isles ;
    They 'll follow every fisher—ah ! they 'll haunt the
        fisher's dream—
    When billows toss, oh ! who would cross the Blue Men's
        Stream ? "

DONALD A. MACKENZIE.

XIX

A LAST WISH FULFILLED

A TALE OF HARRIS AND THE MINCH

Ailein, duinn, I have watched by the tide for thee long,
Where the seal-woman croons her mysterious song:
The fishes are waiting by pale candle-light,
And the lone seagull floats on the waves of the night.

To-DAY it is my desire to conduct you across the Minch to Harris, in order that you may learn something of the origin of that old-world Harris Lament.

Long ago there dwelt on Scalpay a fair maiden named Ann, whose father was the tacksman or tenant-farmer of that Isle. He it was who entertained Prince Charlie when the latter found himself in Scalpay. Now, Ann loved and was beloved by a certain Alan Morison, who was a native of Crossbost, in the Lewis, and the captain of a sailing vessel that plied between Stornoway and diverse southern ports. Alan, besides having been an estimable man, was one of the deftest mariners of his time. He could pilot a three-masted schooner through the treacherous Sound of Harris during a storm as could no one else ; and this is saying a good deal, because Lewis was, and indeed still is, renowned for the proficiency of its sea captains. For generations Stornoway was famous for its nautical school. Its seafarers, like the desperate

pirates of Barra, were mental repositories for all
things maritime.

One has only to glance at the Admiralty Chart
of this area, or for that matter at an ordinary " half-
inch to the mile " map, to realise the consummate
helmsmanship that is required, particularly at night-
time, to navigate without mishap this Hebridean
waterway. By the unskilled and unwary mariner
the Sound of Harris is to be avoided : the current-
swept reefs that beset it are as fine a test of seamanship as one could select. Dr. MacCulloch
described the Sound of Harris as a chaos of rocks
and islands ; and he regarded the navigating of it
as the most formidable operation he had ever
witnessed. And, by the way, I have been reading
in the latest issue of my Lewis *Gazette* that the
lighting of the beacons and buoys erected about
eighteen months ago in the Sound of Harris and
at Obbe (Leverburgh) Harbour has been discontinued, and that all appliances and fittings in connection therewith are being removed, consequent
on the abandonment of the schemes promoted by
the late Lord Leverhulme. Incidentally, let me
say that, since Leverburgh has been dismantled,
and since we have no desire to perpetuate the
memory of what, after all, was a regrettable fiasco,
there is no reason why now we ought not to revert
to the ancient and poetic name of Obbe.

You must bear in mind that at the moment we
are dealing with the days when communication between the Hebrides and the mainland, as well as
between the several groups of the Outer Isles themselves, was very much superior to what it is to-day :
despite our modern mania for speed and our improved and accelerated travelling facilities, relatively

speaking, transport conditions in the Western Isles were never so inadequate as they are at the present time. Before the advent of the steamship the family of almost every Islesman had its small boat in which, when the weather permitted, it was possible to visit friends and relations living on adjacent islands, and to reap its own harvest at sea ; and every crofting township near the shore could muster at least one crew of skilled seamen, and provide at least one boat large and safe enough to convey between the Hebrides and such mainland ports as Kyle, Glenelg, Lochinver, Mallaig, Oban, and even Glasgow, traffic of every desired description. And, parenthetically, it is to be regretted that to-day a race of sailors has become so dependent upon a steamship company with monopolistic propensities that it can transport neither its members nor its live-stock to and from the mainland marts except by paying fares and freightage rates which are almost prohibitive !

ALAN MORISON IS LOST AT SEA.

Now, to return to the main theme of our story, shortly before their marriage was to have taken place, lo ! Alan's vessel was overwhelmed by a storm in the Minch ; and never again was he seen in human form. Eagerly watched Ann for Alan's winding sail : there by the tangled seashore would she linger at eventide, and when the day was parting from the night. Immeasurably great was her distress : like the sister of Iain Garbh MacLeod of Raasay, she sat by the lonely shore of Scalpay Isle and mourned the loss of her loved one with tears and lamenting, and would not be drinking of the rich, red wine of Spain (" *Cha b'ann a dh'fhionn dearg na Spainne* "). Nothing could console her ; and to Heaven she prayed daily and nightly that she might be taken and laid to rest beside Alan in the purple sea.

Nor was it long after her bereavement that Providence placed on her, too, that kindly hand of death for which she had waited so earnestly : peacefully, though broken-hearted, Ann passed away in her home on Scalpay Isle. And deep was the compassion felt for her not only in her native Isle of Scalpay, but also in Skye and in Uist and in Harris, for in all these Isles she had a wide and scattered kindred.

And one day there bore away from Scalpay Isle an immense procession of boats on a voyage to Rodil, in Harris, where Ann was to have been interred. But, when the funereal fleet was half-way across the Minch, there suddenly arose a terrible storm ; and sorely troubled became a sea that a few moments earlier had been as smooth as glass.

A LAST WISH FULFILLED.

So violent was the tempest that the company was filled with fear and consternation ; and so imperilled by its raging was the foremost boat of the procession, in which Ann's remains were being conveyed, that it was decided to lighten its burthen by reverently lowering the coffin overboard, thus giving her a sea burial. And no sooner had the chest left the gunwale than there arose out of the sea the tall, brown-haired figure of a man, who clasped it in his arms and bore it down to the depths of the sea. This was none other than the spirit of Alan : here a few years previously he and his brig had perished.

When the storm abated, the funeral fleet, without its dead, slowly moved on that matters might be explained to the sorrowing kinsfolk, who anxiously had been keeping vigil by the shore of Rodil all this time.

And there was held in the now venerable Cathedral of Rodil a service to which the Islesfolks came from far and near, that they might offer prayers and observe the last obsequies for the beloved and departed who never occupied a Harris grave.

Thus fulfilled was that last wish expressed in the old Hebridean Love Lament, and in the line, " *Ailein, duinn, o hi shiubhlainn leat !* "—Oh, Fair Alan, it is I that would be wandering with thee !

> O lay me to sleep in a wild, Hebrid sea,
> That my last resting-place beside Alan may be—
> Where the grey seal still lists for the drip of his oar,
> And the lap of his old, empty boat on the shore.

Within St Clement's at Rodil, showing part of Alasdair
Crotach's Tomb—one of the sweetest interiors I know.
(See *Behold the Hebrides !*)

XX

TWO PLOTS THAT FAILED

BIG RORY'S REVELRY AT RODIL

DONALD GORM STORM-STAYED AT DUNVEGAN

FAIN would I detain you with tales of Rodil, in the Harris : there is so much to tell of this place. Was it not here that was fought the protracted campaign between cats and rats, in which the cats were so overpowered by the rats (the latter having numbered twenty to one) that they would have been routed utterly, had it not been discovered by one of the natives of Rodil that a little warm milk after an encounter with a rat readily restored a cat's strength and courage ?

It was in Rodil, and on a night of nights in 1601, that Ruairaidh Mor revelled with his retainers after he had carried fire and sword into Trotternish, " sparing no living thing," in return for which invasion the MacDonalds laid waste much of his territory in the west of Skye. And, moreover, it was a night on which Roderic declared that even his fiercest enemy might be admitted to the banquet without endangering his life.

As luck would have it, a galley of Clan Ranald with Donald Mac Iain Mhic Seumais on board was driven ashore that very night on the coast of Harris, not far from Rodil ; and Roderic, suspiciously eager to carry out his declaration, having already received

word of the misfortune that had befallen his hereditary foes, sent a henchman to meet the straggling,
storm-delayed crew and to persuade its members
to join his revelry and accept of his hospitality.   He
even went the length of directing that a wooden
outhouse be erected, wherein the MacDonalds might
take shelter until daybreak.   Justly apprehensive
were his Clan Ranald guests that night, for Roderic
had set many a trap, and had trapped many an
unsuspecting foe.   And, so, when the wind changed
its direction during the early hours of the morning,
they betook themselves to their galley.   No sooner
were they afloat than they observed that the improvised outhouse was ablaze.   But the birds had
flown ; and the MacLeods were long in disgrace for
this treachery.

Probably this is the incident that was in Scott's
mind when he composed the lines—

> " When, if a hope of safety rest,
> 'Tis on the sacred name of guest,
> Who seeks for shelter, storm-distressed,
> Within a chieftain's hall."

Canon Roderic MacLeod of MacLeod (who possibly knows more about Skye and the MacLeods
than any living man, and who at Dunvegan is
affectionately referred to as " Mr. Rory ") tells me
that Donald Mac Iain Mhic Seumais afterwards
became a drover, and was the first man to take a
drove of cattle from Skye to the mainland.   Probably in his time the animals were driven to Kyleakin
or Kylerhea, whence they were compelled to swim
across to the opposite side, as was long the practice.
After Donald had set the example, droves from
Skye were sent yearly to the Falkirk Trysts.

ALASDAIR CROTACH'S TOMB AT RODIL.

At Rodil is the interesting Priory Church of St. Clement—" a church of ancient and tolerable architecture." This sanctuary is attributed by some to David the First ; but its age and origin long have been in dispute. At any rate, it escaped destruction at the time of the Reformation, and was actually repaired during the sixteenth century by Alexander MacLeod of Harris. Another restoration scheme is believed to have been begun in the year 1787.

Rodil has been aptly referred to by our Highland historian, William Cook MacKenzie, as the " Iona " of the Siol Tormod. You will remember that on the south side of the chancel of St. Clement's Cathedral at Rodil is the wonderful tomb Alasdair Crotach prepared for himself nineteen years before his death (vide *Behold the Hebrides !*).

Alasdair Crotach's tomb is reminiscent of one that at a much more recent date was prepared on Eilean Chaisteal, a small islet off Eigg. There the proprietor, who preceded the late Sir William Petersen, actually superintended his own tomb being hewn out of the rock several years before it was required, and directed that, when he was interred, it should be sealed up with a marble slab expressly reserved for the purpose.

DONALD GORM STORM-STAYED AT DUNVEGAN.

Not unlike the attempt of Rory Mor to ensnare the crew of a Clan Ranald birlinn, that on a night of nights had been cast ashore in a storm at Rodil, was the scheme that MacLeod had devised to capture Donald Gorm, who, when on a return voyage to Uist, was forced through stress of weather to seek a haven in Loch Dunvegan.

Great was the rivalry between Rory Mor and Donald Gorm of Sleat.

At this time Dunvegan was hardly the place that Donald Gorm would have selected by choice, and in less compelling circumstances, for in a quarrel resulting from his having repudiated his wife (who was MacLeod's daughter), in order that he might enter into matrimony with a Kintail MacKenzie, he had killed the previous Chief of MacLeod by tipping him over a precipice in the Cuchullins.

Now, from the seaward windows of Dunvegan Castle (Oh, that you might gaze and gaze from these windows !) MacLeod saw Donald Gorm's galley making for port in the storm ; and, with the traditional civility of the Highland host, he despatched a messenger to the shore to convey his greetings to the crew, and to invite it to accept of the Chief's hospitality at the Castle.

And, with the splendour and graciousness that in those far-off days characterised the Talla of the MacLeods in the Dun of the Hospitality of the Winecups (*Dun Flathail nan Cuach*), Donald Gorm and his sea-weary crew were received.

DONALD GORM DECLINES MACLEOD'S INVITATION.

But, when MacLeod invited his illustrious guest to be seated at his own table, Donald Gorm replied : " When from home Donald Gorm never sits but in the company of his men." Hard did the Chief of MacLeod try to persuade his obdurate guest by assuring him that his men would receive plenty meat and drink in another apartment of the Castle. The more MacLeod cajoled him, the more emphatic became Donald Gorm's declination. So MacLeod, eager not to create suspicion unduly, came to the conclusion that the only way out of the difficulty was to extend the invitation to the crew as well ; and this he did.

The termination of the meal that evening marked the beginning of a prolonged carouse. Before long MacLeod was warmed up to the occasion ; and, having turned casually to Donald Gorm by way of vague recollection, he enquired of him whether it was not he who had killed his father.

To this blunt interrogation came the ready-tongued retort : " It has been laid to my charge that I killed three despicable Highland lairds ; and I reck not of adding a fourth to that list this very night ! There's the dirk (*biodag*) that laid your father low : it has a point and a haft ; and its edge is, oh, so sharp ! And, what's more, it is held by the second best hand in Skye ! "

" And whose hand is the best ? " enquired MacLeod, with a faint hope that, out of courtesy, the guest might accord to the host's hand the foremost place.

Thereupon Donald Gorm alertly changed the dirk to his left hand, raised the weapon in the air, and exclaimed : " There it is ! "

MacLeod, who was not a little surprised at this unexpected *dénouement*, did not accept the challenge, and discreetly disregarded an innuendo that in ordinary circumstances was pretty certain to have led to bloodshed.

THE MACDONALDS ESCAPE WITHOUT INJURY.

When it was time to retire for the night, Donald Gorm was offered a separate apartment in Dunvegan Castle ; but to MacLeod's wheedlings that he should have a quiet and undisturbed night's rest he replied : "When from home Donald Gorm never sleeps apart from his men."

And, much as they enticed him with offers of comfortable and luxurious quarters, he so steadfastly declined that in the end it was found necessary to provide accommodation for him and for his men in the kiln (*ath*), a capacious, thatched erection, such as in olden times was possessed by almost every township for the preparation of corn prior to grinding.

Tired were his men that night ; and they slept the sleep of the storm-worn and weary. But Donald Gorm never closed an eye. And, stealthily, there came a friend to the kiln at the first flush of dawn to advise him and his men to evacuate the place with all haste, but with as little pother as possible, and to close the door of the kiln behind them, so as not to betray their departure.

By this time the wind had fallen considerably ; and down to the shore they ran to launch their galley. This they accomplished without mishap ; and when steering down Loch Dunvegan they noticed the kiln was a mass of shooting flames.

But Donald Gorm and his men were well out of MacLeod's grasp by this time ; and without scaith they reached their belovèd Uist.

CRUELTY OF THE HEBRIDEAN CLANS.

Without a doubt, the clans of the Hebrides during the sixteenth, seventeenth, and eighteenth centuries completely eclipsed their mainland brethren in barbarity and ferocity. In those rebellious times an island chieftain, though ever so daring and powerful, often had to think twice before participating in a foray because of the cunning and relentlessness of his foes, or because of the treacherous proclivities of his friends. As illustrative of the character and disposition of the Islanders, the following contemporary passage occurs in the *Historie of King James the Sext*—" Trew it is, that thir Ilandish men ar of nature verie prowd, suspicious, avaricious, full of decept and evill inventioun each aganis his nychtbour, be what way soever he may circumvin him. Besydis all this, thay ar sa crewall in taking of revenge that nather have they regard to person, eage, tyme, or caus ; sa ar they generallie all sa far addictit to thair awin tyrannicall opinions that, in all respects, they exceid in creweltie the maist barbarous people that ever hes bene sen the begynning of the warld."

It would be impossible to measure the quantity of innocent blood that between them, and on the most trivial of pretexts, the warring septs of the MacDonalds and the MacLeods have spilled.

Nevertheless, it is worthy of commendation that, in pursuance of the obligations placed on the chiefs of Highland and Island clans by the Statutes of Iona, the MacDonalds and the MacLeods actually make a genuine endeavour to come to an amicable understanding, as is proved by a most interesting and comprehensive document in the Dunvegan charter-chest. The document in reality is the record of a contract of friendship and mutual forgiveness of injuries between Donald Gorm MacDonald, Sixth Baron of Sleat, and Rory MacLeod of the Harris. It is dated 1609. The signatures of the high contracting parties were affixed in the presence of competent and respectable witnesses, among whom were the minister of Duirinish, Lauchlan MacKinnon of Strath Swordale, and one or two personages who were illustrious in their time, but whose names at the moment I fail to recall. Canon MacLeod is of the impression that Rory Mor was the first Chief of his clan who could write, earlier chiefs having affixed their names to bonds and agreements with their hands " led at ye pene of ye notar."

An Expert Galley-Builder.

Perhaps, I might mention here that in piratical seamanship the MacDonalds were second only to the MacNeils of Barra, from whom they learned many useful tips pertinent to roving. On the other hand, the MacDonalds sometimes instructed the MacNeils : Donald Gorm Mor (who, by the way, was one of the best all-round men of his day) was widely recognised as the soundest judge of a galley throughout the length and breadth of the Western Isles ; and on one occasion he actually went to Kisimul Castle on the express invitation of MacNeil, who sought his expert advice while building a new birlinn.

Several of Donald Gorm's relatives were inde-fatigable pirates. In the year 1600, the Privy Council considered a lengthy complaint lodged by Thomas Inglis, a merchant-burgess of Edinburgh, and Robert Sinclair, a Leith skipper, who were joint-owners of a vessel called *Jonas of Leith*, to the effect that, while fishing in Loch Shell, in Lewis, " ladint with certaine merchandice guidis and geir," a kinsman of MacDonald of Sleat and others came to the said complainers' ship, and by violence " away tuke fra thame the foirsaid schip with the haill merchandice guidis and geir being thairintill."

Photo. by R. C. MacLeod of MacLeod.

Our Pirate Lugger at anchor in Loch Follart.

152

For this act the defenders were denounced as rebels and put to the horn.

* * * * * * *

And, yet, if conditions again made it either necessary or possible, who be he that would be so mean-spirited, so craven-hearted, so unimaginative as to decline the offer of becoming an honourable, chivalrous, Hebridean pirate on a birlinn designed and owned by Donald Gorm Mor of Sleat ?

If my friend, MacNeil of Barra, were to come home from New York and re-fortify Kisimul Castle, and construct in Castlebay two or three full-sized galleys similar to those once possessed by his pirate ancestors, I would sign on to-morrow with one of his sea-rieving crews !

TWO PLOTS THAT FAILED   153

For this act the defenders were denounced, as
rebels and put to the horn.

*   *   *   *   *

And, yet, if conditions again made it either
necessary or possible, that he he that would be so
mean spirited, so craven-hearted, so unimaginative
as to decline to add his mite to the honourable,
chivalrous, Highland praise of a Briton designed
and own

If my friend MacNeil of Barra were to come

XXI

MARY OF THE SONGS

WANDERING CELTIC MINSTRELS

Born at Rodil in 1569 was Mary MacLeod, " the
inimitable poetess of the Isles, and the most original
of all our poets." She is better known to us
as Mairi Nighean Alasdair Ruaidh—Mary, the
daughter of Red Alasdair. As a composer and
singer of Gaelic songs Mary takes a foremost place
among the illustrious company of post-Reformation
bards and bardesses. I have thought it fitting to
introduce her here because of her long and intimate
association with Dunvegan Castle : she was a kins-
woman of its chiefs. In one of her unpublished
songs, which concludes with eulogistic references
to Tormod nan tri Tormod (Norman of the three
Normans), she informs us that she nursed no fewer
than five lairds of the MacLeods and two of the
lairds of Applecross. And many a time she
hummed to the infant heir of MacLeod the Dunvegan Cradle Croon.

It was when asked by a dying chief what kind of
lament she would raise for him that straightway
she composed the celebrated poem called *An Talla
'm bu ghnath le Mac-Leoid—*

> *Righ ! gur muladach 'tha mi,*
> *'S mi gun mhire gun mhànran,*
> *Anns an talla 'm bu ghnàth le Mac-Leòid.*

ITINERARY BARDS AT DUNVEGAN.

Mary spent many, many years at Dunvegan Castle, which on account of its harp and song festivals often was referred to as Dun nan Cliar, the Dun of the Poets. The Cliar-Sheanachain (the poetic disciples, some say, of Seanchan, who, himself, was the arch-bard to an Irish king) traversed the country in olden days as a band of wandering minstrels ; and no castle in the land was visited more frequently by such itinerary bards than was Dunvegan. The hospitality offered to these wandering poets and musicians was considered one of the happiest duties that the chief of every Celtic castle was privileged to discharge.

We find a *dun* at Ormsaig, in Ardnamurchan, that was known widely as Caisteal Dubh nan Cliar, simply because the *Cliaranaich*, or wandering bards and minstrels, were wont to sojourn there while on their rounds.

MARY IS BANISHED TO MULL.

But there came a time when Mary gave displeasure to the Chief because of some passages contained in one of her songs ; and so, under the supervision of a relative, he banished her to Mull. During her exile there, and while seated on a knoll, looking towards Jura and Sgarba and under grief and perplexity (*fo mhulaid 's fo im-cheist*), she composed *Luinneag Mhic-Leòid*. And, when MacLeod heard of this lyric, he immediately sent a boat to Mull to bring Mary back to Dunvegan, but only on the explicit understanding that she promised to compose no more songs.

She Returns to Dunvegan.

Great was Mary's jubilation when, gazing wistfully seaward from her accustomed hillock, she descried in the offing between Jura and Sgarba the galley that again was to convey her to the hall of mirth and festive song.

But Mary could not keep from making songs (you see, she had the irresistible impulse of the artist !) ; and not very long after her reinstalment at Dunvegan the indisposition of the Chief's son and heir sorely tempted her to try her hand at song-making again. When MacLeod rated her for having broken her vow, her reply was that she had only made a *crònan*, or lullaby.

In her latter days Mary was never seen without her *tonnag*, a little tartan shawl that was clasped by a silver brooch ; and we read that she aye leaned on a silver-mounted stick, and regret that she was much addicted to gossip, snuff, and whisky.

Most of her poems are in laud of the MacLeods ; but each one of them is elegant, simple, spontaneous, unconstrained. Her versifications, authorities have declared, " run like a mountain stream over a smooth bed of polished granite."

Mary Interred at Rodil.

And Mary MacLeod died at the ripe age of five score years and five ; and she was gathered to her fathers outwith the rambling ruins of Saint Clement's at Rodil, in the Harris. Peace be unto her manes !

Rodil, as already I have told you, is the " Iona " of the Siol Tormoid (the line of Norman) ; whereas Ui, or Eye, not far from Stornoway, is the time-honoured sepulchre of the MacLeods of Lewis, whom we designate the Siol Torquil.

It is computed that as many as nineteen of the Torquil MacLeods lie buried at Eye, where still may be seen a rather remarkable fifteenth-century effigy, supposed to be that of Roderic, the seventh MacLeod of Lewis. And, although Fortrose Cathedral was acknowledged as the tomb of the MacKenzies, William, the fifth Earl of Seaforth, was interred within the precincts of the Church of Saint Columba at Eye. There, too, lies all that was mortal of Roderic Morison, the Blind Harper, of whom I wish to speak with you in a few moments.

EYE THREATENED WITH DESTRUCTION.

As we go to press, I learn from my *Stornoway Gazette* that the encroachments of the sea are threatening Saint Columba's, at Eye. The last efforts to retrieve the neglect of earlier generations was made by Colonel Matheson, a late and honoured proprietor of the Lewis, who so genuinely inter- ested himself in the historic landmarks of that Island. Within living memory there was a road- way as well as a considerable bank of sand between the church and the sea. To-day the bank has disappeared ; while the erosion of the roadway is proceeding so rapidly that the undermining of the north wall of the church is wellnigh imminent, unless something be done immediately to arrest the action of the sea.

It would be a thousand pities were we, by our apathy and thoughtlessness, to allow this, our Lewisian Valhalla, to be swept away, when with a little foresight it might be preserved. We may be able to persuade the Commission for the

Preservation of Ancient and Historical Monuments to take Eye under its care : this old-world place is meritoriously deserving of its consideration.

If, however, it should fail to appreciate such an opportunity, we sincerely trust that loyal Lewis men and Lewis women, at home and scattered over the face of the earth, will see to it that this most interesting relic of very distant days does not suffer destruction.

XXII

THE BLIND HARPER

ANCIENT HEREDITARY OFFICES IN THE HEBRIDES

THE MORISON BRIEVES OF LEWIS

And loved he was, because he used to play
A silver harp, and sing a silver lay.

THE preceding remarks about itinerant minstrels
at Dunvegan and about Mary MacLeod, the
daughter of Red Alasdair and the bonnie singer of
bonnie songs, are reminiscent of another personality in the annals of Gaelic poesy. I refer to
Roderic Morison, the celebrated blind harper (*An
Clarsair Dall*), who also was associated intimately
with Dunvegan Castle, and whose severance with
the festive hall of the MacLeods was an event not
lacking in poignancy and sadness.

Roderic Morison first saw the light of day in
Lewis, and in the year 1646. His father, a clergyman loved and respected by the Lewis people
because of his uprightness of heart, was a descendant of those Morisons who were the esteemed
brieves or judges of the northern part of the Long
Island. Of the brieves and of the ancient juris-
prudential system once obtaining in the Hebrides
I intend telling you something directly.

Roderic Morison and his two brothers, Calum

and Angus, were meant for their father's profession, in pursuit of which they were sent to study at Inverness. There, however, they fell victims to a virulent epidemic of smallpox, as a result of which Roderic became totally blind. Calum and Angus were able later to complete their theological training, and eventually were inducted to charges in Poolewe and Contin respectively.

It was on account of his blindness that Roderic Morison was advised to take up music, a profession to which he was peculiarly adapted by nature. Before long his musical genius became widely recognised. During the course of his apprenticeship, so to speak, he was induced by his minstrel brethren to go over to Erin that he might study more closely the art of the *clarsach* or harp. That Roderic acquired much technical skill while sojourning in Ireland is undisputed : in his day the Irish harpist school was renowned throughout Celtic Europe for the general proficiency of its tuition.

Roderic Meets Iain Breac in Edinburgh.

On his way back to Skye Morison called at every baronial residence within easy access ; but at this time most of the Scottish noblemen and their retinues were in attendance at King James's Court in Holyrood, so that he did not meet many of those whose ears in ordinary circumstances he would have charmed. But the blind harper, determined not to be thwarted in his ambitions, made his way to Edinburgh ; and there he fell in with Iain Breac MacLeod who, having heard him sing his own compositions to the accompaniment of his silver-toned harp, immediately engaged him and brought him back to Dunvegan as his harper. Iain Breac,

Photo. by R. C. MacLeod of MacLeod.

St Clement's at Rodil—the " Iona " of the Siol Thormoid.

L

whose demise occurred in 1693, was the sixteenth Chief; and Canon MacLeod of MacLeod is inclined to the belief that he was the first Protestant Chief of his clan.

THE POSITION OF THE BARD.

Moreover, he is said to have been one of the latest Highland chieftains to embrace in his personal staff a piper, a wit, and a *clarsair* or harper—three clan-officials who in extravagant measure were provided for as long as circumstances permitted, who were held in the highest esteem, and who took precedence of most of the chief's household. If I remember rightly, the bard of the old, Celtic clan ranked next to the members of the chief's family: it was the bard who, prior to the general adoption of the *crann-tara*, or fiery-cross, summoned the clan to arms, and in inspiring songs of war recited pristine deeds of derring-do. In the bard, as a matter of fact, was embodied the whole *esprit de corps* of the clan.

The position of the bard, piper, and seannachie or official recorder and story-teller (the last mentioned is usually known in Ireland as the *fear-sgeulachd*, or man of the tales) carried with them certain unique privileges inasmuch as they were hereditary offices as a rule. The world-famed MacCrimmons were MacLeod's hereditary pipers; and they enjoyed prerogatives similar to those conferred upon the MacArthurs, who were the hereditary pipers to the MacDonalds.

Like privileges were attached to the office of brieve or judge, where it existed.

Of course, the retention of a licensed wit or jester was a fairly common practice throughout the courts of Europe during the Middle Ages. Such jesters survived well into the seventeenth century. Elizabeth and Mary, Queen of Scots, had their fools ; and in the person of Sexton, who was nick-named Patch, a prominent English monarch accepted a fool or patch on the recommendation of Cardinal Wolsey.

A Hereditary Seneschal.

Many Hebridean castles retained a hereditary seneschal or steward " to marshall guests in bower and hall." In the family of an Island chieftain many important duties devolved on the steward. That to every man according to his rank and quality he might assign his place at the chief's table, it was imperative for him to have been more than ordinarily versed in the lineage of the High-land clans, though, no doubt, in the allocation of seats he was assisted to some extent by the bard and seannachie, who prided themselves on knowing the genealogies other than merely those of the ramifications of their own particular clan. The steward performed his function by drawing a score with a white wand before the guest, who thereupon took his seat in the proper order. Occasionally he erred ; but his chief was not held responsible and in no way incurred censure when his seneschal unintentionally denied a guest the precedence that was his due, or placed an inferior visitor above the salt.

The table of a typical Hebridean chieftain was also attended by a cup-bearer who, after having drunk the first draught as a proof that the contents of the cup were genuine, kept it filled and bore it round the company. His office, too, was hereditary, as was the office of the purse-bearer or chamberlain. The latter official supervised the chief's household and personal accounts ; and in lieu of his services he was invested with rights such as were " fairly written on good parchment."

MORISON IS INSTALLED AT GLENELG.

Roderic Morison long enjoyed the patronage of MacLeod of Dunvegan, who at one time maintained him, rent-free, in a farm at Tota Mor, in Glenelg, a part of the mainland of Inverness-shire where of a time the MacLeods held extensive territories. The Glenelg lands passed into the hands of the MacLeods in 1344. About that year David II. bestowed by royal charter upon " Malcolmo filio Turmode Maclode " eight davochs of arable land (the part of Glenelg forfeited by the Bissets), in return for which the latter and his successors were required to keep in perpetual readiness for the King's service a thirty-six-oared galley.

In the art of the *clarsach* Morison had no peer in all the Highlands. It was while in residence in Tota Mor that the sightless *clarsair* composed some of his most beautiful pieces, including the elegiac verses known as the " Spoil of the Hundreds " (*Creach nan Ciadan*). These verses were written on the death of his friend, Iain Breac ; and in his *Beauties of Gaelic Poetry* MacKenzie alludes to this lamentation as being " one of the most pathetic, plaintive, and heart-touching productions we have read during a life half spent amid the flowery meadows of our Highland Parnassus."

The MacLeods certainly had the happy knack of engaging the services of bards and singers of a very superior order.

No Longer Welcome.

On the death of Iain Breac MacLeod there arose in Dunvegan a Pharaoh who knew not Joseph : Roderic, Iain Breac's successor, dispensed with the services of the harper, piper, and fool. Thus it was that the blind harper found himself no longer welcome in the Dun of the Poets. Such were the unhappy circumstances that drove him away from Dunvegan : such were the untoward conditions that led him to reflect on the never-failing kindnesses of his old chief, Iain Breac, and to felicitate himself by dreaming of the festive scenes of former days.

And it was in his bitterness of heart that he composed what, unquestionably, is the most powerful and vivid of all his works ; to wit, *Oran Mor MhicLeoid*—literally, the Big Song of MacLeod. This lament consists of an imaginary duet between the blind harper and *MacTalla* or Echo (of music) who, like himself, is now an unwanted stranger in the harpless and songless Dun of the Hospitality of the Winecups. By some it is thought that this, his last song, was composed just after his ejectment from his holding in Glenelg.

So cherished was this *Oran Mor*, or Big Song, by Sir Alexander MacKenzie of Gairloch that on special occasions he hired a vocalist to sing it to him ; and it was MacKenzie's chiefest regret that for it every Highland laird did not profess a like regard.

Roderic Morison Returns to Lewis and Dies There.

This pathetic story of the blind harper reminds one a little of the last minstrel to sing of Border chivalry, whose " withered cheeks and tresses gray seemed to have known a better day," and who, with wistful eye and faltering step, sought alms in Newark's stately tower. But there was a slight difference : in the *Lay of the Last Minstrel* we read that the hoary and agèd harper was a wanderer, begging his bread from door to door, whereas we have no evidence that Roderic Morison was ever reduced to such penurious straits, or that he even wandered from place to place with his harp. No doubt, on special invitation he not infrequently went as a guest to the mansion of many a notable family ; but he was emphatically a *duin' uasal*—a man of gentle birth—and scarcely required to eke out a livelihood in that way.

When the years were heavy upon him, the blind harper returned to his native Isle of Lewis : in peace and in tranquillity Roderic Morison lived his latter days in the bosom of his Lewisian kinsfolk. And, when he passed, his mortal frame was laid in the mools at Eye, in the belovèd Island of his fathers.

He was the latest of his bardic company.

HEREDITARY JUDGES IN THE HEBRIDES.

From an early period till about the beginning of the eighteenth century Celtic communities were regulated to a large extent by a system of hereditary jurisdictions. In the Highlands and Islands the administrators of the law held their office by hereditary right. They were called brieves, and corresponded very closely to the ancient Irish judges known as brehons. The latter reduced to writing the system of jurisprudence commonly referred to as the Brehon Laws.

It is probable that brieves and brehons alike (both words are derived from the same root, namely, *breitheamh,* signifying an umpire or judge) were assisted in the discharge of their legal duties by competent men who, either traditionally or by personal study, may have acquired a working knowledge of Celtic institutes. This was especially likely to have been the case if a brieve succeeded his father at an early age, for he could hardly be expected to be very conversant with old-time rights and usages.

Celtic jurisprudence was based on the principle of a money compensation for crimes committed. In Ireland this reparation was termed *eric,* and amounted to nothing more or less that a blood-fine paid to the relatives of a deceased by the man who killed him. Such blood-money was called *galanas* in Wales.

We find the almost identical compensatory provision required by Anglo-Saxon law, for the *wergild* was simply the price paid by the kinspeople of a murderer that the criminal might be reprieved. The sum thus demanded went to the relatives of the murdered person. Of course, the *wergild* varied in amount according to the rank of the person whose life had been taken : at one end of the scale you had the fines payable for a king or an archbishop or a thegn, while at the other end were the varying *wergilds* of bordars and absolute serfs.

A Brieve-in-Chief at Islay.

Seldom in early times was the authority of the brieve challenged. In respect of his services he was entitled to an eleventh part of the sum assessed in compensation for damages ; and the remaining ten-elevenths were divided between the person or persons in whose favour the judgment was given (or his relatives, if he were dead) and the chief. As a rule, the latter took only a small, nominal proportion of the brieve's award.

In the days of the Lords of the Isles, when probably each island-community large enough to require a resident judge had a brieve for the settlement of disputes that might arise locally, Islay was the headquarters of the arch-brieve of the more southerly of the Western Isles. In his fascinating *Book of the Lews* MacKenzie reminds us that there existed a right of appeal to the brieve-in-chief, who held his court in Islay. He was, in reality, the Hebridean Lord Chief Justice in Appeal.

THE MORISONS OF LEWIS.

In Lewis the office of brieve was entrusted to the Morisons, who resided either at Bragar or at Habost, in the parish of Ness, and who were known as *Clann nam Breitheamh*, the Kinsfolk of the Brieves.

Referring to the Morison brieves of Lewis, Sir Robert Gordon writes—"The Brieve is a kind of judge who hath an absolute judicatorie, unto whose authoritie and censure they willinglie submit themselves when he determineth any debateable question between partie and partie." In their legal capacity the Morisons waxed strong in the northern part of the Long Island. They were incessantly at loggerheads with the MacAulays of Uig ; and at a much later date they came into fierce conflict with the MacLeods of Lewis.

It was as a result of a deadly feud between the Morisons and a sept of the Siol Torquil MacLeods that a small islet off the coast of Eddrachillis, in Sutherlandshire, got the name of *Eilean nam*

Breitheamh, the Isle of the Brieve. Towards the close of the sixteenth century a Lewis brieve and three or four of his clansmen encountered a party of MacLeods in Assynt. In the mêlée that followed all the Morisons were slain, including the brieve, who met his fate at the hands of the petty chief of that sept. Now, the remains of the brieve were to have been brought home to Lewis ; but they were buried on this Island because the birlinn that was to have conveyed them across the Minch was delayed by unsuitable winds on this part of the seaboard of Assynt.

To the family of Morisons that supplied Lewis with its brieves belonged the aforementioned Roderic Morison, the celebrated blind harper.

Does it not seem a remarkable coincidence that a barren, out-of-the-way island like Lewis was destined to produce in the Morisons and the MacLeods two of the most powerful and numerous clans in the history of the Highlands ?

How the MacKenzies Became Masters of Lewis.

The latter part of the sixteenth century witnessed the gradual extinction of the Lewis branch of the MacLeods ; and by the beginning of the seventeenth the MacKenzies of Kintail had made themselves rulers of the Long Island by a process that, *de facto*, was completed when in 1610 Neil MacLeod and his piratical kinsmen were dislodged from their stronghold in Loch Roag, and when, according to a letter written three years later to the King by Sir Thomas Hamilton, the then Lord Advocate, Neil went to his execution " verie christianlie " (see *Behold the Hebrides !*).

The weakness of the Lewis MacLeods was inherent : Roderic, perhaps the most disreputable of all the MacLeods of Lewis, married in turn three wives—a MacKenzie, a Stewart (whose son was advised by Mary, Queen of Scots, not to marry without her consent " because you have that honour to be by Stewart blood "), and a MacLean—by each of whom he had a son called Torquil, that name having been the distinguishing patronymic of his sept. The rival claims of these three Torquils to the succession promoted an internecine struggle that utterly shattered the power and prestige of the Lewis MacLeods. When, rightly or wrongly, the aforementioned Roderic divorced his first wife, he automatically disinherited her son, Torquil, who, having spent his earlier years with his maternal relatives in Strath Conon, was bynamed Torquil Cononach. Torquil, the son by his Stewart wife, and in ordinary circumstances the rightful heir, was either killed in Sutherland or drowned in the Minch ; and thus Roderic declared Torquil Dubh, his son by the daughter of MacLean of Duart, to be his heir.

However, in 1568 Torquil Cononach carried off old Roderic, Chief of the Lewis ; and for four years he " held him in miserable captivitie in montanis and cavernis of craigis, far distant from ye societie of men," where he " pereist thro' cauld and famine." In durance vile he made a disposition in favour of Cononach, whom earlier he had declared an illegitimate claimant. Later Roderic actually revoked this acknowledgment, and confessed to his having made it under pain of death.

With the valiant assistance of Neil, the Berisay pirate, Torquil Dubh was able to establish himself in Lewis ; but about 1595 he launched a fierce attack on Torquil Cononach and his MacKenzie kinsfolk in the vicinity of Coigach, near Loch Broom. In retaliation, Cononach devised a scheme by which in 1597 Torquil Dubh fell into his hands and was swiftly disposed of. But for some time Neil was successful in supporting the claim to Lewis of Torquil Dubh's sons against Torquil Cononach. Now, both sons of Torquil Cononach were dead; and so his daughter, who was married to her kinsman, a brother of MacKenzie of Kintail, became heiress. Cononach, her father, had conveyed all hereditary rights to her husband; and it was in this roundabout manner that a few years afterwards the MacKenzies urged a successful claim to the ancient patrimony of the MacLeods of Lewis—a claim that old Roderic, by his personal stupidity a generation earlier, had rendered feasible.

But, for all that, the Island of Lewis remains essentially the home of the descendants of Leod, through Torquil, who was his son by the daughter of MacCrailt Armuinn; and, although during the intervening years Lewis has changed hands more than thrice, MacLeods scattered all over the world cherish their associations with the ancient inheritance of the hapless Siol Torquil.

XXIII

FEARCHAR LIGHICHE

HEREDITARY PHYSICIANS IN THE WESTERN ISLES

THE BEATONS OF ISLAY, MULL, AND SKYE

It is not known when first originated the practice among the chieftains of the Western Isles of retaining hereditary doctors ; but from a glance at contemporary records it is patent that as early as the fourteenth century many members of the famous Beaton family had established themselves securely in several notable households in virtue of their medical skill. We might safely say that the Beatons were our earliest recognised medical practitioners in Scotland. Of their origin and early history, however, we know very little. This may be due to a number of causes, not the least probable among them being that throughout the centuries the name, Beaton, has appeared in so many different forms. Some of the more common variations met with in old MSS. and charters are Beath, Beton, Bethune, MacBey, MacBeth, MacBeath, and even MacVeagh.

The controversy that at intervals has raged on the origins of, and connections between, the Beatons and the Bethunes has been an almost interminable one. My own impression is that as an established family the Beaton sept is very much older than the

Bethunes claiming descent from the French adventurer who came over to Scotland from Bethune in the sixteenth century. In fact, documentary evidence proves that in many of the more southerly Isles the Beatons had gained a professional reputation as early as the fourteenth century. All these names, I would respectfully suggest, are derived from the Gaelic, *beatha*, meaning life. This seems quite plausible when we remember that the Beatons were renowned throughout the length and breadth of the Hebrides as savers of life. Beathag, the life-giver, used to be a common Christian name in Hebrides for a woman ; and the word, *beathan*, is sometimes applied by Celtic poets to a young gallant.

SAINT COLUMBA'S SUCCESSOR.

Perhaps the earliest prominent member of this family was Saint Beton, afterwards known as Saint Baithen. You will recall that, when Columba died in 597, Baithen succeeded him as Abbot of Iona. It was a long recognised custom at Iona for the ruling abbot to nominate his successor, who was referred to as the *oighre* (heir) or *Comh-Arba* of Colum Cille (*i.e.* a successor and partner in church lands). Baithen was both Columba's cousin and foster-brother ; and during the latter saint's life he supervised the farming in Iona and was in charge of the monastic farm on Ethica Terra (Tiree), where penitents were sent until they were considered sufficiently purged of their waywardnesses to be permitted to return from semi-exile.

The monks of Iona continued to select their abbots from the stock of Colum Cille (Columba), who himself was related through Conal Gulban to Neil of the Nine Hostages. Neil was High

King of Ireland, and reigned at Tara towards the close of the fourth century. The Beatons, likewise, were of Irish descent. In his introduction to James MacGregor's *Book of the Dean of Lismore* Skene writes—" The Betons, or, as their name was in Gaelic, MacBheatha(n), who were hereditary physicians in Islay and Mull, and who were also sennachies of the MacLeans, were of Irish origin, being O'Neills."

On the third anniversary of Saint Columba's death (9th June 600) Abbot Baithen died at Iona. The traditions of Baithen still lingers in the names, Abbey St. Bathan's, a parish in the Lammermuirs, and in Bathan's Kirk.

Among the other members of the Beaton sept buried at Iona is Dr. John Beton. On the tablet marking the spot where he lies is engraved the following inscription : HIC JACET JOHANNES BETONUS MACLENORUM FAMILIAE MEDICUS QUI MORTUUS EST 19 NOVEMBRIS 1657 AET 63. DONALDUS BETONUS FECIT 1674 (Here lies John Beton, physician to the MacLean family, who died on 19th November 1657, aged 63. Donald Beton made this, 1674.)

On the upper part of this gravestone is a coat of arms, below which are the lines : ECCE CADIT JACULO VICTRICIS MORTIS INIQUAE—QUI TOTIES ALIOS SOLVERAT IPSE MALIS—SOLI DEO GLORIA. (Lo ! he falleth by the dart of victorious, unrighteous death —who himself so oft loosed others from their ills— to God alone be glory.)

THE BEATONS OF ISLAY AND MULL.

More than one historian alludes to the MacBeths or Beatons of Islay and Mull. One of their number found his way to Mull on the express invitation of a chief of the MacLeans of Duart, who bestowed upon him a piece of land at Pennycross, near Carsaig Bay, in return for his medical services. Doubtless, the chief was none other than he whose life was saved from the venom of a poisoned arrow by the skill of his Beaton physician ; and it is reasonable to suppose that the actual physician was the aforenamed Dr. John Beton, who in recognition of his qualifications was granted a lair in the ancient burying-ground of the Scottish Kings. The Beatons of Mull were usually known as MacVeys or MacVeaghs. There is still a number of Beatons residing in the locality of the Ross of Mull.

In order to encourage them to settle in various parts of the Highlands and Islands, quite a number of chieftains and landlords of lesser distinction offered members of the Beaton family extensive stretches of land, free of any kind of burden. Fearchar Lighiche (Farquhar, the Physician), one of the Islay Beatons and King's Physician, accepted from Prince Alexander Stewart in 1379 the lands of Melness and Hope, in Sutherland ; and seven years later King Robert II. added to the heritage of this same Farquhar all the islands from Armadale Head, in Farr, to Rhu-Stoer, in Assynt. Latterly, he became physician to the MacKays of Farr. Farquhar is referred to in the *Old Statistical Account* of the Parish of Eddrachillis as a native of Islay and a prominent healer. In 1511 Donald Mac-Donachie MacCorrachie, who was " descendit frae Farquhar Leiche," made over the lands of Melness and Hope, together with his estates in Strath Naver, to MacKay.

Not the least representative of the Beatons was the branch that found its way to Skye. It claimed descent from Archibald Bethune of Pittochy or Capeldray, in Fife, fifth son of John Bethune, fifth Laird of Balfour. It was in the House of Orr (Balfour House), in Fife, that Cardinal Beaton or Bethune was born. In the fifteenth century one of these Beatons demonstrated such skill in medicine that he was invited to settle and practise in Argyll. Not very long afterwards the MacDonalds and the MacLeods of Skye were soliciting the permanent, hereditary services of the Beatons, and offered them as much land as they desired to possess, without any financial encumbrances. The Beatons accepted the offer, and stipulated that, as long as their sept remained in Skye, one member of each generation should be educated as a doctor.

Farquhar, the seventh descendant of John Bethune, fifth Laird of Balfour, acquitted himself with such distinction as a surgeon and physician at the Battle of Worcester (1651), in which some hundreds of Skyemen took part, that Sir Norman MacLeod of Bernera, who commanded a regiment of Islesmen, commended him for his gallantry.

As hereditary physicians to the Lords of the Isles the Beatons were held in great esteem throughout the Hebrides. One of their number, Fergus Mac-Bheatha, was in 1448 Chancellor of the Isles. With the decline in power of the great MacDonalds the Beatons lost much of their prestige in what we now refer to as the Inner Hebrides, though in 1609 James VI. granted hereditarily to Fergus Mac-Baithe of Balinaby, in Islay, certain territories in that Island in virtue of his having been " *principalis medici intra bondas Insularum.*"

John, Fergus's son, succeeded to his father's properties in 1628 ; but in the ensuing year he resigned them to the Campbells, who by this time had ousted the MacDonalds from Islay. It would seem as though the Beatons deserted Islay with this change in ownership. But their medical skill was not unrecognised even by the Campbells, as is evinced by the following quotations among the accounts of the Campbells of Islay, dated 1638 :—

"Item waireit one Doctor Beatoune for his charges in goeing to Illa and coming from Illa home againe to Edinburgh, £178, 8s.

"Item givin to Doctor Arnot, Doctor Beatoune, and Doctor Sybbald in ane consultatioun concerneing the Laird his seiknes in Edinburgh, £71, 6s."

NEIL BEATON'S PETITION.

In the vast collection of historical papers belonging to the Duke of Argyll there are many references to the famous family of hereditary physicians in Mull, whose name in the eighteenth century took the form of Beaton, though appearing in earlier records as MacBey. Among such papers is a petition dated December 1760 from "Niall Beaton, son of Master John, minister of Kilninian," praying the Argyll of the time to be reinstated in that small possession which for a debt had been made to Lauchlan MacLean, a Glasgow merchant, by the Laird of Duart. From the charters which the petitioner quoted it appears that in October of 1572 Hector MacLaine of Dowart (Duart) granted a charter to "Andrew MacDonil . . . and his heirs, of the pennyland of Peincross in Brolis, of a shilling and 8 pennyland of howl and extent (he being sufficiently skilled and qualified in the medical art) together with supreme and principal medical office commonly called Ardolleraught within the

Photo. by R. C. MacLeod of MacLeod.

Southern Wing of Dunvegan Castle.

bounds of the heritable lands belonging to Dowart, viz., Mull, Morven, Tiree, Islay, Jura, Loyng, Ardgour, and Lochaber, with all the provinces and properties lying within the Sherrifdom of Tarbert." "Ardolleraught" may be the equivalent of *ard*, meaning high (arch) and *ollamh*, a doctor.

Certain technical difficulties arose as to whether or not the holder of the charter was legally entitled to claim medical and surgical jurisdiction over such a vast monopoly ; but it is recorded that in the end the Duke of Argyll gave to the petitioner, Neil Beaton, and to his heirs a new charter, and thereby obviated any subsequent dispute.

FARQUHAR AND HIS KNOWLEDGE OF BOTANY.

Exactly when the Beatons first took up residence in Skye is not known ; but they seem to have been fairly well established in that Island by the end of the seventeenth century. Martin Martin refers to an " illiterate empiric Neil Beaton in Skye, who of late is so well known in the isles and continent, for his great success in curing several dangerous distempers, though he never appeared in the quality of a physician until he arrived at the age of forty years, and then also without the advantage of education. He pretends to judge the various qualities of plants and roots by their different tastes ; he has likewise a nice observation of the colours of their flowers, from which he learns their astringent and loosening qualities : he extracts the juice of plants and roots after a chymical way, peculiar to himself, and with little or no charge." Neil, he tells us further, treated contemporary medical practice and methods of dispensing with disdain, having effected many cures where recognised practitioners had failed. Martin discoursed seriously with him on several occasions, and felt satisfied that this herbalist obtained his ends by means that were lawful. Martin also makes mention of a certain James Beaton, who was a surgeon in North Uist and accompanied some MacLeans in an attack upon a vessel belonging to the Earl of Argyll, who proposed taking Mull by storm.

Legion are the tales that in Skye are told of Fearchar Lighiche and of his son, Niall Og. One day Farquhar happened to be sitting on a knoll close to where some folks were labouring at their harvest. His apparent indolence so irritated the harvesters that one of them rebuked him for his idleness. But Farquhar retorted that his knowledge of the medicinal properties of the minute plants that clothed the knoll was of greater value than all they could gather from their meagre land. In his early days he had served his apprenticeship to a magician who worked miraculous cures in the Hebrides ; and it was while left in charge of the pot that simmered on the fire, the contents of which he was enjoined not to touch—the pot contained a white serpent, a rare creature used by the ancient Hebridean doctors in effecting their cures—that he, himself, actually received the power of healing, for, when it boiled over, a drop or two spluttered on his hands and thus affected him with the skill of the healer. When his master returned to empty the pot, he discovered that, for him at any rate, its contents had lost their efficacy.

As physician to MacLeod at Dunvegan, Farquhar wrought notable cures among the ailing inhabitants of Kilmuir, and, indeed, throughout all the Isle of Skye, because he was never loath to journey to the bedside of any one who was indisposed. And the folks of Skye declared that he was called to his cases by the ravens, whose language he understood, and who conveyed to him intelligence of illness almost as quickly as telegraphy conveys it to-day. Often when on the moors of Skye did Fearchar Lighiche meet a raven on its way with tidings of illness and distress. He was even accredited in Skye with having had the power of raising the dead by the uttering of a few words chosen from a vocabulary reserved for such occasions. One day, they say, he met a funeral moving towards the shore at Carbost ; and, having stopped it, he addressed the coffin, whereat the corpse within immediately came to life again.

It is not recorded where Farquhar died, nor is it known where he lies buried ; but in Skye he was succeeded by his son, Niall Og, Young Neil, who was endowed by MacLeod of MacLeod with a freehold at Sumardale, a now deserted spot above Loch Harport and some miles north of Drynoch. Sumardale passed out of the Beatons' hands long since. No doubt, the Beatons in Skye at the present day claim descent from Farquhar, the Physician, and from Niall Og, his son.

Neil succeeded his father as medical adviser to Clan Ranald, whose Lady had great faith in him. When in the course of time Neil died, she took very ill ; and there was no one in all the Hebrides who could treat her malady. And much did she wish that Niall Og had been alive to make the cure to her. However, one night Neil appeared to her in a dream, and requested her to send a boat as fast as oars and sails could carry it to the west of MacLeod's Country with a trusty messenger who would find growing in a patch below Healaval Mor a plant, an infusion of which, when drunk, would speedily cure her. Having followed these directions, Clan Ranald's Lady was restored to health.

HERBALIST CURES IN SKYE.

Martin gives us a very complete account of the cures and simples used anciently in Skye and throughout the Hebrides generally ; and in a chapter dealing exclusively with the diseases known and unknown in Skye and the adjacent Islands he enumerates many herbalist cures such as were practised by the Beatons. In these the Islespeople had supreme faith, as is seen from the fact that invalids travelled great distances to seek the advice of these renowned specialists. Here, *brevitatis causa*, I cannot go into the multiplicity of remedies that were recognised ; but I would recommend those who are interested to consult the relevant passages quoted by Martin. His survey includes remedies not only for every conceivable ailment to which human beings are liable, but also for such maladies as deafness and blindness in cattle and sheep. In addition, he gives an enormous list of plants and herbs from which various medicinal extracts were prepared with gratifying results. But, as you will readily believe after perusing Martin's account, the cures invariably were many times worse than the diseases.

John MacCulloch also noted several instances in which the Hebrideans resorted to extraordinary curative measures. Were MacCulloch not so painfully condescending and sarcastic, his letters on subjects relating to contemporary manners and customs in the Western Isles would be more appreciated than they are, because we cannot deny that in one or two respects they are quite unique.

The belief in some of the cures adopted by the Beatons still survives : occasionally one comes across a case where the patient has had recourse to such a traditional panacea. During the last few years a young medical friend of mine, who is practising presently in the southern part of Skye, has noted one or two remarkable instances in which his patients have resorted to the weirdest remedies imaginable ; and yet many Highland folks retain an unholy faith in the bottle of medicine that may be given them, believing that without a dose prescribed by a qualified doctor they cannot possibly recover. In such cases, of course, a bottle of tinctured water may be all that is necessary. Organotherapy, electrical medicine, and public health are swiftly displacing the older and more cumbrous methods of restoration ; but how far these advances in medical science are likely to succeed in an island like Skye, where the faith in bottled cures will certainly die hard, remains to be seen.

THE PRINCE AND THE BEATONS.

The story is told that while crossing a moor in the outskirts of Balmeanach, in Bracadale, Prince Charlie and Flora MacDonald and a guide met a certain Beaton and his newly wedded bride, who were in the act of driving home their cows to be milked. Befitting salutations were exchanged ; and in the course of conversation the Beatons realised that the spokesman of the party was a *duin' uasal*—a man of gentle birth. As this casual interview continued, the Beatons, who to begin with were inordinately embarrassed, became quite chatty and insisted on the three wanderers having a drink of milk. All this time they were noticing, however, that two of the strangers were taking great care of the third—a beautiful youth who said very little and seemed very anxious. And more than curious were Beaton and his wife on seeing that, although two of the wayfarers did not object to drinking out of a *cuman*—a little, wooden milking pail rarely seen in the Highlands to-day—they were careful that their charge drank from nothing less becoming than a golden cup carried for the purpose.

When two of the strangers moved off, the spokesman lingered behind for a moment to speak with the couple, and to offer three pieces of gold as mementoes of a memorable meeting. And sore, sore at heart were the Beatons when they learned that the youth whom they entertained was the young Prince of Scotland. Months elapsed, after which the goodwife of Balmeanach bore a daughter who developed into the loveliest child in all Bracadale, and was as unlike her parents as a child possibly could have been. And she was known throughout Skye as Mairi a' Phrionnsa, Mary of the Prince, as though she had been begotten of him, for the Islesfolk declared that her likeness to the Prince was due to the impression that had been made on her mother, when she realised that one of the strangers who drank of her milk on the moor above Balmeanach was the fugitive Prince of Scotland.

The distinguishing byname of Mairi a' Phrionnsa still is applied in a jocular way to the Beaton descendants of this couple ; but Mairi's singular charm and beauty have not been handed down to her posterity.

Many of the Beatons successfully combined the gravity of the divine and the skill of the physician: as minister of Bracadale, John Beaton, who died in 1707, was the first clergyman to dispense, in Skye, the Sacrament of the Lord's Supper after the Protestant manner.

The written history of the Beatons is decidedly scattered, confused, and scanty. In the Advocates' Library, however, a copious work on this famous sept awaits a translator and transcriber.

A MEMORY OF THE GREAT WAR.

During the Great War I became very friendly with a certain Norman Beaton, who was a native of Skye. Norman and I had been in many a tight corner together. I remember one occasion on which he was obliged to leave the best part of his kilt on the Boches' barbed wire because of an enemy sniper, whose post we had failed to locate. On another occasion he and I managed to escape from the German front-line trench by a piece of sheer bluff. Beaton was " No. 1 " on the Lewis machine-gun ; and he could carry his weapon, together with its spare parts when necessary, through an offensive that lasted for days. He could sprint with his machine-gun across a shell-holed battlefield and through the weirdest multiplicity of enemy entanglements as could no one else in the company.

When coming home on furlough, I gave Norman Beaton an old tin watch as a keepsake. Poor fellow ! he had asked for it, although I believe at the time his tunic pockets were full of watches that a week or two earlier had been looted from prisoners. Beaton and I and another Skyeman (whose name it would be indiscreet to mention here, because he now lives in Skye) carried on a roaring trade for a time in German watches. Since these days, however, I have come to the conclusion that the ransacking of an enemy's pockets at the point of the bayonet was a shabby, shabby practice, much as in the height of battle it was deemed an unwritten law among the more fearless and belli-cose. Its only virtue rested in the truth that, in the event of your being taken captive, you were pretty certain to undergo the identical experience. All the same, it was not what one might call chivalrous : the maxim that in love and in war everything is fair is surely threadbare and out of date.

Often I wondered since 1917 what had become of Norman Beaton, until last summer I found his name inscribed on the Snizort panel of the Skye war memorial at Portree. Probably he met his end in the terrific enemy onslaught in the spring of 1918.

Reading the names on that simple, yet graceful, memorial in Portree, reflecting on the awful slaughter that it serves to commemorate, and re-membering the shirkers who grew fat and opulent on the sacrifice of their fellow-countrymen, com-paratively speaking one cannot but have a tremen-dous respect even for the enemy—and for two reasons, firstly, because he was a braver man than the shirker who never left his employment and received promotion in it when the war terminated, and, secondly, because he and you were out there to murder one another as a means of settling a dispute that neither he nor you had created.

And then Europe brags about its democracy !

Photo. by Kathleen.

The Old Kirk of Kilmuir, in Dunvegan.

"Where nightly the hill-wind whispers requiem."

I can see no salvation for civilisation until democracy demands that the piffling handfuls of men composing reichstags and cabinets and councils of war, who by their avarice or crass stupidity sign declarations of war and otherwise render international carnages and desolation possible, are the first to occupy the front-line trench.

XXIV

THE ROAD TO TRUMPAN

THE LAST OF HIS LINE

" Far from the creeks of home and hills of heath,
A boy, he kept the old tryst of his people
With the dark girl, Death."

RAIN, rain, rain ! What a wonderful Island for
rain ; and what wonderful rain ! Seldom do I
venture far afield without being overtaken by a
deluge. But, in that the best quality of Skye or
Lewisian rain soaks one to the skin in a twinkling
of an eye, it has a really pleasant feature, for to
be half wet is miserable, while to be dripping is
philosophically delightful. All anxiety disappears
when you realise that you are as saturated as you
possibly can be ; and there is a great secret in
realising this an hour or two before you actually are.

It was not so much the rain but the terrific
head-wind that drove me, famishing and irritable,
into Allt-na-Chaim, the first tenanted house in
Vaternish that is reached on the road leading to
Trumpan, it being located immediately above Loch
Bay and a mile or so south of the village of Stein.

In Allt-na-Chaim and at the hands of one,
Seonaid MacPhee to name, I gladly received the
hospitality that befitted such a boisterous day. My
bicycle, as red with rust and Skye mud as a disused
ploughshare left lying for a generation or two

about an old farm-steading, creaked and grated below me : so clogged were its wheels that in their present condition they refused to turn a single yard past Allt-na-Chaim.

BATTLE OF THE WALL.

In the end, however, I did reach Trumpan, and found both the lichened stone marking the grave of Lady Grange and the tomb of the MacDonalds of Vaternish. In many ways the old, ruined church at Trumpan, with its crude graveyard, reminds me of a very similar ruin at Dalmore, in the Carloway district of Lewis : only, the latter is closer to the sea and, as its name denotes, is situated in a valley, whereas the ruined church at Trumpan stands on the side of a hill. Included and almost inconspicuous among the stones composing its dilapidated walls is an ancient baptismal font that, doubtless, was used in pre-Reformation times.

A little beyond Stein and on a small, rocky eminence close to the roadside is a creditably modest memorial in granite to the men of Vaternish who, on land and on sea, made the supreme sacrifice in the Great War.

When visibility is good, Beinn Geary, a hill behind Trumpan, commands an unrivalled survey of Dunvegan Head, of Loch Dunvegan with its iron-bound coast and the Islands of Isay and Mingay, of the Minch, and of the more northerly of the Outer Hebrides.

FOUGHT TO A FINISH.

Below and a little to the south-west of Trumpan are the Bay and Point of Ardmore where was fought the celebrated Battle of the Spoiling of the Wall, a conflict to which I alluded when telling you of the Faery Flag and its legends. Vaternish was the scene of many a strife between the MacLeods and the MacDonalds. In avengement of their defeat at this battle a band of MacDonalds forayed MacLeod's Country. But the raiders were pursued and overtaken ; and at the termination of the rencounter that followed only a MacLeod and a MacDonald smith, both clad in heavy mail, survived to sustain the fight. When, through exhaustion and loss of blood, the MacLeod was about to cave in, his wife, they say, came on the scene ; and, by striking the MacDonald with her stick, she distracted his attention for a brief moment during which her husband slew his opponent. Beinn a' Ghobha, the Blacksmith's Hill, is still the name given to the place where this incident is recorded to have occurred. At the base of Beinn a' Ghobha may be traced the huts into which wolves were baited and ensnared in olden days.

In the name, Cnoc Mhic Iain, the Hillock of the Son of Iain, survives the tradition of yet another combat between the MacDonalds and the MacLeods, for it marks the spot where fell a certain Roderic MacLeod (*Ruairaidh Unish*), the doughty son of Iain MacLeod of Vaternish.

In common with other parts of Skye, the Trumpan district can boast a " Hanging Hill " ; that is to say, a hill whereon the less fortunate delinquents were hanged, probably in the days when jurisdiction was heritable.

FLEEING BEFORE THE GALE.

With the wind at my back, my return to Dunvegan was less strenuous and harassing than the

outward journey to Trumpan, though the holes
and ruts and rain-washed chuckie-stanes so characteristic of a Hebridean trunk road demanded caution
and a discreet regulation of speed. Times there
are when one has no objection to splashing wildly
through pools and dashing helter-skelter through
gravelly streams that may intersect the road.

In the undulating harvest-fields, that at Stein
sweep down to the shores of Loch Bay, the wind
had left not a single stook on its feet : sheaves and
hay-stacks lay strewn in every direction. Vainly I
strove to keep up with a ketch that hugged the
further side of Loch Dunvegan and was making
for the Castle ; and, had certain stretches of the
road not been submerged or completely washed
away, I might have succeeded. But I eagerly
watched the ketch as she sped with almost incredible rapidity before a westerly gale until, like
a phantom galley, she disappeared in a storm that
raged behind the lesser islands of the Loch. I felt
so envious of her crew's sea-worthiness !

At various intervals along the elevated skyline
above Boreraig and Colbost were rising columns of
vapour, caused by the wind rushing up in the face
of the cliffs and blowing into powder the numberless streamlets and rills, just as they were on the
point of tumbling off the rocky shelves. At first
sight one might have taken this spindrift for smoke
rising from cave dwellings or, perhaps, from
smugglers' bothies among the rocks.

IN KILMUIR CHURCHYARD.

To carry out a topographical programme on a
day such as this, at least four things are requisite—
to wit, an iron constitution, a will of tempered

steel, an interesting objective, and a reliable bicycle. For the escort of the elements on this occasion I, myself, was entirely responsible, because, had I gone straight to Trumpan on setting out, I would have been back in Dunvegan before the day broke down. But I had spent the best part of the forenoon in the churchyard of Kilmuir, dreaming and dreaming of " old, unhappy, far-off things, and battles long ago." Thither I had been attracted by the uncomely pyramidal stone that Simon Lord Lovat erected over the grave of his father, whose demise occurred while on a visit to his brother-in-law at Dunvegan Castle. Simon was eager " to show to posterity his affection for his mother's kindred, the brave MacLeods, choosing rather to leave his father's bones with them than carry them away to Lovat." On this obelisk is the inscription that Dr. Johnson described as " poor stuff, such as Lord Lovat's butler might have written," and that Boswell thought to be characteristic of a man " who has made some noise in the world."

THE LAST MALE HEIR OF HIS LINE.

Enclosed by an old, drystane and crannied dyke, partially shadowed by two straggling and bieldless trees in which the hill-wind nightly whispers requiem, and heedless of the passing of time, are the burying-ground and roofless Church of Kilmuir, in Dunvegan. When wandering among the weeds and long, wet grasses that stifle its tombstones, irresistibly you are borne back upon the centuries. Kilmuir is one of the mausoleums of the great MacLeods : within its precincts moulders the dust of some of the Normans, Chiefs of the Dunvegan MacLeods.

There, too, in that wayside sanctuary one may gaze with a threnody on the lips and with quickened pulse on a tablet sacred to the dear and honourable memory of Iain Breac MacLeod, only son of Roderic, youngest brother of the present (23rd) Chief. In the spring of 1915, and at the age of twenty-one, Iain Breac was killed in action while serving with the gallant Black Watch. And his body sleeps in a soldier's grave somewhere about Vieille Chapelle, and far furth from the bosom of his fathers.

Iain Breac was the last male heir of his line. *Mo thruaighe !*—My grief !—What a tragedy !

How are the mighty fallen in the midst of the battle !

XXV

COIRE CHATACHAN :
ITS LITERARY ASSOCIATIONS

DR. MACCULLOCH'S INGRATITUDE

> " *Sit memor nostri, fideique merces,*
> *Stet fides constans, meritoque blandum*
> *Thraliae discant resonare nomen*
> *Littora Skiae.*"

Spooks and elves in Strath Suardal there are in untold numbers : you have only to linger by the Sithean or Faery Knoll at sundown to realise this. And I believe that the good folks of Broadford are terrified to pass by the Sithean between sunset and sunrise. When seen in the half-light, the two tiny trees that stand close to the roadside, and whose backs " the burden of the blast had bent," are in themselves weird enough to make one quake and tremble.

Wintry and wild and threatening a storm was the evening that tempted me to revisit Coire Chatachan. The air was keen and clear ; and around Pabbay Isle—an isle that in ancient times pertained to MacKinnon, and was " neyre ane myle in lenthe, full of woodis, guid for fishing, and a main shelter for thieves and cut-throats "—the billowy cohorts were assembling in mad confusion for an impending attack on Broadford Bay, where the mail-steamer lurched so helplessly that at inter-

192

Photo. by Kathleen.   Memorial Tablet to Iain Breac MacLeod at Kilmuir, in Dunvegan.

vals one or other of her paddles was completely raised out of the water. Pabbay, you will recall, had no trees when Pennant passed it in more recent times ; but it retained its notoriety as having been " the seat of assassins " even as late as 1769. This is the island, by the way, which Hugh Miller declared was so rich in geological specimens that, in spite of its limited area, the variety of petre-factions to be collected on its shores would fill a museum, for " they rise in thousands and tens of thousands on exposed plains of its sea-washed strata, standing out in bold relief like sculpturings on ancient tombstones, at once mummies and monu-ments—the dead and the carved memorials of the dead. . . . Every rolled pebble is a casket with old pictorial records locked up within."

Closely was winter following in the steps of the last of the autumn : above the sombre haze obscuring the coastline of Wester Ross the snowy mountain-tops were suspended like a fleecy mirage. Immediately behind Coire Chatachan the Red Hills —thus designated by MacCulloch because they are littered with long torrents of red rubbish—stood out against a softening sunset like giant patriarchs of eld, clad in hoary apparel. They had donned their winter raiment for the first time ; and, indis-tinct as they were in the dusk, they really looked ancestral. Beinn na Caillich is, of course, the most noteworthy of the Red Hills. This is the mountain that the corpulent Dr. Johnson is particular to inform us that he did not climb during his sojourn at Coire Chatachan. Perhaps, it is as well that he is explicit on this point, because no one who knows this mountain would have believed him, had he claimed to have ascended it.

N

CORRIE OF THE WILD CATS.

Such were the conditions that attended my twilit prowl in search for the long disued cart-track that branches off for Coire Chatachan from the Torran road. The Broadford river had to be crossed somewhere ; and, if you expect to arrive at Coire Chatachan in a state of comfort and with dry feet, you had better know exactly where the crossing-place is. Otherwise you may grope for hours in the darkness searching for the rickety planks that bridge it just where the cart-track is interrupted, and where a ford has fallen almost into desuetude since the construction by the Board of Agriculture of a new road to serve the lately settled small-holdings on the other side of the river.

If, on the other hand, you have made up your mind to visit Coire Chatachan (or Corrie, as it is usually designated by travellers who have partaken of its hospitality in past generations), it will not matter a whit whether or not you discover the afore-mentioned planks, because the best time to go to this place is at the witching hour when, in any case, it would be difficult to light upon such an improvised means of crossing, unless you should happen to be familiar with the neighbourhood.

Coire Chatachan, as its name suggests, is the Corrie of the Wild Cats ; and to-day it does not belie its name. Is it not a source of pleasure to know that there is at least one spot in Scotland where as yet the ruthlessness of professional trappers and taxidermists has not exterminated these rare creatures? But, I pray you, do not divulge this secret to any one whom you think may be likely to go there one day for the purpose of capturing or destroying the last survivors of this magnificent species.

To-day the ruins of Coire Chatachan, standing naked and gaunt between a byre and stable on one side and a barn on the other, are exactly as they appeared fifty years ago : so I was informed lately by the shepherd's mother, who has returned to this neighbourhood after an absence extending over half a century.

PENNANT AT COIRE CHATACHAN.

Among the earliest litterateurs to visit Corrie was Pennant, who, when journeying in Skye with his fellow-traveller, was approached by young MacKinnon, a gentleman who overtook him in a boat and pressed him to accept the entertainment of his father's house at Coire Chatachan. Pennant gladly complied with MacKinnon's request ; and remarks in his *Voyage to the Hebrides* how kindly were his quarters. Here he witnessed the waulking of the cloth : here, also, he listened to the singing of songs at the quern, and observed that, with the introduction of water-driven mills, the practice of singing at the quern-grinding was almost out-of-date. In Scotland, as in England, the landlord was invested with the power of compelling his tacksmen and tenants to abandon the old-fashioned method of grinding grain by the quern. Indeed, the miller was authorised to " search out and break any querns he can find, as machines that default him of the toll " ; and you will remember that during the reign of Alexander III. it was enacted that " na man sall presume to grind quheit, maisbloch (maisloch, *i.e.* mixed grain), or rye, with hand mylnes, except he be compelled by a storm, or be in lack of mills quhilk sould grind the samen. And in this case gif a man grindes at hand mylnes, he sal gif a threttein measure as multer, and gif the man contraveins this our prohibition, he sall tine (forfeit) his hand mylnes perpetuallie."

Pennant, moreover climbed Beinn na Caillich to investigate on its summit the enormous cairn that was reported to him to have been the sepulchre of a gigantic Fingalian woman. This cairn is gener- ally believed, however, to mark the site of burial of a Norwegian princess, who died at Ord. On her death-bed this princess commanded her attend- ants to convey her when dead to the top of Beinn na Caillich, in order that her remains might lie in the wake of the winds from Norway. MacCulloch, referring to this cairn in his *Description of the Western Isles of Scotland*, asks to be excused from repeating any of the traditions respecting it, since he con- sidered them, one and all, to be unworthy of regard. But Pennant and his companion enjoyed their sojourn at Corrie ; and they left its hospitality "after experiencing every civility of the family."

The Liberality of Coire Chatachan.

Never a wayworn traveller failed to find kindness and beneficence at the hands of MacKinnon of Corrie and his cheerful wife, who long tenanted the old farmhouse there. Thither, as I have this moment told you, came Pennant. And, after a short stay at Armadale, where they were met on the sands by Sir Alexander MacDonald and after- wards saw a fox of a size undreamt of in their meagre philosophy, Johnson and Boswell found their way by night to " a house pleasantly situated between two brooks with one of the highest hills of the island behind it." This hill, obviously, is Beinn na Caillich.

At Coire Chatachan the English wayfarer and his Scots factotum were treated with liberality and in a company more numerous and elegant than they had believed it possible to have collected in the Hebrides. Old MacKinnon, Johnson tells us, was a man of letters, for he alludes to his substantial bookshelf, and remarks, as though he were surprised, that literature was not altogether neglected by the more enlightened Hebrideans. Nor did MacKinnon's table lack either variety or quantity.

General Stewart of Garth makes a somewhat similar comment on the educational propensities of the Hebridean people, for he remarks that the clergy, whom he met at Armadale and Ostaig and elsewhere, were zealous, learnèd, and exemplary in their conduct. Furthermore, he reminds us that even Dr. Johnson, in spite of his prejudices against the Presbyterian clergy in particular, and the Scottish nation in general, could not conceal his amazement at finding in Skye so much learning and so many well-selected libraries.

Dr. Johnson's Flirtation.

At all events, judging from Boswell's account of his own ongoings, whisky was plentiful. Was it not at Coire Chatachan that he sat up carousing until 5 A.M., and came downstairs at noon the same day (Sunday !) with a splitting headache, only to be abused by Dr. Johnson for his unseemly conduct ? In his *Journal* Boswell, himself, records how vexed he was that he should have been guilty of such riotous behaviour, and how, on entering Dr. Johnson's room, he picked up his hostess's prayer-book and accidentally opened it at the text : "And be not drunk with wine wherein is excess."

One may guess that MacDonald of Knockow and MacLean of Coll, who also were MacKinnon's guests at the time, did not miss the opportunity of doing themselves well at their host's expense ; and, no doubt, Dr. Johnson was not loath to have his share of what was going and to reel with the others, despite the fact that he is reported to have gone early to bed.   Here, moreover, he actually took. a matron on his knee and kissed her : here, too, on September 6, 1773, the idea seized him of composing to Mrs. Thrale some Latin verses that he embraced in his *Oda Scriptum in Skia*. Boswell reveals that Johnson had been conducting a somewhat lengthy correspondence with the said Mrs. Thrale, "whose enchantment over him seldom failed."

It was at Coire Chatachan that Boswell was informed of the custom whereby a man in the Hebrides, as soon as he made his appearance in the morning, swallowed a glass of whisky. Yet he is judicious in adding that the Hebrideans were not a drunken race, though no man, he continues, was so ridiculously abstemious as to refuse his morning *skalk* or dram.   You will be reminded that after a night's rest at the hostelry in Kylerhea Dr. MacCulloch, impatient to break his fast and to set out for Duntulm one fine morning, learnt to his disgust that " the fearful schalch of camomile whisky was first to be drank : drank—aye, and digested ; and then in two hours came the breakfast ! "   Fortunately, this is a formality that to-day in Strath is almost completely unobserved.

Boswell's description of Corrie is by far the more

entertaining. Among other things, we learn from him that so large was the company that he could not for the life of him imagine how it was lodged, even although the sexes were segregated and husbands and wives slept in different apartments.

ALEXANDER SMITH'S ERROR.

In *Scotland and the Scotch*, a volume published in 1840, yet another writer alludes to Strath as having been a locality of unqualified kindness, where to the letter the inhabitants carried out the biblical injunction to " use hospitality one to another without grudging." Reference herein is made also to the elegant drawing-room at Coire Chatachan, where at the ripe age of ninety-five the venerable Mrs. MacKinnon—the " lady-like woman " who acted as hostess in the time of Johnson and Boswell —was the centre of attraction.

When staying at Ord, Alexander Smith, the author of the ever-popular *Summer in Skye*, made an endeavour to visit Corrie, while attending a hectic cattle market at Broadford ; but he never really found the celebrated ruins. He was directed how to proceed to them ; but he had not traversed very far in the direction of Torran when he arrived at the " confused pile of stones " known as the Sithean. Unwittingly, he thought this Faery Knoll was Corrie, and wrote about it in the belief that he had poured out his soul where more than a century previously Johnson and Boswell had been regaled with unusually large libations of wine. He declared that he wandered around these stones more reverently than if they had composed the cairn of a chief.

Dr. MacCulloch's Ingratitude.

Sir Archibald Geikie, among the many anecdotes contained in his *Scottish Reminiscences*, tells us that, after the publication of MacCulloch's *Description of the Western Isles of Scotland*, a series of volumes in which the author, having accepted in good faith the hospitality of the natives, taken advantage of the Islesfolks' horses and carriages and boats, and generally made use of them during his geological excursions, ridicules their manners and customs, old MacKinnon of Corrie was so indignant that, when he went to Glasgow shortly after the appearance of the account, he took an engraved portrait of MacCulloch to a crockery-dealer, and commissioned him to make a set of hardware with a likeness of the geologist on each piece.

To say the least of them, some passages contained in MacCulloch's letters anent Skye and its people were " caustic, censorious, epigrammatic " ; and, in all fairness to those whom they ridiculed, their publication certainly deserved the resentment they occasioned.

The Ghost of Corrie.

Seldom has the Sithean ghost been seen ; but innumerable and eerie are the tales associated with it in this vicinity. At Old Corrie, however, there is a ghost of whom the people of Strath Suardal live in dread. It takes the form of a very tall lady known to have lived in the neighbourhood of the farm nearby, and to have worn a long, black coat and a white mutch with waving flappers. She is said to roam in the twilight and dark among the peat stacks that line the Portree road, only a mile or so from Coire Chatachan. And I have been

Photo. by A. B. Paterson.

Coire Chatachan and Beinn na Caillich.
"Beneath the lofty shadow of the Red Hills."

told that those who have been bold enough to speak to her have been " met by a stony stare and no response "—an experience sufficiently terrifying to terminate the interview abruptly !

This ghost was thought to have been laid long ago ; but a wit in the locality of Broadford, having once or twice indulged in a little innocent sheet-walking, gets the credit of having restored the ghost to its wonted haunts.

The Corrie Man.

But Coire Chatachan will aye be associated affectionately with old MacKinnon, that public-spirited Highland gentleman who has gone down to history as *Fear a' Choire*—the Corrie Man. MacKinnon, in addition to having been tacks-man of Coire Chatachan and sometime factor to MacDonald of Sleat, occupied the honoured position of Brieve.

Though a man of unusual ability, Lachlan Mac-Kinnon of Corrie was at all times kind and con-siderate ; and he could even spare an occasional hour with the harmless gowk, Gillesbuig Aotrom, who lived close at hand. One day Gillesbuig thought that he would play a trick on his friend, whom he familiarly called " Lachie." So, at a time when MacKinnon's grieve was seriously ill, a loud and agitated knocking was heard at the door of Old Corrie House. " *Am bheil Lachlan an stigh ?*—Is Lachlan in ? " enquired Gillesbuig of the maid who answered the door. Thereupon she hurried away for her master, who, on coming to the door, was greeted by Gillesbuig with such lamentations : " *O mo naire, mo naire, Lachlainn !*—Oh, for shame, for shame, Lachlan ! Your grieve is on his death-bed ; and you have in your press what will save him."

"What will save him ?" asked Corrie. "A good, stiff dram," replied Gillesbuig.

So Corrie quickly departed, and returned in a jiffy with a tumbler overflowing with the best whisky he had in the house, in the hope that it would revive his dying grieve. Gillesbuig had not gone far with his pretended cure when Corrie shook his fist after him, and cried : "You rascal ! my grieve will never taste that whisky, for you will be drinking it yourself." To this Gillesbuig retorted : "I would be sorry that your father's son should prove to be a liar ; and so I am taking you at your word." Thereupon he drank the draught to Lachlan's health ; and, when handing back the empty tumbler, promised to see that the dying grieve got the next dram. Gillesbuig had fewer bats in his belfry than the folks of Strath were prepared to admit.

Some time after this, MacKinnon of Corrie had occasion to be in the village of Broadford where he knocked up against Gillesbuig, who was munching away at a huge bone and apparently in the seventh heaven of delight. "You should be thinking shame of yourself, Gillesbuig, going along the public road in that unseemly manner," said Corrie. "Give that bone to the first dog you meet !"

"Ah, well !" replied Gillesbuig, "you 'd better be taking the bone now, because it may be a long time before I meet another dog."

On another occasion, when Gillesbuig happened to be present at Sligachan where the cattle market used to be held at regular intervals, he was compelled by the inclemency of the weather to seek

warmth in the inn, which at the time was chock-full
of lairds and well-to-do farmers, who, having dis-
cussed the business of the day, were sealing their
bargains with a nip or two. Crowded to its utmost
capacity as was the inn, Gillesbuig succeeded in
squeezing into a corner where he was noticed by
Corrie.

"And where have *you* come from, Gillesbuig ? "
asked Corrie, who was not a little surprised to find
his light-headed acquaintance so far from home.
"I came from hell ! " retorted Gillesbuig in a
manner that was received with a round of applause.
"Oh, Gillesbuig ! " replied Corrie, "that's terrible
swearing to be using. And how do they spend
their time in hell ? "   "Just the way the gentry
spends its time in this inn," said Gillesbuig—"keeping the place so full that there's not a corner for
poor, shivering people."

This Gillesbuig is none other than the half-wit
who, at the time of the Disruption, used to sneak
down to the church at Broadford on Sundays, and
provoke the shepherds' dogs, that awaited their
masters outside, to fight one another.

*   *   *   *   *   *   *

Many are the yarns told in Skye of the grand
old Corrie Man ; and long will those ruins at
Coire Chatachan be sacred to his memory. He is
gone : the ruins of his Highland home are gaunt
and desolate ; but there they are, nestling peacefully beneath the lofty shadow of the Red Hills.

There the wild cat still prowls, unmolested and
at will, by night : there by day the wintered
ptarmigan, shy and gentle, can coorie down among
the bleakest places of the mountains, and be
sheltered from the blood-thirstiness of men.

XXVI

RONA

ISLE OF THE SEAL

A REFUGE FOR PIRATES AND SMUGGLERS

Not to be confused with Rona, a still lonelier island
many leagues northward from the Butt of Lewis,
" inhabit and manurit be simple people, scant of
ony religione," and producing an " aboundance of
corne . . . by delving onlie," is the Isle of the
Seal that in olden days used to be " full of woodis
and heddir with ane havin for heiland galeys in
the middis of it, and the same havein is guyed for
fostering of theives, ruggairs, and reivers, till a nail,
upon the peilling and spulzeing of poure pepill."
This is one of the Inner Hebrides that MacLeod
of Raasay once held by force, and that by heritage
pertained to the Bishop of the Isles. I believe that
long ago the heir to MacLeod of Raasay actually
was styled " Rona."

To distinguish it from the northern whaling-
station now referred to as North Rona, the Rona
that forms the subject of our sketch is generally
spoken of as South Rona.

Etymologically, the name, Rona, has given rise
to controversy at various times. The most widely
accepted, and certainly the most reasonable, origin,
however, is from the Gaelic, *ron*, meaning a seal.
In two respects does the Island answer to this

name : in the first place the shape of Rona is not at all unlike that of a seal ; and, in the second, its shores are the veritable haunt of seals. Though in recent years the seals have been greatly reduced in numbers, owing largely to the barbarous demands of a certain class of indolent women, the seal still frequents the wild, indented coastline of Rona. Only the other day four seals, dripping wet and sleeky black, glistened on a sun-kissed reef at low tide as our small fishing-craft glided into Acarseid Thioram (Dry Harbour) with a limp sail and a gently throbbing engine. We sailed quite close to them ; and they did not seem to mind our intrusion in the slightest degree, though their sparkling eyes followed us intelligently as we cautiously navigated the greenlit skerries that beset our channel.

When we manœuvred out of Dry Harbour an hour or so later, these seals were a little more suspicious of us, for they raised the forepart of their bodies and glanced around as though they had never before seen human beings. One of their number thought discretion the better part of valour, and quietly slithered into the sea. Frequently have I descried seals when sailing close to Eilean Garbh, an island that at the entrance to Big Harbour (Acarseid Mhor) rises sheer and almost shoreless out of the ocean. To-day Eilean Garbh is houseless and desolate, though such was not always its lot.

The last-named Island is to be differentiated from Garbh Eilean, the " Rough Isle " lying in Kyle Rona, the narrows separating Rona from Eilean Tighe and Raasay.

Dr. Johnson says that at the time of his tour Rona was uninhabited, and only on very rare

occasions saw the shepherd who periodically in-
spected the sheep pastured there and on Fladda.
I can scarcely accept the accuracy of this statement.

The name, Rona, also appears in various places
and at various times as Ronay, Rauney (cf. *Hraun*),
Rourhae, and even as Raneira. Some authorities
on the etymology of Gaelic place-names have put
forward what, I fear, is rather a far-fetched deriva-
tion, namely, *robh muir*, which, being translated
literally, signifies " too much sea."

A SMUGGLERS' DEN.

Rona was once notorious for its smugglers, who
in its rock-carved bonded-warehouses stored the
whiskies and brandies they often intercepted from
passing vessels, as well as the special blends that
were distilled in the remoter creeks of Rona itself.
The favourite retreat of the Rona smugglers was
a cove on the east side known as Acarseid Fhalaich,
the Hiding Haven. This creek was also frequented
by mainland smugglers, especially when rumours
of an organised raid along the deeply indented
shores of Sutherland and Wester Ross forced them
at a moment's notice to remove themselves and their
stores and apparatus to safer quarters. Smugglers
in those days were usually willing to accommodate
one another. The Rona smugglers never knew
when their own hidie-hole was likely to be raided ;
and so they always kept on good terms with those
smugglers, to whose dens at any time they might
be compelled to betake themselves and their be-
longings. Indeed, to some extent these smugglers
conducted their business on the lines of a sort of
reciprocity treaty by guaranteeing to succour each
other in the hour of danger.

How closely in this respect have the gigantic liquor combines of our own generation followed their example !

Even the Skye smugglers on occasions were obliged to conceal themselves in the secret crevices of Rona. The whisky-makers, who had their still in a pit at MacQuarrie's Land (Feriniquarrie), near Loch Pooltiel, were acquainted with the excellent possibilities that Rona presented, if ever they were hounded out of their distillery in Sloc a' Ghrundaire, the Distillers' Hollow.

It is not so very long since Rona boasted at least two stills that for the best part of the year were in steady employment. One of the most notorious smuggling places on this Isle of the Seal was a spot above the Clay Port (*Port a' Chreadh*) known as the House of the Black Pot. Long had the excise officials bided their time for a favourable opportunity of paying this den a surprise visit. At length the opportunity came ; and the smugglers, who were in the throes of preparing a very special " brew," were caught red-handed. Many of them were forcibly detained ; but one of their gang, having grabbed the pot and hoisted it on his shoulder, made off with it, and hid it in a peat-bog behind Meall a' Gharaidh—the old dyke that kept the sheep out of the corn. Though a thorough search was organised, the revenue-officers never discovered the pot ; and, doubtless, when the scare was past, it was again in use.

Near the House of the Black Pot—which was nothing more than a bothy—ran a tiny streamlet that, when required, was let into it by a craftily concealed channel. In this way, while distillation was proceeding, the smugglers could remain under cover all the time, and thus reduce to a minimum the risk of disclosing by visible movement the locale of their distillery.

LEGEND OF A NORSE TOMB.

Rona is not without its archaeological interest, inasmuch as the ruins of a temple may be traced on it. Here it may be noted that the inlet in Rona nearest to Raasay, and through which most of the land communication goes, is termed Port an Teampuill, the Haven of the Temple. The flat stones of which this temple was built are thought to have been brought across the Inner Sound from Wester Ross, as no such stones are to be found on Rona. Possibly they may have been consecrated stones from the locality of Maolrubha's shrine at Applecross.

Parenthetically, it might be mentioned here that the name, Inner Sound, denoting the stretch of water running between Rona and Raasay and the mainland of Ross, is strictly speaking a misnomer. The Skye fisherfolks call it Linne an Ear, the Eastern Sound, thus distinguishing it from Linne an Iar, the western *linne* (linn) or pool, that lies between Rona and Skye. " Inner " in this case, I humbly submit, is just a corruption of *linne* and *ear*, meaning eastern pool. Of course, in the sense that the Inner Sound is *inner* relative to the Minch, the name is reasonable ; but the adjective, " eastern," was given originally to distinguish it from the " western " pool, or what we now call the Sound of Raasay.

To a stone on a hilltop south-west of the light-house and in the neighbourhood of the Retreat of the Cunning One (? fox) the name of Leac Nighinn

Photo. by Farquhar MacKenzie Matheson.

Sea-sparkle—The Coolins from Plockton.

Righ Lochlainn has been given. According to its legend, the son of the King of Greece went to Denmark to attend a royal banquet and, incidentally, to woo the daughter of the King of that country. On his arrival in Denmark he met the son of the King of Sweden and other suitors. So jealous did he become that he eloped with the princess. But the son of the King of Lochlann (Sweden in this case) pursued the couple and overtook it at Rona, where he challenged the son of the King of Greece to mortal combat. In the contest that ensued the Greek was slain; and for his corpse a grave was prepared on the summit of a hillock above Blarain, in Rona. And it was at the request of the daughter of the King of Lochlann the grave was made wide, that she might leap in beside her slain lover. This she did; and the folks of Rona placed a *leac* or slab to mark the site of this mysterious burial. And ever since this spot has been identified as Leac Nighinn Righ Lochlainn—the Tombstone of the Daughter of the King of Denmark.

OLD-FASHIONED AGRICULTURAL METHODS.

Agriculturally speaking, Rona is very far behind the times, though I doubt very much whether the introduction into that Island of the most scientific agrestic methods would produce much more than at present is raised on its rocky, barren soil. Mac-Culloch thought Rona one of the most unfertile and unproductive spots in the Western Isles, offering nothing else than a refuge for coasting-vessels in a storm. Notwithstanding that he and his geologising company were able to purchase a couple of cows hereabouts, he subjoins the following subtle reminder—" You gentlemen of Scotland, who live at home at ease, must not imagine, however, that you are to cruise round the Western Islands upon beef steaks ; no, nor on fresh mutton neither." While referring to its barrenness, it may be mentioned that *hraun*, an Old Icelandic word denoting a wilderness (particularly of lava or igneous rocks), has been suggested as the origin of the name, Rona. Thus, Rona would mean the isle of the rough, rocky surface. This description is amply borne out by Martin, who writes—" This little isle is the most unequal rocky piece of ground to be seen anywhere : there is but very few acres fit for digging : . . . most of the rocks consist of the hectic stone, and a considerable part of them is of a red colour."

Rona possesses neither a harrow nor a horse. The crofters still use a two-handled rake with wooden teeth. Some years ago a man *did* bring a horse to the Island ; but it was so restless and recalcitrant (and little wonder !) that the people could not manage it. So one day the strong man of the Island took hold of the horse and felled it to the ground. Thereafter no horse was retained on Rona. The strong man was none other than he who sprinted off with the distilling pot, when the revenue-officers appeared at the door of the House of the Black Pot. Locally he was known as *Iain MacMhurchaidh*, John, the son of Murdo ; and at the present day his son lives on Eilean Tighe, the little Isle of the House that lies in the channel flowing between Rona and Raasay, and is so close to the latter that at low tide it is separated by a dry, rocky ridge a few yards in width. At high tide a fishing-boat of ordinary dimensions can pass between Raasay and Eilean Tighe. The last time I visited this locality we had been detained so long on Eilean Tighe that, when we returned to the shore, the tide had receded so far as to compel us to sail right round that Island. On this occasion we were bound for Fearns, a picturesque hamlet by the south-eastern shore of Raasay.

Martin has very little to say about South Rona, so that we cannot tell whether or not the Island pastured a horse in his time. He gives us a certain amount of information about Rona, off the Butt of Lewis, however ; and he mentions that the inhabitants, when visiting Lewis, were astounded at seeing so many people, and were " mightily pleased at the sight of horses." One Rona boy, on hearing a Lewis horse neigh, asked if the animal were laughing ; while another lad, on seeing a pony bolt, leapt with fear into a " bush of nettles, where his whole skin became full of blisters."

Though Eilean Tighe is an island of no mean extent, its entire resident population, human and infrahuman, at present consists of one family, a cow, a flock of sheep, a pickle of hens, a few odd puffins and guillemots and cormorants, and the loveliest shaggy-haired collie you ever beheld. The collie usually keeps watch on a small knoll, and warns the inmates of the only house when the doctor's barge is making for the narrows between Eilean Tighe and Raasay, and is likely to pay a call in passing. Never a boat touches the shore of Eilean Tighe that this beautiful creature does not dash down to welcome in a manner that is positively overwhelming.

The only person on Rona who owned a harrow was the old schoolmaster, Angus Murchison, who

resided on this Island for over seventeen years.
Even *his* harrow, he tells me, was a home-made
contraption. In the course of a conversation I once
had with him, he informed me that on Rona it was
directly contrary to custom to commence sowing
grain until after May 6th of each year. Despite
varying conditions, this is still the recognised date,
since the Rona folks have a firm belief that not
until after May 6th can they possibly hope for
dry weather.

The ancient foot-plough is used extensively on
Rona, as is to be expected on an island that knows
the use in agriculture neither of the harrow nor of
the horse.

Population Declining.

The natives of Rona are particularly hospitable,
and at all times are ready to entertain any stranger
who may chance to find his way to their shores.
Having, themselves, often to depend on the kindness of others when away from home, since frequently they experience difficulty in getting back
according to plan owing to such causes as stormy
weather at sea, lack of roads, and general remoteness, they make a point of welcoming every one.
Moreover, they are very clannish, most of them
being closely related to one another.

A few years ago more than half the population
of Rona went in a body to raid lands at the southern
extremity of Raasay. The Board of Agriculture (a
department that not infrequently is subjected to
unreasonable criticism) generously yielded to the
demands of the raiders, and, with a view to settling
them comfortably there, purchased the whole of
Raasay Isle, with the exception of the mineral

rights in the proximity of Inverarish. So there is less congestion on Rona now. But, for all that, the difficulties of obtaining supplies from without, the fact that among the remaining three or four families there is not a sufficient number of sea-worthy men to man the boats, and the serious handicap that, owing to winter storms, it is some-times impossible to leave the Island even for the purpose of replenishing food supplies, render the existence of the remaining islanders very precarious indeed. Howbeit, I believe that a movement is afoot to induce them to take up their abode on some less remote and more remunerative territory.

In addition to being extremely kind-hearted, many of the natives of Rona have the " second-sight " in a pronounced degree. During his pro-fessional residence on the Island, Mr. Angus Murchison noted the following rather remarkable instance that ought to disarm the sceptics. One evening two of his younger pupils came to him in a state of alarm, and declared that they had observed a crowd of people following a funeral to the church-yard in Raasay, a considerable distance away. They even named the men who bore the coffin, and described the order in which they proceeded : a fortnight or so thereafter a young woman belonging to the township of Dry Harbour was dead ; and her remains were conveyed along the very same route, and by the very same people whom these children, a couple of weeks earlier, deponed to having seen.

The Widow's Cot.

Before the erection of the lighthouse at the northern end of Rona, seafarers were guided beyond the treacherous rocks and reefs defending this wild,

Hebridean coast by a light that was kept burning in what was known as the Widow's Cot. One night, while the husband and sons of the agèd occupant of this place were fishing in the Little Minch, there arose a great storm. When she went out to see if there were any signs of their returning, she noticed the boat to be making for the rocks and for its doom : they had lost their direction in the darkness and storm, and perished within ear-shot of home. And thereafter, and until the light-house was built, the lonely widow nightly kept a lamp burning in the window of her cottage, lest other Rona fishermen should be uncertain as to the exact whereabouts of their bourne.

RONA VIEWED FROM THE STORR.

If you wish to view Rona and Eilean Tighe and Fladda and the northern part of Raasay from a unique position, I would suggest that you follow as far as the Storr the road that from Portree leads towards Staffin and the tempest-splitten Quiraing. It is a dull, dreary road, I admit : but for the croft that crouches into a hollow on the hillside, and that from certain angles is barely noticeable because its grey walls and rain-sodden thatch merge so perfectly into its bleak, rocky surroundings, there is precious little to acquaint you with the existence of a dwelling-place within miles, unless you proceed as far north as Tote or Rigg.

Nevertheless, at the southern end of Loch Fada— a blue, fresh-water lagoon passed on the right-hand side as you journey towards the Storr—there is a lodge. But, as a rule, it is untenanted, and has its windows boarded up. Moored close to the shore of Loch Leathan, a little further on, is usually a small boat, indicating that occasionally human beings do pass this way. Then, of course, those beautiful shaggy herds of Highland cattle with their long hair combed over their eyes are constantly straying across your path ; and *they* must have an owner who visits them from time to time.

When visibility is good and the day is mild, one gets a magnificent panorama from under the lanky shadow of the Old Man of Storr. Never do Raasay, " Rona of the Ships " and of the Seals, and the tall, majestic, world-old mountains of Applecross and Torridon appear in grander sheen than when they are wet and gleaming in the slanting sunshine that follows rain.

XXVII

RAASAY REVISITED

TRAMPING THROUGH A HEBRIDEAN SOUND

> " Here beauty reigns on ev'ry hand,
> From woody slope to pebbly strand."

" RAARSA is ane Ile of five myle lang and thrie myle braid, perteining to the Bischop of the Iles; but it is occupiet be ane gentleman of McCloyd Lewis kin, callit Gillechallum Raarsa. His offspring bruikis the same yit, and are callit Clan Gillechallum of Raarsa. He hes ane strange little castell in this Ile, biggit on the heid of ane heich craig, and is callit Prokill (Brochel). It is but 8 merk land, and will raise 80 men. It payis yeirlie to the bischop 16 merks, but to the capitaine thairof it payis of sundrie tributes better nor 500 merks. Thair is na woodis, but great heich craigis in this Ile. It is commodious for corn and all kinds of bestiall, and chieflie horses."

Thus runs an old account of the Island that, more than any other, I should like to possess, were I given an opportunity of becoming a landed proprietor in a small way. Though the actual date of the above description cannot be fixed with any degree of certainty, there is every reason to believe that it was written between 1577 and 1595, because it records the massacre of the MacDonalds by the MacLeods in the cave on the Isle of Eigg, and also makes mention of John Stewart of Hoping (Appin), whose demise occurred in 1595.

Raasay's Variety of Scenery.

To the stranger among the Isles Raasay presents a weird, yet pleasant, series of surprises : it is, indeed, a Hebridean wonderland. The road that from old Raasay House leads north towards Glam and Manish is perhaps the most charming and varied with which I am acquainted. At one moment you are treading along a path so dark and dense when the trees are full-leafed that you might be penetrating through the heart of a great, tropical forest, where at night one might hear

> ". . . the lion roar,
> And the hyaena scream ;
> And the river horse as he crushed the reeds
> Beside some hidden stream."

Raasay at present is devoid of such ravenous fauna ; but, when meandering in the darkness through its wooded labyrinths, you can quite well pretend for the time being that the owls, screeching and whirring uncannily overhead, are a species of tropical bird with gorgeous plumage. Raasay, by the way, has a most interesting bird life. Beyond the sylvan parts lies a region that is characteristic of the typical Norwegian fiord or of the upper environs of a Swiss lagoon. Here one meets with pine-clad slopes sweeping down to a sparkling sheet of water below : here in winter neither the elk nor the chamois would seem the least out of place.

Under certain aspects a Raasay sunset is strangely reminiscent of Hammerfest with its midnight sun. A little to the north of the fiord country you pass into a belt that is undulating, heath and bracken covered, and loamy, where the grasses have an almost arid semblance, where the bushes and shrubs are puny and stunted and have the appearance of scrub, and where one might reasonably expect to meet a steenbok or a timid, dark-eyed gazelle. This region is traversed by a bridle-path, twisting and turning down a hillside into a deep gorge below, whence in zig-zag fashion it ascends to a glorious ridge afar off. About this part there is a decided suggestion of the American canyon country. The scenery is extraordinarily like that with which the cowboy is familiar. I have several times thought that the Isle of Raasay would make a most fascinating setting for a historical novel, or even for a wild-west film drama. Why cannot our film-producers select settings such as this and utilise them for the propagating of beautiful ideas, instead of foisting on an innocent, unthinking public these hideous travesties invariably depicting one of three extremes—sex, squalor, or obesity and opulence? To my mind the average " picture " is a gross insult to the intelligence of the British people.

LIFELESS, EMPTY, AND BARE.

You can imagine my delight when first I explored this wonder Island on the back of a tough sheltie, one minute climbing a saddle-path with a steep precipice on either side, and at another descending into a defile to gain the sandy-coloured track that, as it were, lay perpendicularly before me. I felt exactly like a cow-boy or like one who on horseback had travelled into a far country. The last time I made this excursion, however, the track was so slippery with ice that I was compelled to lead the horse most of the way.

With the exception of the few sheep that graze on its emeralded oases, the territory to the north of the cowboy region is bleak, barren, rocky, and closely resembles the sister Island of Rona. This part of Raasay might be likened unto a stretch of Patagonia. The moor, though not without its interest, lies empty and bare ; and, but for the seabirds that haunt the creeks and for the spluttering of a few burns, the northern end of Raasay is cold and lifeless.

ENTERTAINED AT RAASAY HOUSE.

Of course, were I ever to become the laird of this Isle (the probability, alas, is remarkably remote !), Raasay House, a mansion that a hundred and fifty years ago was described as " a neat modern fabric," would become my country seat. Here it was that the reception given to Dr. Johnson far exceeded his most sanguine expectations : here both he and Bozzy " found nothing but civility, elegance, and plenty " : here the carpet was rolled off the floor, and along with the rest of the company the burly doctor danced and tripped with the nimbleness of a faery.

Oddly enough, Johnson remarks that in Raasay there is little that can detain the traveller. Yet he appears to have observed a good deal when residing there. He mentions Oar Cave (*Uamh nan Ramh*), for example, and with some hesitation reminds us that herein the Islanders hundreds of years ago used to conceal their oars after their return from a rieving expedition. Hidden among a clump of trees, Oar Cave is still an object of interest in Raasay. He also comments on the old custom of graddan, whereby the Hebrideans destroyed their fodder with the genuine improvidence of savages. But he actually states that in Raasay he saw a barn, the first he had observed during the whole of his sojourn in Skye. Speaking of gardens in the Western Isles, he writes : " Few vows are made to Flora in the Hebrides."

An Island of " Maney Deires."

Johnson informs us further that there were no deer, hares, nor rabbits on the Isle of Raasay in his time. That a century prior to this Raasay was entirely devoid of deer seems improbable, for at Duntulm in September of 1628, along with Sir Donald MacDonald of Sleat, Colin, Earl of Seaforth, Sir Lauchlan MacKinnon of Strathardell, and Alexander MacLeod of Dunvegan, Alasdair MacLeod of Raasay entered into a somewhat lengthy written agreement before competent witnesses for the mutual preservation of deer and roe on their respective estates, and for the punishment of trespassers in pursuit of such game. Though in Dean Monro's day Raasay boasted " maney deires," it is very possible that at this time deer on that Island were on the verge of extinction, or at any rate were becoming extremely scarce.

Raasay's Water-Horse.

Boswell recites somewhat inaccurately the story of a fierce water-horse that on a time inhabited Loch na Mna, a lochan near Dun Caan, in Raasay. One day this monster devoured the daughter of a native who, in order to avenge himself, lighted a great fire and roasted a sow on it in the hope that by the smell thereof the creature would be tempted to pass through an avenue of large stones that purposely he had arranged. The water-horse in this manner was inveigled into a trap and met its death ; and the very avenue of stones was pointed out to Johnson and Boswell (as the latter tells us when not over-anxious lest he should lose any of the " gold dust " of the conversation that fell from Johnson's lips) by a man who did not laugh when he told the story.

A Subtropical Climate.

About the brambled track that winds through the larch and birch groves behind Inverarish there is something delightfully refreshing. Raasay is one of the very few islands in the Hebrides where, when the honeysuckle is in berry, one might spend a profitable day picking brambles from the sturdy bushes that scramble wildly among the tufts of long, shaggy heather and bog-myrtle, and even besiege the unshaded patches between the clumps of frost firs and dwarf Scots pines. One can also gather nuts in Raasay. But what struck me most was the height to, and profusion with, which fuchsia hedges grow in the southern part of this Island. From Inver, a township lying almost opposite Portree, to Oskaig and Inverarish the lower ground impinging upon the sea exhibits a fertility which even after a bad spell of weather is nothing short of amazing for an Island situated in a region that, botanically speaking, suffers so much from the inclemency of the climate.

In the late summer or early autumn the variety as well as the abundance of flowers to be seen in the old, walled garden adjoining Raasay House is really astonishing. There the lover of flowers may discover masses of clematis and roses and columbine, and every flower that goes to make a garden a thing of peace and of joy. And I have never seen finer hollyhocks than the giant white and maroon ones that in Raasay are sheltered from the searing winds by spreading deciduous trees and tall, handsome conifers feathered to the very ground.

Looking westwards and southwards from Raasay House in the direction of Ben Lee and Glamaig and Loch Sligachan one has, I think, perhaps the most pleasing prospect I know. In autumn, when the rowans are red and the brackens are bronzed and an occasional leaf is whirled across the grassy lawn in front of your windows, the colouring here surpasses description. And, should you chance to be gazing seaward from the windows of old Raasay House at tea-time, a tiny bit of modern life is added to this panorama when the mail-steamer paddles past on her way from Suisnish, in the south of Raasay, to Portree. Raasay House is the edifice by the shore that Pennant alluded to as making a pretty figure.

A FAERY LOCH.

If you meander around the home farm, whose clock-tower is surmounted by a weather-vane in the shape of a fleeing fox, you soon come to a sweetly scented woodland path leading to the most exquisite, artificial lochan you have ever cast eyes upon. This little loch is surrounded by fir trees and bushes and reeds and shoulder-high rushes. It is gemmed with a number of circular islets which to human beings are impenetrable because of the gigantic rhododendra that cover their entire area, and in some cases grow to a height of twenty feet and more. So dense is the vegetation on these islets that I can scarcely credit a rabbit's being able to penetrate through its undergrowth. The shadow effects on this loch are wonderful. It ought to be visited in June or July, when against a dark green background everything is pink and mauve and heliotrope, and great masses of water-lilies are spreading themselves upon the surface of the loch. At eventide, while the fishes are spinning their wide, concentric circles and are leaping to snatch an odd insect that, haply, may be piloting close to the water's face, this mirror of nature is so complete that one sees the rhododendra-smothered islets more distinctly when looking at their reflection than when gazing directly at them.

Nothing is wanting here—in a reedy channel that is overshadowed by alders and fringed by long, drooping grasses even an old boat is to be found. But my epistolary vehicle fails me utterly when I endeavour to describe to you the charm and the poetry of this secluded lochan in so sweet an Isle.

TOMB OF THE MACLEODS OF RAASAY.

Behind Raasay House and likewise embowered is an ancient burying-ground, a ruined church " callit Killmolowocke " (Kilmoluag), and two roofless, sepulchral chapels with young saplings sprouting from their crannied walls. To-day there is no trace of the image of the Virgin Mary that once stood above the door of the older chapel ; but over the lintel of the more recent one you may still examine in a fair state of preservation a coat of arms and a motto carved on an oaken panel. The burying-ground is simply packed with graves. They are marked by small, unshapen stones ; and to-day many of them lie hidden among a wild profusion of mosses and grasses and buttercups, and nettles and dead leaves. This is the hallowed resting-place of the old MacLeods of Raasay (*Mac Gille Chaluim*), a cadet branch of the Siol Torquil which, when the MacLeods of Lewis became extinct in the direct line, succeeded to the chiefship.

Pursued with Fire and Sword.

On the death of Torquil Dubh MacLeod of Lewis, according to Sir Robert Gordon, MacKenzie of Gairloch pursued " the Clan-wick-Gil-cholm with fyre and sword . . . macking them participant of the calamities of the Seill Torquill." The MacKenzies gained a decided advantage over the MacLeods of Raasay in 1611 when, at the termination of a fracas on a vessel chartered by the Laird of Gairloch and detained possibly by contrary winds in Raasay waters, MacLeod of Raasay, who innocently had gone on board for the purpose of purchasing some wine, was killed, but only after he had vanquished Gairloch's son, Murdo, and others. From what the chronicler tells us, it appears that in the end Raasay met his death at the hands of the only three men left to sustain the fight, and that, after having killed MacLeod, even *they* had to retire to die in seclusion from the mortal wounds he had inflicted. The MacLeods of Raasay were renowned for their strength and courage : the name of Iain Garbh—John, the Strong—was long a household word throughout the length and breadth of the Western Isles.

The Laird of Raasay was one of the many proprietors brought to destitution by the crisis of 1846. In that year the Raasay estates were sold, when, I

Photo. by Percy Donald.

Raasay from Beinn Dearg Mhor.

225

believe, the Chief went to Australia. It was at the hands of one of the MacLeods of Raasay that in 1773 Johnson and Boswell fared so well.

CASTLE BROCHEL AND ITS MEMORIES.

My last trip to Raasay was made from Portree on the *Brothers' Pride*, a boat thus dubbed because it is owned and manned by three brothers. The object of our cruise was threefold : we had a call to make on Eilean Tighe, a vaccination at Glam, and, incidentally, a cargo of hay and flour to be unloaded at Clachan on the way home. With a fresh wind astern and a sail hitched as high as was compatible with safety, we soon reached Eilean Tighe, where the sun-flecked tide was so low that we were obliged to drop anchor some distance from the shore and launch our small boat. On that Island we were detained sufficiently long to enable our crew to prepare for us a warm meal in our cosy " dining-saloon." Thus refortified, we sat in rotation at the steering-wheel, successfully navigated the dangerous channels, zealously eschewed all reefs and submerged rocks, and struggled through the Sound of Raasay against a steady head-wind until we arrived at Clachan after a wearisome, though by no means uneventful, voyage. At Clachan we disembarked. While our crew was engaged in un-shipping the cargo, we made our way to Raasay House where, as aforetime, we were graciously received and enjoyed a cup of good cheer (tea !). There a vehicle was thoughtfully placed at our disposal which enabled us to execute our professional engagement at Glam with a minimum of inconvenience. With the customary kindness that everywhere is met with in the Hebrides, we were each presented at Glam with a glass of beautiful Raasay cream, and learned from the donor that she cherished with no small pride the fact that her seventeen children are all alive and thriving.

Had time permitted, we would have continued our journey two or three miles eastwards across the Island, so as to have revisited old Brochel Castle. In that long impregnable stronghold, capable, it used to be said, of accommodating six or seven hundred souls (the entire population of Raasay at the time), resided the gallant MacLeods of Raasay. Thither Iain Garbh and his doughty kinsmen frequently repaired in time of siege. During the " Forty-Five " Brochel suffered at the hands of the Hanoverians because, as you will recollect, the MacLeods of Raasay espoused the cause of Prince Charlie, and even raised men on his behalf. There is no place in the world that has captivated me as Brochel Castle has done. And I cannot explain why !

OUR SILENT CREW.

It was pretty dark when we returned to the causeway at Clachan, where now the tide was full and our boat had been brought alongside. All hands were required on deck to weigh the anchor that in the interval had become inextricably entangled among the great clusters of seaware that make this shore a real sea-garden. But before long our engine was restarted, and the *Brothers' Pride* was forging ahead with the wind astern again, with Kennie at the steering-wheel, with Fair John leaning over the manhole above his engine, and with Black John, the third brother, lying across the bow, keeping a look-out in case of our running down small craft in the darkness and, incidentally, on the alert for herring shoals which, we are now convinced, he locates by smell as well as by sight and sound. They were a silent trio! Never a word did they address to one another from the time we passed the Narrows of Raasay until the launching of the small boat a couple of hundred yards from the quay at Portree harbour. Had I not asked Kennie a ridiculous question as we steered clear of MacMillan's Rock, I am very doubtful whether he would have broken the crew's traditional taciturnity. Black John was too engrossed in smelling for herring at the bow to be disturbed ; and Fair John, rather than suffer his musings to be interrupted, quietly ducked below the manhole and commenced to tinker away at his engine whenever we showed our heads above the cabin hutch. For all that, one could not wish to go sailing with a more courteous and kindly crew. And never have I met three brothers who, when not too conservative about communicating their knowledge and the results of their experience, were better informed on topics of maritime interest.

HOME TO PORTREE.

Between Clachan and MacMillan's Rock the Sound of Raasay was as smooth as glass. Thereafter, however, it became squally ; and while seated round the stove in our cabin we could hear the sea racing past our timbers and every now and then giving our starboard such a thud ! We went on deck once or twice ; but our presence in no way influenced our crew, each member of which was still engaged in his allotted task. Before us the "Northern Lights" danced brightly and merrily ;

and a phosphorescent wake streamed some hundred yards abaft. The sky overhead was not without stars ; and the long shadow of Ben Tianavaig enveloped us as we swerved westwards into Portree Bay at the conclusion of a memorable voyaging. There was not a sound in Portree when we returned ——nothing to greet us save the lamps that, in the windows down by the water's edge, sent out across the dark, glittering loch their streaming rays of warmth and of welcome.

Throughout the whole of Raasay Isle there is only one eyesore. I refer to the long, crimson, monstrous structure at the pier. Iron-ore may have its uses ; but it seems barbarous that on so romantic an Island as Raasay the requirements of commercialism (and such progress as some say it promotes) should justify the erection of a contraption of this hideous order. What a shock Iain Garbh would receive were he now to wander down Loch Sligachan towards Sconser to find this ugly affair destroying the sanctity of his fathers' Isle. Even on the summit of Glamaig or Marsco you cannot get away from its ungainliness.

But, when this structure offends my vision and wars against my conception of propriety, I try to console myself by imagining that even yet the tree-fringed and mossy meads fornent old Raasay House are the recreation-grounds of gnomes and fays and other species of the faery tribe.

XXVIII

WITCHES AND THEIR WAYS

WAS there ever an island that harboured so many witches as the Isle of Skye? No matter where you go in Skye, you will meet some one who either believes in the present-day existence of those evil and elusive hags, or can tell you something of their exploits in olden times. As late as 1880 witches were giving trouble in Skye. In the autumn of that year many prominent members of the Free Church at Uig petitioned against a mother and her daughters who "by evil arts take the milk from the neighbours' cows." In the following year an office-bearer of the same congregation declared before a justice of the peace at Uig that everything he possessed was bewitched by a sinister woman, who lived next door to him.

In the township of Camustianavaig there lived three witches, whom the Skye folks consulted whenever they wished to do an enemy a bad turn; and seldom were these witches slow to be hired for such a purpose.

EFFICACY OF A DRAM.

Now, the skipper of a well-found fishing boat was very anxious to have his revenge on a rival crew; and so, one evening, when his boat happened to be replenishing its stores at Portree, he took the opportunity of going round to Camustianavaig in order to consult the witches as to what form his retaliation should take. When he arrived at their house, he found that only two of the witches were at home ; but, anxious to have his malicious intentions executed without further delay, he thought it wise to transact his business at once, for no one knew how long the third witch, who at the time was engaged in her noctivagant devilry elsewhere, was likely to be absent. Thereupon the skipper produced his bottle of whisky—always a welcome companion in this part of the world—and negotiations were entered into immediately.

After a protracted discussion, which only terminated when his bottle was dry, he thought he should be returning to Portree, for he feared that his crew would be wondering what had detained him so long. And, just as he was about to leave the witches' house, in walked the third witch who, in all conscience, was annoyed on learning that the conference had taken place during her absence, but who became obstreperous when she caught sight of an empty whisky bottle on the table, and found that they had not reserved the proverbial droppie for her. Nothing would appease her : the more they tried to excuse themselves, the more clamorous she became ; and she swore by all the gods that she would clype on them, and thus upset their plans. What could the poor skipper do to avoid this contretemps ? His whisky was done ; and he had no prospects of getting another bottle for some time to come. As you may imagine, he returned to his vessel feeling very uneasy that his interview with the Camustianavaig witches had ended so unhappily.

On the following evening he was sailing past

Camustianavaig before a pleasant breeze ; and the people who were tending their cattle on the slopes of Ben Tianavaig were watching his boat, when suddenly there arose a black squall that enveloped him and his crew.

And (to put it in the words of the credulous person who told me this story), if you are not believing it, you have merely to sail from Portree to Camustianavaig with a west wind to experience such a squall, even on the calmest day.

A Recent Case of Alleged Witchcraft.

The above story I got from a native of Camustianavaig who declares that in his youth he knew one of the witches ; and she actually had interfered with him. He and some companions had been fishing out from Camustianavaig when, after having set several barrels of nets, they were obliged to hasten for the harbour owing to a sudden change in the weather. Anxious was the crew at daybreak to set out in order to see whether the nets were still where they had been cast ; but sailing was delayed because one member did not turn up at the appointed hour. At length two of the crew, whose patience sorely had been tried, went to the house of this witch, where the late-comer lived, and found that she had still to prepare his breakfast.

In response to their pleadings that she should buckle to, since they were particularly desirous of inspecting their nets, the witch coolly retorted : " You need be in no hurry to-day, for you won't be getting your nets for several days to come." But she consoled them by adding that, when they did recover them, they would in no way be damaged.

Despite her forecast, however, the crew made a

gallant attempt to reach the fishing-grounds where the nets had been cast, but again a squall compelled it to beat a hasty retreat into Camustianavaig.

When the tempest had subsided after a raging that had continued for several days, the teller of the story got word that the nets had been sighted a mile or two beyond Ollach, in Braes; and, on going to look for them, he recovered them in perfect condition.

So the Camustianavaig witch's forecast was correct!

It was a prevalent belief among fisherfolks that witches could raise storms at sea. As late as 1590 a certain Agnes Sampson, commonly known as "the wise wife of Keith," was beheaded, having deponed in the presence of James VI. and his Council that, while the King was returning from Denmark with his bride, she seized a cat, christened it, and then "bound to each part of that cat the chiefest parts of a dead man and several joints of his body." And, furthermore, she confessed that on the following night she and her witch companions, having sailed out in their baskets into the Firth of Forth, cast the cat into the midst of the sea, "and so left the said cat right before the town of Leith."

The declared result of these acts was that a storm swamped a vessel conveying sundry jewels and gifts that were to have been presented to the new Queen of Scotland on her arrival at Leith.

THE THREE CATS.

There is a witch story associated with a haunted house that once upon a time stood on the moor between Dunvegan and Stein, in Vaternish. In this house there lived a woman and her son. Now, one day, while the mother was out at the peats, and her son was having a snooze on the *seiseach*, or wooden settle (a piece of furniture almost invariably found in the typical Hebridean home), three black cats came in through the window and instantly took the form of women. Nefarious was their intent : they had come hither to hold a regular " Witches' Sabbath " ; and had entered the house as cats so as to conceal their identity.

A prolonged consultation ensued ; and it was only when their conspiratory deliberations were nearing an end that the witches realised the boy on the settle had been feigning sleep all the time, and had overheard their malicious plans. Thereupon one of the witches addressed him sternly ; and warned him not to repeat to any one a single word they had uttered, for she added that, if he did, he would surely regret it. Having intimidated the boy into promising that he would not betray them, the three witches again assumed the form of cats and departed as they had entered, there having been no glass in the Skye windows in those times.

But, when he thought that all likelihood of the witches carrying out their threat was passed, the boy felt constrained (as good boys sometimes feel !) to reveal their evil secret to his mother, who, having listened attentively, vowed that she would divulge it to no one. But, unfortunately, some time afterwards his mother and one of the witches had a violent quarrel ; and with feminine earnestness they indulged rather freely in mutual slander and recrimination. In the end the witch became so abusive that the boy's mother completely lost her temper and let the cat out of the bag, so to speak, for she thoughtlessly accused the witch and her confederates of planning evil against a neighbour.

WITCHES GET THEIR OWN BACK.

That night the witches held in camera another of their sinister conferences ; and a motion was adopted to waylay the boy in the dark. Successful in its object was their ambush, for on the morrow there was found between Faery Bridge and Stein the lifeless body of the unhappy lad who innocently had confided in his mother. "And"—to put it in the artless words of the raconteur who told me the story—" if you don't believe it, there's a sign on the roadside between Faery Bridge and Stein to prove it !"

The people of the vicinity raised a cairn to mark the spot where the foul deed had been committed ; but to-day the Lad's Cairn (*Carn a' Ghille*) is no longer conspicuous, it possibly having sunk down into the peaty soil. This *locale* is said to be haunted ; and even yet young children, who have been told how the three witches ambushed and murdered the little boy, do not care to pass this way at night. Indeed, I actually have met elderly people who deliberately avoid this crossing-place in the darkness, if they can. And sometimes it is not easily avoided, because most overland communication between Dunvegan and Vaternish must of necessity cross there.

Hebridean witches frequently took the shape of cats. It was through the schemings of such bewitched cats that one of the MacLeods of Raasay lost his life. He was greatly disliked by the Skye witches, because he was in the habit of meting out such rough justice to them when they defaulted in any way. So they arranged to assemble by the shore at the Narrows of Raasay, not far from Braes, and to watch for him when he was likely to be sailing from Clachan to Portree. This they did ; and, whenever they observed his boat to be conveniently far from the shore, a select contingent of them was transformed into cats, and made for the boat, which it capsized by huddling together at the poop.

Thus MacLeod was drowned ; while the cats swam ashore in great exultation, and resumed their human appearance once more.

The Drowning of Iain Garbh.

Then, you will recollect that in a chapter dealing with the Laments for MacLeod of Raasay in *Behold the Hebrides !* I made reference to Iain Garbh, who was drowned in the Minch while returning from Stornoway. The story is told that a raven flew ominously round Iain's boat, and eventually perched on the gunwale. And young Raasay, having drawn his dirk, made an attempt to kill the raven. But he missed his prize ; and so colossal was his strength that the point of his dirk clove the timbers instead, with the result that the boat rapidly made water and sank with all hands.

And the raven, they say, was only a witch in disguise, who had been hired by Iain's stepmother. She was inimical toward him, as stepmothers often are towards stepchildren who have succeeded, or may be likely to do so one day.

But Donald Gorm of Sleat is said to have had a hand in the drowning of Iain Garbh MacLeod of Raasay to the extent that he promised the witch a profitable strip of land in Trotternish, if she carried

out his directions.   The witch, as we have seen,
implemented *her* part of the agreement ; but Donald
Gorm, who seldom was particular about keeping his
promises, changed his mind.   At any rate, the witch
was drowned close to the shores of Raasay not long
after she had sent Iain Garbh to his doom ; and
the Skye folks had a shrewd suspicion that it was
Donald Gorm who had planned her death.

CAUGHT IN THE ACT.

A dairymaid in Sleat was continually pestered
by a cat that, for its size, had an abnormal capacity
for milk.   This cat had been helping itself to the
milk for years ; and every precaution to exclude
it from the dairy by keeping the door properly
snecked and the windows carefully closed proved
futile.   Likewise, all attempts to capture the cat
were unsuccessful.

At last the long-suffering dairymaid got her own
back, for one day the cat, having drunk so much
milk that it could scarcely crawl, was caught red-
handed.   In revenge the dairymaid sliced off one
of its ears with a chopper.

Not long afterwards she was aghast at finding
that a woman living a few doors away had lost an
ear.   And so ashamed of herself was the victim
that she would not venture out unless her head
was completely muffled.

"WITHOUT EVEN A BUTTON TO HIS SHIRT."

The witch story that I am now about to relate
was told me at Glasnacille, in Strathaird, last
autumn.   A shepherd, who resided at Elgol, had
jilted a girl.   One black night shortly afterwards
he was returning home from a *ceilidh* at a friend's

house ; and, when he arrived at the bend of the road between Glasnacille and Elgol, a hare crossed his path and described a circle round him. The shepherd declares that, when the hare completed its circle and passed in front of him again, it was transmuted into a horse that neighed wildly, and that in turn was changed into a woman who attacked him, scratched him, and left him " without even a button to his shirt." And he earnestly avers that the witch-like termagant threatened to repeat the assault, should he tell any one in Strath that he had been victimised in this way.

Moreover, she added that he was fortunate in having had with him his dog, and not his bitch. The obvious inference is that, had the latter been present, she would have taken sides with the assailant.

And to this day the folks of southern Strath will tell you that they hear the strains of faery pipes issuing from the hillock close to the spot where this strange incident is believed to have occurred.

SHOD WITH HORSE-SHOES.

Loch Bracadale, also, has its witch story, for Angus, the favourite manservant of the tacksman of Ullinish, had a most extraordinary experience. Angus and his employer were at all times the very best of friends ; but, although they had the utmost confidence in one another, Angus was loath to tell his master why he always looked so bedraggled and exhausted before the day's work had begun. In course of time the state of Angus's health gave the tacksman such real concern that he approached him in a fatherly way, and persuaded him to reveal the secret. And it turned out that poor Angus was the dupe of a woman whom he declared to have been a witch. When he came in from his work at night and was eager to lie down to rest, she used to throw a halter round his neck and transform him into a horse, on whose back she galloped all over Skye to attend witch meetings during the night-time. They never returned till morning, with the result that Angus was usually too tired to be able for his daily duties about the farm. Greatly perturbed was the tacksman of Ullinish when he heard Angus's story ; and so, without breathing a word to any one, they both decided that the next time the witch bothered Angus he would take the bridle forcibly from her, and reiterate to her the phrases she had been in the habit of repeating when transforming him into a horse. In addition, the tacksman directed Angus to shoe her with real horse-shoes whenever she was changed, and to restore her to her normal condition after he had had a jaunt with her round the countryside.

To be sure, that very night the witch again was at her devilish art ; and Angus did not fail to carry out the instructions he and the tacksman of Ullinish had decided upon.

Next morning, when the family was assembled for breakfast, the tacksman kept on wondering and wondering why his wife was so long in making her appearance. He went to look for her at last ; and found that she was ill in bed. So he straightway sent for a physician, who on arrival discovered a pair of horse-shoes so firmly nailed to her feet that neither of them could be removed. And before long the tacksman of Ullinish was lamenting the loss of his wife, who, to his chagrin, had been a witch all the time.

A DUNTULM WIDOW AND HER COW.

In Trotternish long ago there lived a celebrated witch who on more than one occasion came into conflict with Coinneach MacUilleim, or Kenneth Williamson. Kenneth, a solicitor in a small way, was employed as factor in the north of Skye at the beginning of the sixteenth century. According to the *Collectanea de Rebus Albanicis*, Kannoch Wilyameson was granted the rental (six merks) of two fairly productive farms at Baramosmor, in Trotternish— " to hald the said Kannoch at the skolis, and for to lere and study the kingis lawis of Scotland, eftirwart to excerce and use the samin within the boundis of the Ilis." This document is dated " Strivelin, the xj day of Aprile, the yere of God, I^m v^c and viiij yeris, and of the kingis regne the xxi yere" (11. 4. 1508).

I should think that this must constitute the earliest extant record of a Scottish educational scholarship.

Now, it so happened that in the execution of his duties Kenneth one day found himself in the neighbourhood of Duntulm. Thither he had gone in order to mulct a poor widow named MacRuairi, who was considerably in arrearage with her rents. Nor had this cratur's troubles come singly : her husband had been drowned at Duntulm ; her two sons had met a similar fate a week or so later, while rowing a load of seaware over from Tulm Island ; and, owing to the severity of the winter, she had been deprived of all her livestock with the exception of one cow. As she had nothing whatever to offer the factor in lieu of her rent and previously incurred debts, he robbed her of her precious cow, and drove it off to Duntulm, where earlier in the day he had arranged to dine with the gamekeeper.   Bitter were the lamentings of the poor widow ; and her neighbours, on hearing of the heartlessness of the factor, were so enraged that they devised a scheme by which both the widow's cow and Kenneth's horse (which in the meantime had been placed in the same field) were clandestinely ferried across to Fladda-Chuain, a pastoral islet a few miles away, and concealed there.

WITCH REBUKES THE TROTTERNISH FACTOR.

At the termination of his visit to the house of the gamekeeper, Kenneth naturally made for the field where, a few hours previously, he had left the cow and his horse.   But to his astonishment he found that both animals were gone.   Those who stood by protested their innocence, and swore that no one had passed since he entered the game-keeper's house.   And they advised him that the wisest thing to do was to consult, without further delay, Ishbel, a spaewife, who lived by the shore at Duntulm.

"Fetch her !" said Kenneth hastily to the lad in whose bright mind the idea had originated.   So the lad hurried away for the spaewife, and told her the story of how the factor had robbed poor widow MacRuairi of her cow, the only thing in the world she possessed.

In a second or two the witch draped herself in her mystical attire, and with a magic distaff in her hand accompanied the lad to the field, where Kenneth, the factor, was gnashing his teeth with rage.

When he saw her approaching, he cried out to her : " Where are the horse and cow I left in this field only a few hours ago ? "

Photo. by J. Skelton.

View from within the Ruins of Old Duntulm.

Q

"Whose beasts are they?" enquired the witch.

"The horse is mine, and the cow belongs to the king," replied Kenneth.

"And how did the king's cow find its way into a Duntulm field?" she pertinently asked.

"Oh," said Kenneth, "a woman at Kilmuir gave it to me in place of her rent."

But the witch was not believing Kenneth's story, for she had been told the right way of things by the lad who ran to fetch her.

And so, without making any bones about it, she candidly informed the factor that he had stolen the cow from poor widow MacRuairi at Duntulm, and that a band of little men had driven both the cow and his horse over the hills to a corrie, whither it would be unsafe for him to follow.

Coinneach MacUilleim speedily took his departure; and never again had he the temerity to collect the king's tax from a helpless widow in the Parish of Kilmuir.

FLADDA OF THE OCEAN.

When he had retired a reasonable distance from the township, the young men, who had transhipped the animals to Fladda-Chuain (and who, by the way, had executed this piece of strategy with such alacrity that their boat was again drawn up on the beach below Duntulm before the factor emerged from the gamekeeper's house), rowed over to Fladda-Chuain, and brought back both the horse and the cow, and presented them to the poor widow, whom the factor would have oppressed.

Fladda-Chuain, or Fladda of the Ocean, an islet measuring roughly fourteen hundred feet in length and with a mean breadth of three hundred feet, is situated about six miles off Rudha Hunish, the northernmost point of the Isle of Skye. On it is the site of a Columban chapel, where, as I have told you in *Behold the Hebrides !*, fishermen detained in olden times by contrary winds bathed, with gratifying results, a round, blue stone that was always moist. This "weeping stone" possessed a further property in that it had the power of removing stitches, when applied to the ribs of persons affected.

Martin speaks of the interment near the chapel of a monk called O Gorgon, whose grave was made conspicuous by two stones five feet in height that stood one at each end of it. To-day on Fladda-Chuain we look vainly for O Gorgon's grave. In addition, Martin declares coulter-nebs performed the *deisul*, or sunwise turn, round Fladda-Chuain before settling on it in March, and before leaving it in August—a custom that in his day the tenant of the Island was equally careful to observe with his boat, each time he put out to sea. He also mentions a whale that frequented the shores, whose eyes were so big as to petrify with fear whosoever beheld them.

Anciently Fladda-Chuain had three burial-places ; and within recorded times it could boast a Druidical circle consisting of nine stones. One or two interesting relics have been dug up here on various occasions.

WITCHES HAVE NINE LIVES.

Superstition dies hard, for, as Bacon has written, " it erecteth an absolute monarch in the minds of men." From some of the foregoing remarks you will see that in many parts of Skye the witch tradition is far from dead.

And the witches that were most feared in the Western Isles were those who had the power of transforming themselves not into hares, but into cats. I suppose this may be explained by the fact that to kill such a witch was asking for trouble, because cats were each believed to have had nine lives.

The superstitious connection between cats and witches is of very ancient origin, and may have sprung from the Grecian legend of Galinthias, who was transmuted into a cat and became a priestess of Hecate, an instructress in all matters appertaining to sorcery and witchcraft.

Those of us who are conversant with the works of Shakespeare will remember that, in *Romeo and Juliet*, Tybalt puts to Mercutio the question : " What wouldst thou have with me ? " To this the latter replies : " Good king of cats, nothing but one of your nine lives ! "

And, again, do we not read in the old collection of adages and proverbs known as *Gnomologia* that a cat has nine lives, and a woman has nine cats' lives ?

An alleged case of witchcraft was brought before the stipendiary magistrate at Glastonbury only the other day, when an almsman of seventy-seven summers applied for a summons on a charge of witchcraft against another almsman, who, he declared, had not only bewitched him, but also his clock, which consequently ticked three times louder than usual, and stopped at the same hour every night. The complainer further averred that his enemy only visited him when he sat by the fire, and that, after having thoroughly bamboozled him, he always disappeared in a ball of smoke. The case occasioned much amusement ; but, needless to say, it was dismissed.

XXIX

A HEBRIDEAN TEMPEST

DUNTULM AND ITS REMINISCENCES

> "The cloud-capt towers,
> The gorgeous palaces,
> The solemn temples,
> The great globe itself,
> Yea, all which it inherit,
> Shall dissolve,
> And, like the baseless fabric of a vision,
> Leave not a rack behind."

LOUDLY are "The Guns" reporting in Bagh nan Gunnaichean, the Bay of Armaments; and the northern sea-cannons are levelled against the Headland of the Ferry (Rudha na h-Aiseig) and Rudha Hunish. Though actually only a few miles away from the latter, Gearran and its twin satellites—including Lord MacDonald's Table, that sea-girt outpost on which, for reasons of safety, Sir Donald of that Ilk deposited his deeds and charters prior to joining the earlier Rebellion—might be undistanced leagues away on such a stormy day as this! And Eilean Flodigarry and Staffin Isle are smothered in a confusion of mist and angry spume.

Further south the Storr frowns portentously upon the solitary passer-by; and the Quiraing, the herdsman's calendar, and one of the most reliable barometers in all the Hebrides, is enfolded in rolling waves of vapour. Nowhere do the misty battalions deploy more mysteriously than among the topmost crags of the Quiraing.

The stone-strewn moors to the east are as dismal as anything possibly could be : not a soul treads the rough mountain-road : not a bird intrudes itself upon the weary lochans in the sodden plain below. What an eerie, eldritch, repellent scene ! A streak or two of lightning and a prolonged peal of thunder verberating and reverberating among the spray-drenched sea crags, and in the tinnient hollows of these world-old hills are all that are required to complete the utter desolation of this place-before-time. How meaningless, futile, ridiculous are the disputations of men in comparison with the warring of the two great forces of nature attacking and defending in turns, one armed with the wieldy weapons of heaven and the other mailed in the iron-bound armour of earth ! Think of the tragedy of having died in ignorance of the splendour of such a conflict ! Here engage two armies that are never vanquished. Their armour neither rusts nor tarnishes, even though they spend half the year in the luxury and laziness of winter-quarters.

One's mind could not be idle in an environment of this bewilderment. Such a scene would stir the stoutest hearted ; and, yet, the Lords of the Isles must have witnessed even more awesome storms from the seaward windows of old Duntulm.

Down the Quiraing the rain blobs, manumitted from the bondage of a clouded sky, are pelting like a hail of bullets ; and its ribbed and fluted sides and tumbled screes and fragments are runnelled with frothy, wriggling streamlets too numerous to be counted. Its " Prison," its " Needle," its " Table " are lost in the chaos of a typical Skye storm. To give you some indication of the magnitude of its riven and flood-washed chasms, it has been calculated that in the most capacious hollow of the Quiraing no fewer than four thousand head of cattle could be impounded. No doubt, in the days when raids were rife the inhabitants of the plains stretching to the south and east frequently concealed in the vast pits of the Quiraing both themselves and their livestock.

Even when not wreathed in rolling mists and drizzling rains, the prospect from the elevated platform crowning the Quiraing fills you with awe. To these rocks a million years are as a day : yet the pitiless onslaught of unnumbered winters of rain and sleet, of wind and frost and ice, have wrought havoc with this basalt plateau, for at last it is beginning to break and crumble under the eternal recurrence of these dynamics. When exploring the Quiraing, it suddenly flashes across the mind that one is engirdled by rocks about as old as the world itself,—a terrific thought, is it not ?

But the eagle still has his eyrie in the yet impregnable " Castles " of the Quiraing ; and you should see him soaring into the spaceless blue of a summer day, or swooping down into the valley below with a noise as of the rushing of a mighty wind.

THE GRANARY OF SKYE.

If for a mile or two you follow the north-going road of doubtful classification that runs below the Quiraing and within a few hundred yards of the sea, you arrive at Flodigarry House. Flodigarry is one of the fertile bits of land that Pennant thought justified his referring to the parish of

Kilmore (Kilmuir) as " the granary of *Skie*." At garner-time the western side of Kilmuir, with its intensively cultivated hill-slopes, certainly answers to this description. Here the tiller of the ground is recompensed for his toil and industry in a measure almost unknown elsewhere throughout the Western Isles. I vividly recollect having witnessed a rather remarkable harvest scene round the hill-sheltered bay of Uig a year or two ago. Uig, one might confidently say, has maintained its reputation as a locality that in due season is " laughing with corn." It should be added that, in virtue of their productive-ness even in ancient times, Glen Uig and Glen Hinisdal, a few miles to the south, were included among the four pasturages upon which the legend-ary grey goat of the Feinne browsed. In the days of long ago Uig Bay was populous with boats : to-day its piers are seldom visited.

You will remember that for some time the husband of Flora MacDonald tenanted a farm at Flodigarry, and that the heroine lies buried in the old churchyard of Kilmuir in company with most of the MacCrimmon pipers and many other celebrities. To-day there is not a vestige of the ancient Church of St. Mary ; but the site is still proudly referred to as the *Reilig Mhor Chloinn Domhnuill*, the great burying-place of the Clan Donald.

Saint Moluag's Crosier.

Before you reach as far as the Bay of Armaments, the road, veering gently westwards and passing through Kilmoluag, brings you to the western sea-board of Trotternish within earshot of the historic Castle of Duntulm. Kilmoluag has been spelt in so many different ways that often it is unrecognisable at first sight. It is said to have got its name from the fact that Saint Moluag, the patron saint of Appin and the " Great Garden " (Lismore), settled here and erected a place of worship. Kilmoluag is still the name applied to the Argyllshire parish from which he came originally.

The godly Saint Moluag had a wonderful *bachall* or crosier that was entrusted to a hereditary custodian who, in return for his services as keeper, was endowed with a freehold in Trotternish. Saint Moluag's crosier had the power of healing whomsoever was touched by it. When he died in the latter half of the seventh century, one of his goodly apostles took the *bachall* with him from Lismore to Appin, whither he had journeyed to minister to a dying man. In his haste to re-cross to Lismore so as to avoid an impending storm, he arrived back without Saint Moluag's magic crosier ; but, just as he was about to step on the threshold of the church, something whizzed past his ear. What was this but the *bachall* or crosier returning of its own accord to the proper place in the church ! In common with many small bells that, because of their healing properties, were used either privately or in churches, this crosier had the miraculous power of finding its way back in the event of its being stolen or forgotten. The touch of a *bachall* and the sound of such a bell alike were held to heal afflicted persons by dispelling the evil spirits of which they were possessed. Saint Moluag's crosier wrought many a cure in northern Skye : hence the little hamlet of Kilmoluag was consecrated to his memory.

A healing bell accidentally left by the bedside of

a sick man at Kingussie is claimed to have returned
of its own accord to the church to which it belonged.
And, while Prince Charlie's enemies were in pursuit
of him, they searched a green islet in Loch Shiel
whereon stood a tiny chapel, on the altar of which
lay such a magical bell. One of the pursuers,
having thought the bell a fine piece of loot, picked
it up ; but, they say, it began to screech so weirdly
that he straightway dropped it and fled. No one
since has attempted to remove that bell ; and I
believe it remains on this islet in Loch Shiel.

THE GHOST OF DONALD GORM MOR.

A couple of miles due west of Kilmoluag and on
a green eminence overlooking the Minch stand
the empty, forlorn ruins of Duntulm Castle, the
Dun of the Grassy-Green Knoll. To-day it is but
the mere fragment of a typically Hebridean fortress
that of a time was unassailable by land or by sea.
Though a little fantastic in minor details, the old
print of Duntulm Castle and its enclosed garden
to be found in one of Pennant's volumes conveys
a fair impression of how this stronghold appeared
presumably about 1774. At the present time the
site is garden-less and barren. The soil of Duntulm
garden was supposed to have been brought from
seven or eight different European countries.

Erected on the site of an older Viking fortress
known originally as Dun Daibhidh (David's Fort-
alice), Duntulm for at least two centuries was the
chief seat of the doughty Lords of the Isles, who,
it is alleged, were driven out of it round about 1715
by the haunting ghost of Donald Gorm Mor.
After having vacated Duntulm, Sir Alexander Mac-
Donald and his family betook themselves tempo-

rarily to an ordinary dwelling-house at Mugstot (Monkstadt), six or eight miles further south. There the MacDonalds resided before the completion at the beginning of the nineteenth century of Armadale Castle, though many of them had transferred themselves to Sleat long before the end of the eighteenth century. Johnson and Boswell in 1773 were greeted on the sands of Sleat by a MacDonald who conveyed them to his then unpretentious house of " Armidle." The MacDonalds occupied in succession Islay, Mull, Trotternish, and finally Sleat ; and to each of these places they brought a most interesting tradition.

The deserting of Duntulm by the MacDonalds has never been satisfactorily explained. Some say the accidental death of a child that fell out of a western window into the sea was regarded by its inmates as an event sufficiently grievous and unpropitious as to warrant their evacuating it ; but the more generally accepted explanation is that the MacDonalds dreaded the restless ghost of Donald Gorm Mor.

For all that, this same ghost on one occasion proved invaluable, and in the following manner. The year after Donald Gorm Mor was succeeded by his nephew, Donald Gorm Og (Young Blue Donald), an important family document went amissing. On the recovery of this document a great deal depended. Now, at this time there frequently had been seen in the neighbourhood of Castle Duntulm three ghostly forms, whom Young Donald Gorm had made many unsuccessful efforts to accost. One day, however, they were seen to have entered the Castle ; and a wiseacre in the locality suggested that seven men, bearing seven staves with fire at their ends, should follow them. These directions were carried out; and whom did the seven men discover in the wine-cellar of the Castle but Donald Gorm Mor and two carousing clansmen! And Donald Gorm told the intruders where the much-sought document was to be found.

Excessive Revelry in the Isles.

The wine-red contents of many a cask were heartily consumed within the walls of grey Duntulm; and the story I have told you this moment relating to Donald Gorm Mor's ghostly revelry brings to mind the steps taken by the Privy Council to enforce upon certain drouthy Highland chieftains a measure of sobriety. Historical records supply us with ample proof of the passion for wine among the Western Islanders in the early seventeenth century. An Act of 1609 prohibited the importation to the Isles of wines and spirits from the mainland; but this measure did not restrict the use of either, and even admitted the right of persons resident in the Isles to brew for personal consumption their own aqua-vitae and other drinks. Furthermore, special barons and " substantious gentlemen " were at liberty to send to the Lowlands for such additional supplies of liquor as they might desire.

A more decisive step was taken when in 1616 the Privy Council forbade the free use of wines in the Isles under high penalties, and summoned a number of chiefs to appear in Edinburgh on what in modern phraseology we would term charges of disorderliness and drunkenness. At this convention it was deponed that " the great and extraordinary excess in drinking of wyne, commonlie usit among the commonis and tenantis of the Yllis, is not only ane occasioun of the beastlie and barbarous cruelties and inhumanities that fallis out amangis thame, to the offens and displeasour of God, and contempt of the law and justice ; but with that it drawis nomberis of thame to miserable necessitie and povartie sua that they are constraynit . . . to tak from thair nichtbours."

Through indisposition Donald Gorm was unable to answer the summons of 1616 ; but he found the necessary surety, ratified the treaty, so to speak, and named " Duntullim " as the residence to which any further communications should be addressed. The Privy Council, besides having made a number of minor stipulations into which we need not enter herein, granted Donald Gorm permission to retain six household gentlemen, and to consume annually a wine supply not exceeding four tun. Three tun were prescribed for the other branches of Clan Ranald ; whereas the allowances to MacKinnon, Coll, and Loch Buidhe (Lochbuy) were each assessed at one tun—a considerable reduction, no doubt !

That this limitation failed to produce among the wealthier classes the sobriety desired is borne out by an Act passed by the Council of Scotland in 1622 to place a restriction on the importation of wines. From the preamble to this *Act that Nane send Wynis to the Ilis* we learn that, on the arrival of a vessel with liquor on board, the people wasted " bothe dayis and nightis in thair excesse of drinking and seldome do thay leave thair drinking so lang as thair is ony of the wyne restand sua that being overcome with drink thair fallis oute mony inconvenientis amangis thame to the brek of his maiesteis peace. . . ."

A Slipway for Clan Ranald's Galleys.

The locality of Duntulm is steeped in legendary and historical lore. Close at hand is Cnoc an Rola, the hill of wheeling or marching, so called because hereon Donald Gorm Og, on learning that Mac-Leod's galleys had set sail from Dunvegan and that an attack on Duntulm Castle was imminent, accepted the counsel of his father's wit and collected every available person in the neighbourhood, whether capable or not of bearing arms. He then marched his battalion round and round this hill to give the MacLeods the impression that a mighty host awaited their arrival. Fortunately for Duntulm, this hoax had the desired result, for at the time the garrison of the Castle was engaged elsewhere. Just below Cnoc an Rola is Cnoc a' Chrochaidh, literally the Gallows Hill. Here many of the victims of Clan Ranald's wrath breathed their last. By the shore of Score Bay, and skirted by the road a little south of Duntulm, is the well that in olden times supplied the Castle with water. Then, at Bornaskitaig we have the characteristic "Cave of Gold" in which the MacDonalds were said to have hidden their treasures in times of danger ; while on the rocky shore immediately below Duntulm Castle may be seen the natural slipway up which the birlinns of Clan Ranald were hauled. The straight groove is still clearly discernible ; and at the present day the local fishermen draw up their craft at this *Barr nam Biorlainn*. In close proximity to the Castle one may still examine Cairidh Ghlumaig, the ancient weir that retained flat fish after the tide had ebbed. Along the shores of Skye any number of disused " cairidhs " are to be found.

Near Duntulm, too, is a hillock called Cnoc an

Eirig. An eighteenth-century writer entitles it
"the Hill of Pleas," since it is thought to have
been one of the knolls from which the MacDonald
chiefs dispensed the law and pronounced sentences
upon those who disregarded it. Another seat of
jurisdiction associated with the sovereignty of the
MacDonalds is Cnoc a' Mhoid or Cnoc a' Chomh-
airle—the Knoll of the *Mod* or Assembly. The
names of all the hillocks in the vicinity of Duntulm
Castle testify to the departed glory of the great
MacDonalds of the Isles.

An Artful Nephew.

Some miles south of Duntulm and at a point
overlooking the sea are the ruins of another fortress ;
and hereby hangs a gruesome tale. Donald Gorm
Mor of Sleat had no issue ; and so about 1580 his
nephew, Hugh, the son of Archibald the Clerk
(*Uisdean mac Ghilleasbuig Chleirich*), devised a scheme
to deprive those who, in ordinary circumstances,
were likely to succeed him. With this object in
view, Hugh commenced to build at a point close
to the shore of Loch Snizort, but some considerable
distance from Duntulm, a tower that he never lived
to complete, and that ever since has gone by the
name of Caisteal h-Uisdein, Hugh's Castle. This
stronghold was constructed with neither door nor
window : a ladder reaching to the top of the tower
and conveniently hauled up at will supplied the
only means of entry. Little did Donald Gorm
suspect that, by assisting his nephew to erect
Caisteal h-Uisdein, he was heaping coals of fire
upon his own head.

Now, it happened that a year or two later Donald
Gorm had occasion to visit his kinsman at Dunyveg,

in Islay. On his return to Duntulm, his birlinn was forced to take shelter in the leeward of the territory belonging to the Duart MacLeans. By some strangely suspicious accident Hugh, the son of Archibald the Clerk, simultaneously found himself in this neighbourhood. Here he "lifted" some of MacLean's cattle, and made away with them so quietly that his uncle's crew was accused of having stolen them. In a skirmish that ensued between the MacLeans and the MacDonalds one or two of Donald Gorm's men were slain ; and he and the remainder of his crew escaped to Skye only after having experienced the roughest treatment at the hands of the ireful MacLeans.

Yet another conspiracy did Hugh arrange against his unsuspecting uncle ; but this time the crafty nephew was taken by surprise, for Donald Gorm, having been in Uist when the plot came to his ears, entrusted the arrest of the perpetrator to a couple of reliable henchmen, who came upon Hugh unawares, and brought him to Duntulm Castle. Into the dark dungeon he was cast. There he was fed with the saltest of salt beef : there he died of thirst. The native of Glen Hinisdal, who recited this story to me some time ago, insisted that, so as to make his sufferings the more terrible, he was chained to the centre of the dungeon wherein, but beyond his reach, was placed a brimful dish of water.

Hugh's remains were committed to the parish burying-ground ; but it is alleged that his bones were exhumed as curiosities, and that they lay for years about the walls of the old church, until some humane person re-interred them.

Photo. by R. C. MacLeod of MacLeod.

All that remains of Duntulm Castle.

The Oystercatcher and Its Legend.

The storm that beleaguered the Quiraing, when last I visited it, had abated somewhat by the time I tramped through Kilmoluag to Duntulm, although the great Atlantic tide boomed and resounded in the hollowed fiords of Loch Snizort, and the wind of a Hebridean storm whistled and moaned through the paneless windows of the Castle. As I peered seaward from this august coign of vantage, there flew before me two oystercatchers, uttering their weird warning—" *bi glic, bi glic ; bi glic, bi glic,*" meaning " be wise," " be prudent," " take care." By mariners this cry is usually regarded as the sign of an approaching storm. No bird has occupied a more prominent place in Celtic mythology and legend than the oystercatcher ; and Hebridean folklore is full of references to this beautiful creature. In Gaelic the oystercatcher is known as *bridean* or *gillebridean*, for it is associated with Saint Bride (Bridget), the foster-mother of Christ. It is said that originally its colouring was black, and that in recognition of its services to mankind it was awarded a white plumage on the breast in the shape of a cross. This cross of white is very noticeable when the oystercatcher happens to be flying towards one.

Adrift in a Coracle.

It is narrated that in the Island of Eigg the oystercatcher won its saintly reputation by having rescued three motherless infants, who were adrift in a storm in a small *curach* or coracle. Two oystercatchers, having heard the children's cries as they flew past, hurried off to tell Saint Bride, who came immediately to their aid, and guided them on the inflowing tide to a place of safety, where a warm bed of bog-cotton and down had been prepared for them.   It was said, too, that when Christ was being pursued from one Hebridean island to another, He was hidden at low tide by two oystercatchers, who covered Him with seawrack and kept watch over Him until his adversaries had passed.   For this act it was supposed that the oystercatcher was selected to be the *gille* or servant of Saint Bride, Christ's foster-mother.

Few birds excel the oystercatcher in its pains-taking and thorough research of the seashore ; and in Gaelic we have a phrase, " *Cho eolach 's tha 'm bridean 's an traigh*," meaning " as well acquainted as the oystercatcher is with the shore."   Then, this bird is noted for its swiftness and alacrity, as the phrase " *Cho luath ri bridean* " denotes.

* * * * * *

The grim shell of Duntulm Castle is storied with mysteries.   Whether it is emeralded by grass and moss and lichen, whether it is etched against a sombre, dismal sky, whether it stands faintly in the dimness of daybreak, whether it dreams in the day of the noontide sun or gleams in the night of a silver-mooned autumn, its appeal to the imagina-tion is ever present, and cannot be denied.

Here is a place—eerie, ghostly, solitary, once impregnable by sea or by land—where, upon the crumbling mortar over a window, one yet may trace the weathered galley of the brave Clan Ranald.

And I would that you tarried at Duntulm when the lightnings are being made for the rain, and when the wind is being brought out of his treasuries.

XXX

IN THE HEART OF THE COOLINS

MOUNTAINEERING IN SKYE:
ITS THRILLS AND ITS PERILS

> " Oh, the far Coolins are putting love on me,
>   As step I wi' my cromag to the Isles."

SLIGACHAN, the Place of Shells, must surely rank among the premier mountain-climbing centres in the world : its far-famed Inn occupies a position at the mouth of a wilderness of chaos that, to say the least of it, is unrivalled. Sligachan is an oasis in a desert of riven mountain and undressed stone, of dark linns and dark corries. It is a tiny bit of human life amid indescribable sterility, barrenness, bewilderment.

In some ways, however, Sligachan is uniquely central. From it the hill-climber may strike out in any direction—northward through Glen Varragill to Portree, southward through Glen Sligachan to Coruisg and a hundred other eerie corries, eastward by the shore of Loch Sligachan and under the shadow of Lord MacDonald's Forest to Sconser, and westward through Glen Drynoch to Loch Harport and Bracadale and Glen Bretil. A great part of the Coolins is approached more easily from the Glen Bretil side. In each of these directions, with the exception of the second, one may follow a road or at any rate a beaten and unbroken track, lonely and lifeless as it may be. If you go by Drynoch to Glen Bretil, you are pretty certain to meet the shepherd whose hirsel is at Treen. He may be driving a flock of sheep from Talisker by the Glen-under-Road (Gleann-fo-Rathaid), or collecting sheep on the slopes of Eynort. And, if you halt for a moment and get into conversation with him, he will give you his name in an indirect manner by making a remark of this nature : " Well, there's no many Camerons in the Lewis ! "

PANORAMA FROM GLAMAIG.

So far as the Coolins are concerned, the road through Glen Varragill does not interest us, except in that from it one receives a splendid conception of the magnitude of Glamaig and Marsco when descending into Sligachan. From the road leading towards Sconser Glamaig may be ascended, though, no doubt, experienced climbers prefer to follow the course of the Oaken Brook (Allt Daraich) and attack it from the southern side. No one sojourning at Sligachan, who has any power of physical endurance, should omit to climb Glamaig—though my advice to any one intending to do so is to keep clear of the long, sloping screes where the detritus is so broken that you find yourself sliding back two steps for every one you take forward. The summit of Glamaig is grassy and mossy. There, if the wind be high and piercingly cold, as it usually is, one may draw breath in the leeward of a cairn that year by year is being added to at an ever-increasing rate. Glamaig may be descended in comparative comfort on the north-east side, whence one may return to the Inn by following the road through Sconser and along the shore of Loch Sligachan.

Nothing of its kind in the world can excel the panorama around Glamaig ; and likewise no language can portray its thrill and immensity. You must needs bear in mind that here you are at an altitude three times that of Arthur's Seat and rising almost immediately from sea-level. Looking southwards and between the peaks of the Red Hills one gets interrupted glimpses of the Sound of Sleat ; and further round to the south, where Marsco does not obstruct the view, may be seen Canna and the mainland of Argyll. To the west and north-west lie a corner of Loch Harport, the whole of Loch Bracadale with all its larger islands, " MacLeod's Maidens " at Idrigil, " MacLeod's Tables," part of Loch Dunvegan, and the greater part of Loch Snizort.

To the south, Strathaird is almost entirely hidden by the majestic peak of Blaven ; but, should you descend a little to the north and east, nearly the whole of Loch Ainort comes into view. Broadford is easily discernible ; while, looking in a northerly direction, Portree resembles a tiny hamlet at the side of an inland loch, the entrance to its commodious harbour being concealed behind Ben Tianavaig. Though Sligachan, itself, is tucked away far below, as it were, a remarkable idea of the watershed of the impinging country may be gained from the summit of Glamaig.

A Goorkha's Feat.

My chiefest regret about Glamaig lies in that Loch Bretil, and Rudh' an Dunain—that wild headland stretching seaward as if to meet Clan Ranald's galleys from Canna—are obscured completely by Sgurr nan Gillean and Bruach na Frithe. Oh !

I love Rudh' an Dunain ; and one day I mean to tell you why.

Towards the close of last century a barefooted Goorkha climbed to the top of Glamaig from the bridge near Sligachan Inn and returned in fifty-five minutes. Think of it ! This stupendous feat was witnessed by MacLeod of MacLeod and other gentlemen still living. It may convey to you some conception of what this undertaking entailed when I tell you that it would take most people twice fifty-five minutes to arrive at even the base of this mountain from the bridge at Sligachan. And the people at Sconser will describe to you how, on descending the mountain, the Goorkha straightway made for the river to soak his feet in it.

THE WILDNESS OF GLEN SLIGACHAN.

When you have wandered a few hundred yards past the deep, ferny ravine just where the Oaken Brook gurgles noisily in its anxiety to join the brimming Sligachan River, you are actually treading on one of the wildest and most fascinating hill-tracks in the world. I used to think that under certain aspects nothing could be dreicher than parts of the Moor of Rannoch ; but it is tame and civilised after experiencing the solemn loneliness and remoteness of the heart of the Coolian with its tremendous rock-mountains. It is hard to believe that the Coolins and the obnoxious, perfume-smelling loafing-places of the modern city, where at any hour of the day are to be found the painted dolls and the fops of humanity, could possibly be within ten thousand miles of one another—so wild, so remote, so terrifying are the Alps of Skye.

In the beauty and magnificence of their bleakness the Coolins are without parallel. But their sombreness is oppressive when the day is so dark and wet that you may pass within a yard of the mountain-hare that conceals himself in the canach of a sodden morass, and remains motionlessly there in the hope that he may be unnoticed. Many creatures are bolder and more confident in bad weather : they seem to know instinctively when the passer-by is too preoccupied in selecting the least irksome route to trouble about disturbing them. See how tame deer become in severe weather. They soon play havoc with your January cabbages when driven down from the mountains by heavy falls of snow.

Through Trackless Wastes.

Ere you have wandered very far into Glen Sligachan, the narrow hill-track, that between the Allt Dearg Mor and the Allt Dearg Beag is fairly well defined, becomes irregular and broken, gradually disappearing as would a river in the heart of the Sahara. Travelling, indeed, begins to get disagreeable and tiring now, especially after torrential rains, when in order to avoid pools and bogs one is often obliged to take circuitous detours that add considerably to the day's journey. At one time you are treading along the gravelly ridge laid by a stream that in spate was too swollen and impetuous to have been contained in its legitimate watercourse : at another you are selecting the most suitable stepping-stones across a river in an endeavour to reach a great rock capped by an odd chunk of peat, on which grows a healthy cluster of heather and blaeberry. And you commence to enquire how this tuft found its way up there—whether originally it was wind-borne or bird-borne, and whether it increases in size, as does a sand-dune, from a temporary obstacle. And then you begin to wonder how the vegetation thrives so well on such a thin, barren clod of peat ; and you immediately reflect on the supplies of animalcula carried aeolian-wise and by rains.

This is the place for stags and hinds ; and eerie is the bell of the disconsolate stag in the corries separating Marsco from the Red Hills. Should you be on the windward side of a Coolin stag, your chances of seeing him are very small, because he "gets wind" quicker than any other creature in the world. A superstitious person passing by Lord MacDonald's Forest might readily be inclined to believe that the roar of the unseen stag was really the voice of a gruagach or of a water-kelpie, or perhaps of a banshee foretelling death. At first hearing, the bay of the stags in the fastnesses of Marsco brings to mind the caged ferae on Corstorphine Hill. Far be it from me to say anything of a derogatory nature about the Scottish Zoological Park. It is a place where the observant may learn something of what is the merest fringe of nature ; but, oh, how antonymous are the words "wild" and "caged" ! After all, any form of deliberate captivity is a contradiction, when we realise that the whole Universe is groaning for freedom.

How a Baptism was Performed.

Somewhere behind Marsco are the ruins of a shepherd's house. There upon a time dwelt a family that scarcely ever saw a stranger. If a human being appeared anywhere in sight, the

The Sligachan in spate, and Glamaig.

children swiftly flew into the steading to conceal themselves. Before any one of them was baptised, the youngest child was well on his legs, while the eldest was about fourteen years of age. When at last the minister called to christen the children, he found the whole clan seated in readiness for him in the kitchen. However, when he started the ceremony, the children were so scared that they sought refuge behind pieces of furniture and under beds. So agile were they that their parents found it impossible to collect them again. In the end a brilliant plan was struck upon—when the door of the house was unsnecked to permit of the startled youngsters rushing out into the open, the minister, having stood to one side with a basin of water in readiness, drenched them *en masse*, and called their names as they dashed out. There are still living many members of this family.

MAGNITUDE OF THE COOLIN PEAKS.

To get a proper idea of the strength and magnitude of the Coolin peaks, they ought to be viewed from a comparatively low eminence. When on the summit of a very high mountain such as Sgurr Alasdair or Blaven, you cannot raise your eyes to the hills whence cometh your aid, with the result that there is a tendency to lose that sense of proportion without which a day in the Coolins is misspent. It is only when a sheep or a deer is detected on the hillside that one to whom this chaos, this place-before-time, is unfamiliar receives any real indication of the stupendousness of these mountain masses, and of the unbelievable distances that must be traversed to reach them.

Very few artists really get the magnitude and

distance of the Coolins.   One artist whom I know, and to whose pictures of Skye the term, magnificent, would be merely gratuitous, always brings out this bigness by looking at his picture from time to time, and asking himself whether any one climbing the mountain depicted would be fatigued ere he reached the top.   You could *not* ascend Sgurr nan Gillean in half an hour without feeling tired ; and, if your picture leads you to imagine that you could, then you may be certain that something is wrong with its distance or its altitude or with both.   Again, into the picture you may have introduced too much detail : all artists are aware that detail diminishes distance, space, and magnitude.

HARTA CORRIE.

No hill-wanderer journeying between Sligachan and Coruisg should be disinclined to enter Harta Corrie and Lota Corrie, both of which are comparatively accessible by turning round the southern shoulder (the " Castles ") of Sgurr nan Gillean and following upstream and from a bend immediately below a black lochan called Loch Dubh the headwaters of the River Sligachan.   Just here is the water-parting.   The overflow of Loch Dubh runs in a northerly direction into the Sligachan ; whereas another lochan a little to the south of Loch Dubh supplies the river known as Amhuinn Srath na Creitheach which, before reaching the loch of the same name, enters and emerges from Loch an Athain.   The overflow of Loch na Creitheach finds its way into Loch Scavaig at Camusunary (Camus Fhionnairidh), and near the celebrated stepping-stones.

FIVE MAGNIFICENT CORRIES.

There are five corries in the Coolins that every artist should see on account of the fact that in formation, as well as in colouring effects, they are all quite different from one another. They are Harta Corrie, Lota Corrie, Coir' a' Ghrunnda, Coire Lagain, and Coire na Creiche. The last two corries mentioned may be approached more conveniently from the Glen Bretil side of the Coolins. Coire na Creiche, the Corrie of the Spoil, got its name through having been the hollow where in 1601 the MacDonalds concealed and afterwards divided the sheep and oxen they had taken from the MacLeods in a successful skirmish. From Sligachan it may be visited by following the Allt Dearg Mor and striking over the Bealach a' Mhaim (Pass of the Mam) towards the easterly watershed of the River Brittle. The ground here is very soppy and broken, being kept in an almost continual state of bog by the great number of springs that diversify it. Between Corrie Lagain and Coir' a' Ghrunnda is the Great Stone Shoot, by way of which one may ascend the majestic peak of Sgurr Alasdair (3309 ft.), and review Sgurr Dubh, Sgurr Mhic Coinnich (the latter is named after John MacKenzie, the famous Coolin guide) and its other satellites.

THE COOLINS AND COLOUR.

To paint the Coolins successfully some knowledge of geological formation is essential. There you get colourings that are to be found nowhere else in the world—as for example the curious green of the screes. Coolin colour is a colour quite by itself. Sligachan offers an infinite variety of subjects to the artist's brush ; and almost every day one sees Glamaig from a different aspect.

Few pictures of Lota Corrie adequately convey its wildness and remoteness, hemmed in as it is between the steep, mist-robed flanks of Bruach na Frithe and the gigantic citadels of Sgurr nan Gillean. When there recently, it was so enveloped in mist and rain that I barely could see five feet in front of me. I would have been there yet but for the head-stream of the River Sligachan that guided me to the Bloody Stone at the entrance to Harta Corrie, whence I regained the discontinuous bridle-path somewhere under Marsco. But, curiously, while one part of the Coolins is being deluged with rain and palled by mists, the corrie a mile or so round the corner is frequently bathing in the brightest of sunshine.

The Weirdness of Coruisg.

My last journey through Glen Sligachan to Coruisg was made in anything but pleasant circumstances. I had climbed out of Harta Corrie, and was forced by mists and driving rains to descend into the valley about three miles from the head of Loch Coruisg. Thence I trailed along the side of that Loch towards Camusunary, and ascended above Loch a' Choire Riabhaich to the ridge known as Drumhain.

The weirdness of the scene around Drumhain I shall never forget. Marsco, Trodhu, Blaven, Sgurr Alasdair at the four cardinal points of the compass fill one with a sense of magnitude and desolation that is sometimes depressing, nay, appalling. Below, Loch Scavaig rolled furiously before a driving gale. That day Coruisg bore a sulky countenance, and was attired in the wildest, fiercest, gloomiest apparel to be found in its extensive wardrobe.

Coruisg, where

> " . . . all is rocks at random thrown—
>   Black waves, bare crags, and banks of stone,"

ought to be seen on a dull, foreboding day, when the lowered clouds almost rake its inky-black water and the incalculable talus of shattered rock with which its shores are bestrewn. Oh, the sullen solemnity of this chasm ! Who would not be superstitious about a place like this ? How marvellous is the craftsmanship of the ice and the denuding handiwork of Time !

HOME TO SLIGACHAN.

By some lucky accident I found my way back to Loch Dubh, and there regained the track leading more or less directly to Sligachan that I had stupidly forsaken to enter Harta Corrie. I was utterly drenched with rain and weighed down with mud by this time, having been up to the hips in quagmires and pools and streams more than once. The brooks that between Sligachan and Marsco previously trickled across my path were raging torrents when I recrossed them about five hours later ; and the sides of the mountains were white with gushing rivulets. Scarcely audible for the reverberance of tumbling and spluttering water was the hollow roar of the stag.

To visit Scavaig and Coruisg from Sligachan Inn and return thither the same day (as one must needs do !) one would require to tramp almost continuously for six or seven hours. Everything for an excursion of this nature depends on the day : the wanderer among the Coolins cannot be too careful about choosing his day. My day broke down, as I have already told you ; and so, partly from anxiety of being lost in the mist, I was obliged to complete the entire detour without a single halt. To drink I did not require to pause, because the rains were running over my lips much faster than I could consume of them. At one point, to my disgrace, I nearly lost heart—and, indeed, would have done so, had I not realised suddenly how idiotic it would have been to have given way on the side of a storm-beaten, untrodden mountain at least seven miles from the nearest human habitation. In any case, if you feel you must collapse, it is a mistake to do so until you have arrived at the side of a track or footpath, where, if you be lucky, you may be discovered eventually in a state of semi-decomposition. Better far to be found dead by the side of a track in the Coolins than not to be found at all !

The ideal way of exploring the Coolian is to take with you a sturdy Highland pony that can manœuvre any " Bad Step " and that has a real sense of humour. Certainly the most comprehensive way of reaching Lochs Scavaig and Coruisg from Sligachan is by hiring a pony as far as Camusunary, and thence walking along a very rough path under the southern base of Trodhu towards Port Sgaile.

THE PERILS OF THE COOLINS.

Beset with perils are the serried ranks of mountains composing the Coolian ; and deep and treacherous are the valleys and lochs that penetrate them. Even those who are well acquainted with these mountains should observe certain maxims. One should never wander far from Sligachan alone, even when familiar with the topography of the region. Any mishap might befall an unaccompanied person : after a good drenching, the next easiest thing to get in the Coolins is a sprained ankle or a dislocated thigh. Set out on your expedition at an hour that will give you a sufficiently long spell of daylight to enable you to return before nightfall ; and always bear in mind during the outward journey that, as a rule, you will have to cover exactly the same distance to get home again.

Into the heart of the Coolian no one should venture without a haversack containing food : you never know how many hours you may be delayed, waiting for the mists to clear. No one need carry water to the Coolins, for even in the hottest summer its burns are never dry.

Frequently at Sligachan are search-parties organised ; and for unreturning hill-wanderers many an anxious vigil has been kept in that very same Inn. If you knew the boundlessness of this wilderness, you would realise how remote the chances of discovery sometimes are. A needle in a haystack and a human being lost in the Coolins are in very much the same position.

Far From the Madding Crowd.

At times the desolation of the Coolins is positively repellent. There is nothing here but trackless wastes and a colossal welter of rocks and mountains. And the feeling that on every side you are hemmed in by a sodden, mist-wreathed wilderness defies description.

For miles and miles you never see the slightest evidence of anything human in origin—not even a dyke or fence. Such a man-constructed device as a fence would be as out of place in the heart of the Coolins as a bull would be in a china-shop.

And often it is with a genuine feeling of thankfulness that you are again passing by the Eagle Rock, and are within earshot of Sligachan Inn once more.

S

Sgurr Beag, Sgurr na h-Uamha, and Sgurr na Stri from Sgurr nan Gillean.

XXXI

TALES OF RUDH' AN DUNAIN

MACLEOD AND HIS LIEUTENANT OF THE COAST

> Comes a peace to Rudh' an Dunain
> With the first, faint flush of morn :
> Here the birlinns of Clan Ranald
> Oft lay splintered and forlorn. . . .

WEIRD, weird are the tales of Rudh' an Dunain,
that frowning cape at the southern entrance to
Loch Bretil (Brittle), in Minginish, and stretching
seaward towards Canna, the Island in whose
obscurest creeks its fiercest foemen concealed themselves in ancient days. It was at this wild Headland of the Little Dun that, night and day, MacLeod
of MacLeod was compelled to maintain a Lieutenant
of the Coast as a means of protection against the
punitive and predatory raids of the Lochlannaich
and the MacDonalds of Clan Ranald, who sailed
across Cuillin Sound from Canna and Rum and
Eigg. These Islands they conveniently used as
jumping-off places for their attacks on the south-
western territories of MacLeod's Country.

Oft-times in that splendid harbour between Canna
and Sanday did Clan Ranald's galleys share the
peace of quiet waters with the storm-stayed trading
vessels from the Baltic : often, too, in the crevasses
and caves of that Island, where " the fowls hes few
to start them except deir," did the Lochlannaich

divide the spoil they had taken from Rudh' an Dunain and Glen Bretil.

Dangerously near to Rudh' an Dunain were the rieving Northmen when they succeeded in reaching Loch Scavaig, or managed to sneak into the leeward of Soay Island without having been observed by MacLeod's sea-watchman ; and equally hazardous was it for Rudh' an Dunain and Glen Bretil when it became known that the MacDonalds had manned their fleets of war-galleys with the most mettlesome of their Uist sailors, and were assembling in the shelter of the Small Isles. Soay is a little more than a league from Rudh' an Dunain ; whereas Canna and Rum are distant less than three.

A Beacon's Fiery Warning.

At the very point of Rudh' an Dunain is the *gob* or beak, whereon at night, and when necessary, the garrison of the *dun* kindled a signal fire, in order to warn the inhabitants of Glen Bretil and the surrounding country that an invasion was impending, or had just taken place. And, having noticed the fire at Rudh' an Dunain, the sea-watchman on duty at the proximate fort would raise the alarm, and light a similar fire. Within an incredibly short space of time the coast would be a line of glowing beacons, sending forth their fiery message through the darkness, and summoning all men capable of bearing arms to muster by the shore, that the invader might be repelled.

In Skye may still be seen the ruins of several *duns* that were utilised in this and in other ways : for example, a few miles due north of Rudh' an Dunain, and near the mouth of Loch Eynort, is a *dun* that in this manner was in telegraphic communication with Rudh' an Dunain, on the one hand, and with a *dun* whose ruins stand near Talisker, on the other.

THE MACASKILLS COMMAND MACLEOD'S GALLEYS.

Loch Eynort was a favourite landing-place of the MacDonalds during the centuries that the Mac-Askills were in command of MacLeod's galleys. They landed there about 1395 when they suffered defeat at the Bloody Stone in Harta Corrie, and retreated to Loch Eynort to discover that in their absence MacAskill had captured their birlinns. Again in 1490 the Clan Ranalds disembarked on the shores of Loch Eynort and ravaged MacLeod's Country up as far as Glendale where, after a desperate struggle, they were beaten back. On this occasion the remnants of their force made good their retreat to Loch Eynort. It was in this battle that Alasdair Crotach became *crotach*—hump-backed —the muscles of his neck having been severed by a swoop from an enemy's sword.

THE THREE BANSHEES.

Without number are the tales of Rudh' an Dunain ; and not unwitch-like is the following tale. Upon a time there lived at Rudh' an Dunain a certain Tormod MacSweyn. This Norman was shepherd to the tacksman of Rudh' an Dunain, who leased extensive stretches of moorland in the locality of Glen Bretil, and owned large flocks of sheep. One day Norman's wife chanced to be reclining in a dreamy way on her bed, while her young child was seated on the lap of a kindly neighbour, who crooned to it by the fire. The neighbour, too, was feeling a little drowsy ; and before long she was quite overcome with the sleep induced by the warmth of the fire.

Now, though dovering, the mother of the infant was sufficiently awake to be conscious of everything that was going on around her ; and, on glancing casually in the direction of the fire, to her amazement she espied three little women gathered round the sleeping neighbour and the babe : they had entered the house surreptitiously. Having been unable to recognise them, she concluded that they were banshees bent on mischief. Nor was she far wrong, for she overheard the senior of them whisper to the one who stood near her : " Raise the babe, and we 'll depart with it ! "

" Oh ! " she heard the other banshee say, " leave with the poor woman MacSweyn this one babe, as already you have had so many of her children ! "

It was not till then that the third banshee broke silence by expressing a similar desire, having had compassion on the poor mother.

Angry, indeed, was the senior banshee that her sisters had thwarted her plan ; and to their suggestion that the child should be left she responded : " If, then, I must yield to your entreaties, we will not bear the child away ; but this I declare— when the *caoran* (a *peatag*, or little peat) I see smouldering on the hearth before me shall be burnt out, the child will surely die."

The three banshees then crept out of the house in the order in which they had entered, the senior of them having led the way. Little did the kindly neighbour know of what had taken place during her snooze. But no sooner had the banshees taken their departure than the mother of the child, having listened breathlessly to their conversation and altercation, rose speedily and poured over the fire the contents of a large jorum—the utensil that lay nearest to hand. The sodden *caoran*, to which the banshee had referred, she snatched up off the hearth ; and, having wrapped it carefully in a cloth, she hid it in a kist, after which she returned to her sleeping-box.

To Church at Eynort.

Years passed during which the child—Oighrig MacSweyn to name—grew into a beautiful young woman, who eventually plighted her troth.

Those were the days when the now ruined and moss-covered parish church of Eynort was the place of worship to which all the Glen Bretil folks went : those were the days, moreover, when in the Isles the bride-to-be did not attend church between the time of her betrothal and her marriage. It was a long, long way from Rudh' an Dunain to service at Eynort ; but Norman MacSweyn and his *cailleach* thought nothing of a twelve-mile tramp to church, even in the most inclement weather. And any one who is at all familiar with the locality of Glen Bretil knows how fiercely the storm can rage in this part of Skye.

Well, one Sabbath, when Norman MacSweyn and his wife had gone over to worship at Eynort, Oighrig was tempted to examine the contents of the kist that for so many years her mother had guarded so jealously. Naturally, the lassie was curious about it ! So, having forced it open in her parents' absence, she teemed out everything until she found at the bottom of the kist a strange piece of cloth, in which was wrapped a *caoran*, or little peat. Oighrig could not conceive what had possessed her mother to keep in her kist such a common thing as a *caoran*, for, apart from the fact that it would burn, she knew of no other use to which it might be put—though, by the way, a little peat frequently was used in the Hebrides as a nucleus round which wool or yarn was wound. And, therefore, Oighrig innocently threw the little peat on the hearth, where it soon became ignited ; and, as it continued to smoulder away, she began to feel very ill.

When the folks returned from church at Eynort, they found their beautiful daughter in the grips of death, and the kist lying open beside her with all its precious contents scattered higgledy-piggledy about the room. Nowhere to be found was the *caoran* that the wicked banshee had cursed ; and ere long the fate, that by her mother's presence of mind had been avoided in her infancy, overtook Oighrig.

And Oighrig's remains were interred with dool and wae in the old burying-ground at Eynort.

THE ROBBER-WOMAN OF RUDH' AN DUNAIN.

There was a time when the inhabitants of Glen Bretil were sorely oppressed by the cruelties of a strong, powerful woman, who begged from door to door. She was an unholy terror in the land— so much so, in truth, that, rather than provoke her to anger, the poorer people parted cringingly with whatever she demanded.

One fine day the goodwife of Rudh' an Dunain repaired to her shieling, where her maids were herding the cattle and engaged in the making of butter and cheese. So congested was the shieling becoming that she filled a couple of panniers with dairy-produce, placed them on the pony's back, and sent her maids off with a consignment to Rudh' an Dunain, while she awaited their return. And in their absence who should have arrived on the scene but the wandering robber-woman, who proceeded to help herself lavishly to such produce as had not been sent down in the panniers. Vainly did the goodwife of Rudh' an Dunain remonstrate ; but her protestations were of no avail. In the quarrel that ensued the robber-woman killed her and speedily fled away into the hills above Glen Bretil, having put a piece of cheese between the lips of her victim to make believe that she had been choked by it.

On their return to the shieling the maids found that their mistress had been strangled. Great was the hue and cry in Glen Bretil that day. Suspicion immediately fell on the robber-woman, who aforetime had committed heinous crimes in the district ; and without delay a search was made for her.

LIEUTENANT OF THE COAST KILLS THE ROBBER-WOMAN.

Wrathful on learning what had befallen his mother was Iain Mor MacAskill, who at this time was Lieutenant of the Coast at Rudh' an Dunain against the invasions of the Clan Ranald. And, as it happened, one holy day, when the people of the neighbourhood was skailing after service from the old church at Eynort, who should accost Iain Mor but the bold robber-woman, who coolly informed him that she had been hearing of the threats he had uttered against her.

But Iain Mor, at all times a man of few words, and on this occasion in a mood for anything but an argie-bargie, swiftly drew his sword and beheaded her in the presence of the people assembled round the door of the church at Eynort.

And overwhelmed with joy were the poor folks of Glen Bretil and Rudh' an Dunain that in Iain Mor MacAskill the vagrant robber-woman, who for years had kept them in a constant state of terror, at long last met her match. The robber-woman has a parallel in the robber-man who haunted a cave at Fiadhairt, in Loch Dunvegan.

Donald Dubh Frustrates a Raid.

Numbered among the more dauntless Lieutenants of the Coast at Rudh' an Dunain is Donald Dubh MacAskill. We have heard many stories about MacKendrick and his six archer sons, who practised their nefarious archery at Ardeonaig, above the shores of Loch Tay; but not one of them was more adept in the use of the bow than Black Donald MacAskill.

One day Donald Dubh perceived a Clan Ranald barge in the Sound of Canna, as if making preparations for a raid on MacLeod's Country. He had extraordinarily good eyesight, as, indeed, was required of any sea-watchman, because in those times field-glasses and telescopes were undreamt of. As the barge drew nearer to Rudh' an Dunain, Donald Dubh recognised it to be on plunder intent, and manned by twelve sturdy MacDonalds. So he crept into the *dun* to collect an ample supply of arrows, and then hid behind a rock from which he fired twelve arrows that killed twelve rowers. And soon Clan Ranald's barge, with its lifeless ballast, came ashore and was smashed against the very rocks at Rudh' an Dunain that it had hoped to make in kindlier circumstances.

Photo. by Percy Donald

Sgurr Dubh and Loch Coruisg.

I cannot vouch that Donald Dubh MacAskill's bow was bent from the famous yew at Easragin, in Lorn, or that his bowstring was burnished with yellow wax from Galway. Nor can I say for certain that his arrow-heads were fashioned by Mac-Phedran, the renowned archer-blacksmith, or that his arrows were trimmed with feathers from the mighty pinions of the eagles that never forsook the fastnesses of Loch Treig. But, in any case, Donald Dubh's arrows were as swift as Diarmad, who was swift as the swiftest arrow from the yew ; and, forby, his arrows sped surer than the hazard of the die.

It may be of interest to mention that, while digging in his garden at Soay Isle recently, a gentleman came upon a flint arrow-head that puzzled him very much. Perhaps it was fired from Black Donald MacAskill's bow !

REGALED WITH BREAD AND CHEESE AND WHISKY.

The last tale of Rudh' an Dunain I propose telling you concerns a Lieutenant of the Coast who was known generally throughout Minginish by the simple appellation of *Mac Dhomhnuill Duibh*—Son of Black Donald. In the course of his duties this Lieutenant apprehended a man who previously had been convicted of an endless series of crimes, including murder, cattle-lifting, and fire-raising. The Son of Black Donald did not detain him long in enthralment, but tried him on the spot. Before the actual execution took place, however, he brought the prisoner to his own house and regaled him extravagantly with bread and cheese, and filled his quaich with whisky, many many times, that he might be the more hardened for his last experience on earth.

Thereafter, he marched him up a steep brae above the sea ; and with his own sword, I suppose, cut off his head. And the head rolled down the steep brae, crying out as it rolled : " *Faire, Faire, Mhic Dhomhnuill Duibh !*—Beware, Beware, O Son of Black Donald ! "

This is a typical incident in the ancient government of MacLeod's Country.

Glen Bretil in a Storm.

When last I visited Rudh' an Dunain a terrific thunder-storm overtook me : the thunder pealed in the echoing corries of Sgurr Dearg ; and the deluged crags of Sgurr Alasdair—the noblest and loftiest of all the Cuchullins—were illumined weirdly and magically by nature's fireworks. Shelter there was nowhere. Life terrestrial there seemed none except my drenched and lonely self and a wedge of geese that a thousand feet above me flew seaward out of the storm. I thought the drove road climbing up from Loch Bretil, and twisting to and fro more or less in a northerly direction and over an indescribably desolate moor to Treen and Drynoch, at the head of Loch Harport, would have no ending. From a point on it about a couple of miles west of Coire na Creiche, the Corrie of the Spoil, I looked back to have a final glance at Glen Bretil ; but it was so enveloped in the storm that I could see little except a dreary, sodden plain that might have been a hundred miles away. Not a bird—not a whisper—not even a bleating sheep—nothing but the spluttering of rain, and the moaning of the wind, and the rut of the rebellious stags somewhere in the mists that obscured the almost immeasurable flanks of Sgurr nan Gillean. . . .

And it was with a sense of relief that, having deserted the Glen Bretil–Drynoch road, and having picked my way for a few miles over a moor of pools and quagmires, I located the cairn at the Pass of the Mam (Bealach a' Mhaim), and some hours later arrived at Sligachan by following the course of the *Allt Dearg*, or Red Brook.

How I wished that day my stride had been as gigantic as that of Fingal's father, Comnal, who could place his feet on the tops of two mountains, and stoop down to drink of the river that flowed between them ! And how companionable my dog would have been, had he accompanied me on this excursion ! Here was a situation in which one's dog would have filled a place that no human fellow-mountaineer could have filled. As a rule, you never become crotchety with your dog, even when both you and he are miserably cold and wet and tired, and are equally uncertain as to the best route to adopt. Never in my life did I regret more that my collie was not with me, for a dog has a sympathy and a patience and an understanding that are more to be desired in trying circumstances than the company of argumentative and despondent men.

* * * * * * *

THE THRILL OF RUDH' AN DUNAIN.

And tens of generations hence, when again time will have added its respect to that little, ruined fort by the sea, and made its fragments even more eloquent than they are to-day, the tales of Rudh' an Dunain, that in our younger days some of us are fortunate in having heard recounted by the glimmer of the peat-fire, will have passed far into the mythical and mystical annals of legendary lore. And from ultra-maritime dominions luxurious tourists in their aeroplanes and kindred speedy contraptions will be landing for a moment or two at Rudh' an Dunain, and enquiring of those who then may be dwelling in Glen Bretil—" What mean ye by these stones ? " They are almost certain to outlast, *in situ*, the coming and the going of generations. And these sightseers will be quoting from the fragmentary literature of Rudh' an Dunain ; and they will be reading of the Lochlannaich, of the fierce Clan Ranald, and of the Lieutenants of the Coast maintained by MacLeod. And their children and their children's children will be listening with eagerness to the tales that will tell of the splintering and the breaking of many a proud Hebridean birlinn, where the eternal tide surges around the resounding cliffs at Rudh' an Dunain.

Let us hope that from succeeding generations modernism and all its complementary affectations and insincerities and matter-of-factnesses will not have swept away the delightful art of story-telling, nor stifled the vision that enthrills the child and adult mind.

Who be he that could wander through Glen Bretil to Rudh' an Dunain, or sail past that storied Headland of the Little Dun in a storm, without at once being quickened by its romance, by its chivalry, by its old-worldness ? And, likewise, who be he that would not quaff from the brimming fulness of its sea-tangled alembic ?

One can imagine *anything* to have happened to Rudh' an Dunain during the unnumbered years that MacLeod was obliged to station there a Lieutenant of the Coast, that he and his garrison might repel the invasions of the intrepid corsairs from the distant Land of Lochlann, and might foil the punitive expeditions of Clan Ranald's lion-hearted henchmen who, in stealth and before a side wind, sailed in their birlinns from the geese-haunted shores of Uist.

And, incidentally, I am *so* proud of my Mac-Donald blood, despite the sometimes unwarranted attacks of the Clan Ranald on the territory of the MacLeods !

To be thoroughly thrilled at Rudh' an Dunain you must journey there on a night when the tempest beats unrelentingly against its weathered asperities, and wails, lowly and loudly, a mournful ode, such as in the time of Ossian was sung in the Hall of Winds.

You may inhale at Rudh' an Dunain a breath of the breeze that on a time filled the bulging sheets of the Northman's trireme.

> Would that *thou* to Rudh' an Dunain
> Mightest go at ebbing light,
> To review the phantom galleys,
> As they steal upon the night ;
> Listen there with bated breathing
> For the sweep of oars below—
> Sweet was vengeance to Clan Ranald
> In the nights of long ago. . . .

XXXII

THE BOWMEN OF STRATH

NIALL A' BHOGHA AND THE SHEET-WALKERS

THE incident I have just related concerning the
prowess of Donald Dubh MacAskill, who with his
bow and twelve arrows killed the twelve rowers of
a Clan Ranald birlinn at Rudh' an Dunain, brings
to mind a not altogether dissimilar deed performed
by Niall a' Bhogha, who with the same number of
arrows and within earshot of Old Corry House slew
twelve MacLeod cattle-lifters.   This Neil MacInnes
of the Bow was one of the original MacInneses
who came to Skye from Argyllshire.   Eventually
these MacInneses became the hereditary archers to
the MacKinnons of Strath, a capacity in which they
acquitted themselves with distinction.

Now, it was by the merest accident that the
herculean strength of Neil of the Bow was discovered.   MacKinnon of MacKinnon at the time
of the " Forty-Five " possessed a bow that he
thought no one but himself had the sinews to bend.
It happened that, while in convivial company with
a number of mainland chiefs who had come over
to Skye in order to negotiate with him as to how
best they might support the Stuart cause, Mac-
Kinnon produced his big bow, and challenged any
one present to string it.   Every one made an
attempt ; but no one succeeded.   In the end Mac-

Kinnon turned in a boastful manner to Neil, who at the time was his cowherd, and said : " Here, lad ! see if you can string my bow." And, to the intense surprise of the chiefs in conclave, Neil accomplished the task with the greatest ease.

After the suppression of the Jacobite Rising, Neil and hundreds of his Skye contemporaries enlisted in the Red Coats (*Saighdearan-Dearga*), and took part in many of the campaigns that gave to Skye a martial record unsurpassed by that of any island in the world. It was reckoned that to the French Wars alone Skye contributed six hundred officers, five hundred non-commissioned officers, ten thousand men, and a hundred and seventy pipers. Of course, it must be borne in mind that this was in the days before parasitic landlords and their merciless factors drove the people forth like cattle to the slaughter, so as to make room for deer and sheep.

And the record of the Isle of Skye in the Great War has still to be reduced to writing.

DEEDS OF DERRING-DO.

Before he left Skye, Neil's parents accompanied him to Breakish, where lived a man who, it was believed, had the power of charming one's life. To the blessings of Patrick of Breakish Neil attributed his fearlessness and invulnerability in battle.

The old campaigner spent his latter days in Strath, the parish of his childhood, where he became renowned for his tales of derring-do. But the younger generation was never quite sure whether Neil's accounts of his personal experiences were true, or were merely a brag ; and so the sceptics, having known that after a spree in Broadford he had certain nocturnal tendencies, resolved to put his bravery to a real test.   One evening, therefore, when Neil had gone to Broadford to lift his pension and was likely to be returning home in a state of merriment after a day's damning and dramming with his cronies, a number of youths donned white sheets, and secreted themselves among the tomb-stones in the churchyard of Cill Chriosd (Kilchrist), as it impinged on the road by which he was bound to be returning.

Neil Scatters the Spooks.

When he came within a few yards of the church-yard, there arose from behind a dyke a host of ghost-like figures.   But Neil, undismayed, addressed the apparitions in the following terms : " Spooks, or whatever ye be, if it's a fight you're wanting, you can have it now, for Neil, the son of John, the son of Ewen (*Niall Mac Iain Mhic Eoghainn*), has more friends lying in the churchyard of Kilchrist than you're thinking ! "   Having grasped his stick firmly, he thereupon leapt over the dyke, flew furiously at the sheet-walkers, and dispersed them in every airt.

That night Neil returned home with at least a dozen sheets as the spoil of his victory.

And to this day the old folks of Strath will tell you of Neil, and of the daring exploits of one of his successors, Duncan of the Bow, who was the latest MacInnes archer to win his laurels in the flight of the arrow.

Rudh' an Dunain.

"Here the birlinns of Clan Ranald
Oft lay splintered and forlorn."

XXXIII

THE ECONOMIC DEVELOPMENT
OF SKYE

A GENERAL SURVEY

As I write, London is in the throes of a strike
that in meaning and magnitude is unparalleled in
the history of industrialism. With the exception
of the fleets of private cars dashing about in mad
excitement and of the old, antiquated vans and
lorries and horse-drawn vehicles that for decades
have been hidden away from the light of day, the
entire traffic of " the hub of the universe " is at a
standstill. There are no undergrounds, no 'buses,
no taxicabs, and no newspapers. Many generations have come and gone since Oxford Street and
Piccadilly have been so depopulated : much water
has flowed under the bridge of time since the road,
which my window faces, has been so safe and noiseless. The great thoroughfares of the city, that as
recently as yesterday roared with traffic and depressed one with their endless streams of errandless,
unthinking men and women, are to-day as silent
and deserted as Wentworth Street, Portree. The
change that has been wrought in a night is almost
as incredible as it is pathetic.

And irresistibly my thoughts are turned to the
Isle of Skye where, in the main, economic conditions
have altered so little during recent centuries as to

have left the majority of the populace unencumbered by the national crisis that threatens the means of subsistence of its less fortunate countrymen in pseudo-civilised towns and cities. Skye possesses neither railways nor taxicabs ; and to many of its inhabitants the inability of the press to function will convey nothing. For the very good reason that the conditions giving rise to, and necessitating the effectual continuance of, trade unions have never been required in Skye, the Island—though not without acute economic problems of its own— remains little influenced by those disputes concerning hours and wages and profits that have illustrated the failure of industrialism, as we understand the term, to provide even the necessities of life for vast masses of our people.

MARBLE AND ORE.

Notwithstanding, Skye has witnessed several industrial experiments, and has suffered many vicissitudes and failures. Marble has been quarried with doubtful success in Strath ; and iron-ore mines were started in Raasay during the late war. The cessation of hostilities, however, resulted in a tempo-rary suspension of operations in Raasay, and the consequent displacement of the casual labour absorbed. The ore, I am told, is of an inferior quality ; and the demand for it, therefore, is spas-modic. The mines are still worked at odd intervals, however, for during the past few months I have noticed tramps loading ore at the pier at Raasay. About thirty years ago diatomite works were started on the east side of the Isle of Skye ; but to-day they are derelict and forsaken, though rumours of resuscitating this industry have been persistent during the last year or two. I understand that the quarrying of marble at Kilbride was abandoned on account of its poor quality. At any rate, the company that was formed to exploit the marble resources soon went into liquidation. Of this industry we read in the *New Statistical Account* as follows :—" Free-stone and marble, which abound in this parish (Strath), have been worked by Lord M'Donald, the former for building and the latter for architectural ornaments in his elegant castle at Armadale. The marble quarries have also been worked by the Duke of Hamilton for paving the lobby of Hamilton Palace, and by the Board of Ordnance for powder mill stones ; they were, however, abandoned by the Board from the impracticability of finding blocks sufficiently large for their purpose."

Generally speaking, however, it is to be admitted that, for the discipline and specialisation involved in industry as meantime organised, the Hebridean is temperamentally unsuited. Nature has made him a crofter-fisherman, and a lover of the freedom that is so characteristic of the life he leads.

AGRICULTURE AND FISHING.

To say the least of it, the rural problem of the Western Isles is unique. This, obviously, is due to a number of inherent causes such as those arising from climatic conditions, remoteness, the general infertility of the soil, and the gradual decay of the fishing industry. The economics of the West Highlands cannot be compared in any way even with those of the East Highlands, where we find high farming, excellent steadings, pedigree cattle, and markets. Cattle and sheep breeding now form the only really remunerative industries of Skye.

The line-fishing, that formerly flourished, has been destroyed by the East Coast trawlers ; and Spanish barilla helped to ruin the kelp industry. The consequences of stagnation in trade are that the population yearly diminishes, and schools lack pupils and become increasingly expensive to support. Since the scale of living has improved, steamers bring greater supplies ; but they arrive full and depart empty, with the obvious result that freights to and from the Hebrides are extortionate.

THE PIG INDUSTRY.

With regard to the pig industry, it is well recognised that the Highlander does not like the pig. With some good taste he objects to attending to a pig-sty when he can choose a more fragrant occupation. Hence, the pig population of Skye this year, as generally, is eight. After much exhortation the figure has been known to rise to twelve, but never higher ! Herds of pigs in the open are not only less objectionable, but can be rationed largely on the bracken which, in its decided partiality for the best soil, is rapidly over-running the sheep pastures of the Highlands and Islands. Pigs folded on bracken uproot it, and consume even the rhizomes, leaving the ground tilled and manured and suitable for the growing of almost any green stuff desired. As is evident in Ireland and Denmark, the pig industry is by no means an unprofitable one.

DEPOPULATION AND EMIGRATION.

Each year the retention of the rural population in the Islands seems to become more and more difficult, in spite of the fact that in the most remote and northerly parts the Hebrideans are more tenaciously attached to the soil of their fathers than are the less isolated communities on the mainland. The failure to find profitable employment and the consequent over-population unquestionably have induced many to emigrate who, had a reasonable standard of subsistence been possible, would have remained at home by choice.

As things are at present, emigration is the only course left to those who have the grit and the opportunity to avail themselves of it. This is a confession I make with some reluctance, for the draining of the arterial blood of a people cannot but leave it sterile and impotent. Emigration can never be a cure for unemployment : at the best it is merely a doubtful palliative.

SMALL-HOLDINGS.

In that the amount of cultivable land is limited, the demand for holdings has been keen. A year or two ago the Board of Agriculture established in the centre of their new Bracadale settlements a cheese-making factory. At the outset the possibilities seemed rosy ; but experience demonstrated the weaknesses of the scheme. When a creamery was constructed and operations were about to have commenced, the promoters offered between 5d. and 6d. per gallon for milk—an offer that, as was pointed out in the *Glasgow Herald*, sealed the doom of the undertaking so far as the community was concerned, since milk for ordinary purposes was fetching 6d. per quart at the time. It was an unfortunate experiment. The land-holders could not be persuaded to accept the Board's proposals ; and, to put it in the words of the esteemed paper already referred to, "after a colossal expenditure from the start to its inglorious finish, the Ose Creamery sounded the retreat without ever making one pound of cheese."

The small-holdings settled by the Board of Agriculture in Skye have been more successful, however ; and as a casual onlooker I take this opportunity of saying that few government departments have been more unfairly criticised than this Department. Doubtless, it has had its shortcomings, as can be said of every form of administration ; but I do feel that it has shown a sincere desire to assist the Highland people, and that it is more deserving of gratitude and appreciation than many of us are willing to accord it.

HOUSING AND HEALTH.

In Skye the last few decades have witnessed the complete displacement of the old " black house." To-day I am sure you could count on the fingers of one hand all the " black houses " in the Isle of Skye. As to the hygienic benefits resulting from the improvement in housing conditions, medical authorities are at variance. If I may be permitted to say so, my own impression is that, as a place of human habitation, the old " black house " has been painted blacker than it really is. That in the past strong, healthy, beautiful families have been reared in " black houses " is unquestionable ; and it is of importance to note that, according to the Registrar-General's Report for 1923, the infantile mortality for Lewis (where a census in 1919 revealed that the proportion of " black " to " white " houses was 3 to 1) was 28 per thousand births. The corresponding figures for Aberdeen, Glasgow, and

Edinburgh during the same period were 104, 90, and 82 respectively. As Dr. George Gibson puts it in an article to be found in a recent issue of the *Caledonian Medical Journal* : " I can almost imagine the Old Black House laughing as it hears the record of the cities."

In addition to this, it is a recognised truth that other ailments and diseases associated with bad housing and the slum conditions of our great towns are comparatively unknown among communities dwelling in " black houses." Dr. Noel Paton has shown rickets to be almost unknown in Lewis where, he adds, in the air space per person and in ventilation the " black houses" compare very favourably with the deplorable slum dwellings of our great cities.

Tuberculosis a New Disease.

To the Western Isles tuberculosis is a new disease. This is amply supported by the testimony of doctors who practised in the Islands last century. In 1860 Dr. Morgan recorded that, during a residence of seven years on the Island of Raasay, he scarcely ever came across a case of pulmonary phthisis. Again, the late Dr. Millar of Stornoway, who practised in Lewis for sixty years (1829-89), expressed himself on the subject as follows :—
" The medical gentleman who practised on this island before me (Dr. MacIver) used, when filling up schedules of insurance of life, invariably to answer the question relating to the death of the proposer's relatives from phthisis : ' No such disease known in the Island.' I have now practised thirty years in this island, and have often been struck by the immunity of the natives from

consumption, but cannot go the length of saying that there is no such disease."

From the bulky evidence at hand there is no doubt that tuberculosis was brought into the Western Isles from the cities ; and I am inclined to the belief that the death-rate therefrom is due mainly to the Islanders' lack of immunity to a disease that is comparatively new to them.

CHANGE IN DIET.

While writing of the health of the Hebridean people, a word or two here on diet may not be out of place. Modern feeding has taken the place of the staple diet of half a century ago : white bread, tea, fancy cakes, sweetmeats, and other productions of the co-operative store are swiftly ousting porridge, oatcakes, potatoes, salt and fresh fish, " crowdie," butter, cheese, eggs, and home-fed meat. The proverbial teapot has displaced the *cuman* or milk-pail. In Skye one finds many hillsides and straths that in past generations were cultivated, which to-day are croftless and deserted. And the number of ruined mills to be seen throughout the length and breadth of the Hebrides testifies further to the decline in agriculture that has accompanied this change in diet. Very few steamers call at a Skye port nowadays without leaving a hamper or two of city bread and mixed groceries. With the additional assistance of light motorcars these commodities are carried with almost incredible rapidity into the remotest parts of the Islands.

There can be little doubt that the change from a wholesome, nutritious diet has produced a certain degree of katabolism, has had an adverse effect on the teeth of the Islanders, and has lowered vitality and the power of resisting disease.

The Little Red Brook (Allt Dearg Beag) and Sgurr nan Gillean.

Decline of the Fishing Industry.

Skye has shared in the reverse that during recent years has overtaken the Scottish fishing industry. On the restoration of fishing a great deal depends ; and, as I indicate in another chapter, the first step to be taken in the direction of putting the industry on its feet once more is effectual protection against trawling in prohibited areas.   If matters be allowed to go on as they are at the present moment, nothing can save the fishing industry from extinction.   After protection, its greatest need is swift and ready transport to and from the centres of population where fish is always in demand.

The Need for Transport.

And this brings us to the brief consideration of a state of affairs that justifiably has been the cause of much dissatisfaction.   Inadequate sea-transport services and excessive charges have been a long-standing grievance in the Western Isles, where the restrictions and curtailments necessitated by the war are still the order of the day.   A comparison of the scales of charges made by the MacBrayne Company for 1914 and 1925, and of the services run during those years, readily illustrates the dire need for a thorough enquiry into the transport conditions obtaining in the Western Isles.

As showing how obsolete is the craft employed, let me mention that a month or two ago the derrick of the *Glencoe* was unable to unload at Raasay half a dozen railway sleepers at low tide.   Many futile attempts to swing the sleepers on to the pier so tried the captain's patience that he interrupted the operations, and declared that they would be landed in the morning on the return voyage to

Kyle.   On a conspicuous notice-board on this same boat occurs the following sentence : " For 90 steerage passengers, when not occupied by cattle, animals, cargo, or other encumbrances."

There can be no improvement in the economic life of the people until better and cheaper transport facilities are established.   Every effort to develop the natural resources of the Islands has been handicapped by the deplorable transport conditions.   Only by improvements in the marketing of natural products and by encouraging traffic of other kinds can we hope to strengthen the economic basis of the Hebrides.

RESPONSIBILITY OF THE STATE.

It would seem that to some extent the Government should be held liable for the maintenance of a system of maritime communication which would do something, at all events, to alleviate the pitiable conditions that at present exist in many of the remoter parts of our country.

In recent years we have seen that to an increasing degree the State has accepted responsibility for the repair and maintenance, and even for the construction of roads throughout the kingdom, wherever it can be shown that these roads are of indispensable value as a means of communication between the great manufacturing and industrial centres and the districts to which the essential commodities of life must needs be transported.

The old economic maxim, that the act of production is not complete until the commodity is in the hands of the consumer, is a maxim the truth of which is only emphasised when a community realises that the means of transport at its disposal, even for the distribution of its foodstuffs, is so deplorably inadequate as to render it economically unprofitable for the local seller to lay his order with the producer, and economically impossible for the local buyer to purchase even those commodities of life to which every member of a civilised community should have a right at a reasonably cheap cost and in a ready and reliable manner.

That some districts on the mainland have profited considerably by the increase in transport facilities is unquestionable : the Government recognised the national value of its investment in the construction of roads as a means of improving trade conditions.

Now it seems not only fair but also logical that, as the Outer Isles and the north-west of Scotland generally are equally an integral part of the kingdom, and contribute their share (certainly in brains and in time of war) to the common weal, they are equally entitled to some consideration in the matter of improving the shocking means of communication which at the moment exist between them and the commercial centres on the mainland.

As successive Governments, acting under the Small Holdings (Scotland) Acts, 1886-1911, have provided large sums of money for the purpose of constituting new small-holdings, or of enlarging already existing ones, it is the duty of the State to see that the ultimate economic success of these small-holdings is not hampered by conditions of transport which render their existence uncertain. And it is for the State to see that the benefits which are expected to accrue from such a huge public expenditure are not outweighed by an obsolete system of transport.

The report of the Rural Transport (Scotland) Committee, which delivered its opinion in the spring of 1919, distinctly urged the dire necessity of improving transport conditions, and referred particularly to the position in the areas now under our consideration, where it considered that improvements in communication were most urgently required. But in the carrying out of the committee's recommendations very little has been done.

AFFORESTATION IN SKYE.

As a means of supplementing a livelihood from fishing and agriculture, more attention might be paid to the tweed industry. Then, most experts are agreed as to the suitability of our waste places for the planting of trees. Colonel Martin Martin of Ostaig consistently has advocated sylviculture for Skye, where many thousands of acres are fit for nothing else. He has pointed out that in time the result of an extensive afforestation scheme would yield employment in a number of ways, as, for example, in the building of small vessels, and the export of timber to the mainland where the demands at present are supplied by foreign countries.

The excessive rainfall, rendering the growing of cereals uneconomic, favours the growth of forests, since trees seldom can have too much moisture. Forestry employs more men than sheep. It is true that the soil is often too shallow, and that in some parts the peat is of a character which altogether precludes the growing of trees ; but there is much land, especially in Sleat, where formerly forests flourished, and where an afforestation scheme would have every possibility of success. In Skye, furthermore, steep gradients and heavy rainfall offer ample opportunity for the creation of cheap water or electrical power ; and, since no point of the Island

is distant more than four miles from the sea, cheap
carriage is assured for timber and any other commodities that might be produced. Of sailing craft
I have made brief mention already. It does seem
rather ridiculous, however, that the Hebrides are
almost the only archipelago in the world that has
not developed their maritime possibilities.

Some time ago there was a Colonial Exhibition
in London, in which Gibraltar was invited to participate. Gibraltar accepted the invitation ; but,
when its industries came to be examined, it was
discovered that its only manufacture consisted of
postage stamps. Skye is in even a worse position,
for Gibraltar, a free port, has a very large transit
trade, and dabbles successfully in smuggling—a
flourishing institution that financially has benefited
every one concerned, with the exception, of course,
of the Spanish Treasury.

Glasgow as a Model.

The Hebrideans make a great mistake in striving
to ape Glasgow with its infinite mineral resources.
They employ Glasgow steamships ; and, even in a
small matter like jam, they think tinned jam from
a wholesale warehouse in Glasgow something very
desirable indeed, and therefore refuse to grow a
few gooseberries and currants to make their own.
Home products, which ordinarily are fresher and
better, they are inclined to despise. For this and
other absurdities our educational system is greatly
responsible. Norway is a much closer model than
Glasgow. I say this without any prejudice, because
there is no city in the world for which I have a
greater regard than I have for Glasgow.

* * * * * * *

But, for all I have said, it must not be imagined that in every way Skye is behind the times. To some extent the advent of the motor-car has compensated internally for the serious deficiency in the means of external communication. As I have remarked, fancy cakes and the like are by no means unknown ; and the betting epidemic has so laid its hands on many of the Islanders that they are kept in touch with all the latest racing tips, and even conduct with ease and promptitude their own sweepstakes. Of course, we cannot blame them altogether when we remember that the very classes which ought to be setting the plebeians an example are gambling away the best part of their lives. Even in the remote corners of Skye it is painfully evident that we have become a nation of bettors and speculators, living on chance and by our wits.

But I feel certain that one of the root causes of our economic difficulties in the Hebrides is the lack of enterprise. Our enterprise has gone to other lands with the best of our race.

XXXIV

STRATH OF THE WHELKS

THE LAND OF THE MACKINNONS

> " Mackinnon's chief, in warfare grey,
>   Had charge to muster their array,
>   And guide their barks to Brodick Bay."

OLD King Autumn has been deposed : his throne
and crown of gold are gone ; and in his stead
King Winter reigns Monarch Supreme.   And this
" ruler of the inverted year " has flung his fleecy
mantle over the shoulders of Blaven ; and, as would
a despot, he holds Loch Slapin and the Great
Strath between the Coolins and the Red Hills in
the grip of his frigid hand.   By the icy shores of
Ob Breakish the gulls and terns are sleeping on
their feet, with their heads snugly tucked away in
their downy bosoms.   The road to Torran lies
buried in snow ; and not a bird's cheep is heard
among the ivy-muffled gables of old Kilchrist, in
whose kirkyard rest the remains of many a Mac-
Kinnon.

CLAN FINGON OF THE WHELKS.

  When first the Clan Fingon of the Whelks came
into possession of this part of Skye is not quite
certain, though one supposes it to have been about
1354.   But we know that the MacKinnons parted
with the last of their Strath properties towards the

close of the eighteenth century, after a tenure that extended over a period of more than four hundred years. They held their territories as vassals of the Lords of the Isles ; and, according to some authorities, they were the hereditary custodians of the standards of weights and measures recognised by their powerful overlords. One family for generations supplied the MacDonalds of Sleat with their standard-bearers. For its services in this connection it was enfeoffed at Duisdalebeg, near Isle Oronsay. The first authentic notice of the Clan MacKinnon, according to Gregory, occurs in an indenture between the Lord of Lorn and the Lord of the Isles concerning the forfeiting and granting of certain lands in Argyllshire.

In a terse account, compiled during what Hume Brown describes as the " Golden Age " of the Western Isles, we read that " ane pairt of this Ile of Sky callit Strathvardeill perteins to ane Laird callit McKynvin, given to him be McConneill for to be judge and decide all questionnis and debaitts that happeinis to fall betwin pairties throw playing at cairtis or dyce or sic uther pastime, and will raise aucht score men. McKynvin hes a castell thair callit Dewnakin." (Dunakin or Castle Maol.)

For the MacKinnons I have a decided partiality since they are descended from Fingon, grandson of Gregor, who was the son of Kenneth MacAlpin, King of Scots. In common with the MacGregors they enjoy the same badge (*suaicheantas*), namely, the pine (*giuthas*) ; while their *cath-ghairm* or war-cry is " *Cuimhnich bàs Ailpein*—Remember the death of Alpin ! " The crest of the MacKinnons is the head of a boar, holding in its jaws the shankbone of a deer. It is said to have had its origin in an

Blaven with Loch an Athain below.

U

attack made by a wild boar upon an early chief of the Clan who, in a cavern of Elgol, thrust the bone of the deer down the throat of the enraged boar.

BONDS FOR MUTUAL PROTECTION.

The good feeling that existed between the Mac-Gregors and the MacKinnons is evinced by a deed that at Kilmorie in 1671 was executed " betwixt the honourable persons underwritten, to wit, James MacGregor of that ilk on the ane part, and Lauchlan MacFingon on the other part, for the special love and amitie between these persons, and condescending that they are descended lawfullie frae twa brether of auld descent, quhairfor, and for certain onerous causes moving, we faithfullie bind and obleise us and our successors, our kin, friends and followers, to serve ane anuther in all causes with our men and servants against all wha live and die, the king's highness only excepted." There is also extant an earlier (1606) bond of manrent between Lauchlan MacKinnon and Findlay MacNab. The former signatory affixes his name thus—" Laughland, mise, MacFingon." *Mise* means " myself." It was customary in rebellious times for clans to enter into agreements with one another for mutual protection against a common foe.

Though at one time the MacKinnons held extensive territories in Mull, Tiree, and Arran, latterly Strathordell, together with the Islands of Pabbay and Scalpay, became their principal residence. In Dean Monro's time Pabbay, an Island famous for harbouring vagabonds, pertained to " M'Kynnoun." As a result of the regulations drawn up at Iona in 1639 enjoining that certain Hebridean chieftains might sustain and entertain in their retinue three gentlemen only, who were prohibited from bearing pistols, hagbuts, and armour, the chiefs of Mac-Kinnon were deprived of much of their pristine independence. MacKinnon's fleet was limited to one birlinn of sixteen or eighteen oars; and his liquor allowance was assessed at one tun of wine per year. Even remembering that bards and seannachies were no longer to consider themselves entitled to entertainment in the houses of gentlemen, we cannot imagine that a tun of wine went very far in the days when every chief's home was the essence of hospitality.

STRATH AND IONA.

That the Clan Fingon had a substantial connection with Iona is seen from the fact that many of them were buried there. Skene tells us that the MacKinnons frequently furnished Iona with abbots. There was interred Abbot Lachlan MacFingon; and at Iona one may still read on a cross erected in 1499 to the memory of him and his son, John, the following inscription: " HAEC EST CRUX LACOLANI M'FINGONE, ET EJUS FILII JOHANNIS ABBATIS DE Y FACTA ANNO DOMINI MCCCCLXXXIX." Pennant mentions that the altar at Iona was made of marble quarried in Strath. I believe that a fragment of this altar is still to be seen in St. Andrew's Church, in Glasgow. There are considerable quantities of marble in Strath, much of which was used architecturally to ornate Armadale Castle, and to pave the corridor of Hamilton Palace. Quarrying here has been abandoned and restarted at different times.

SAINT MAREE'S CELL.

Despite this long association with Iona, Columba was not the patron saint of Strath, as one might have expected. That honour was bestowed upon Saint Maree or Maolrubha, whose headquarters were at Applecross. At Kilmaree, in Strathaird, and not very far from the western shore of Loch Slapin, one may examine the site of Saint Maolrubha's cell or church. He so often sailed from Applecross (Aper-crossan) that anciently the route followed by his barge received the name of *Aiseag Mhaolruibhe*, St. Maree's Ferry ; while *Cladh Aiseig* was long applied to the spot below Kilmaree where the Saint was in the habit of disembarking. Near Kyleakin is a spring from which Saint Maolrubha drank when first he set foot on Strath, and which to this day is referred to as Tobar na h-Aiseig, the Well of the Ferry.

Few parishes in the whole of the Highlands have an ecclesiastical history as interesting and varied as that of Strath.

AN OPPRESSIVE DEATH-DUTY.

The wells of Strath are rich in lore, sacred and secular. At the foot of Blaven is a well where an heir to MacKinnon, while in the act of drinking, is said to have been foully done to death. Not far from Druim nan Cleoc is Tobar Dhomhnuill Ghruamaich, the Well of Sulky Donald—so called because in 1534 he died here while returning to Duntulm from Dunscaith. Near Kilchrist (*Cill Chriosd*) is Tobar Chliamain, Clement's Well. Tradition has it that Clement was a missionary whose *cathair* or seat is now occupied by the glebe at Kilchrist. With Tobar Tath is connected one of the prophetic utterances of the Brahan Seer.

But perhaps the best-known well in Strath is Tobar a' Chinn, the Well of the Head. It was here that a certain Lauchlan MacKinnon avenged himself on Donnachadh Mor (Big Duncan) by beheading him and washing his head in this well. Donnachadh Mor was ground-officer to MacKinnon of Strath ; and in the course of his rounds he exacted from a poor widow the oppressive death-duty known as the *each-ursainn*, it long having been the custom in the Highlands for the laird's factor to remove from the relatives of a deceased tenant their best horse or cow. On this occasion the widow resisted Donnachadh's claim ; but he ill-used her and took the horse from her by force. Now Lauchlan MacKinnon learned as a youngster that his own mother, when left a widow, had suffered similar treatment at the hands of the same factor ; and years did he wait for an excuse to have his revenge on Donnachadh. At last his opportunity came : he fought the tyrant, killed him, decapitated him, and washed his head in Tobar a' Chinn. Thereafter the death-duty known as the *each-ursainn* became obsolete in Skye.

"THE LAD OF THE STONES."

The interesting geological phenomena of Strath at various times have attracted to the Parish groups of eager petrologists. Geikie recites a number of amusing anecdotes about geological pioneering in this part of Skye, and tells us how aggravating it was to find that the local lads engaged in carrying bags containing specimens of rocks frequently teemed out the specimens, and refilled the bags

with stones to be gathered nearer home. The
people of Strath nicknamed Geikie *Gille nan Clach*,
the Lad of the Stones. It was beyond the reasoning
of the people of Strath that any man, who wandered
about the countryside with a hammer and chipped
bits off rocks, could possibly be sane.

STRATH IN OLDEN DAYS.

There was a time when, for reasons of geographical situation, Strath was the busiest part of Skye.
Broadford used to be the rendezvous (as in a lesser
degree it is to-day) for all drovers and shepherds
who conducted their cattle and flocks to and from
the mainland marts. As late as the latter half of
the eighteenth century horses were transported from
Kyleakin and Kylerhea in the same manner as
Hannibal passed his cavalry over the Rhone ; while
horned cattle intended for the markets at Glenelg
swam across the kyles to Bernera in strings of eight
or twelve, the first animal having been roped behind
a rowing-boat.

In those days all overland communication between Sleat and the rest of Skye, as well as between
the north, south, and west of the Island, went
through Broadford. At Sligachan westbound and
northbound men and traffic parted company. There
the former struck off into Glen Drynoch for Duirinish, Vaternish, and Bracadale, whereas the latter
continued their journey northwards through Glen
Varragill and in the direction of Portree.

CASTLE OF THE WHELKS.

On a promontory above Kyleakin and overlooking
Loch Alsh stand the ruins of an ancient keep known
as Castle Maol. When on his way to Largs in

1263, King Haco is said to have anchored his fleet in Kyle Akin or Haco's Kyle, and thus to have given to this strait its name. The walls of Castle Maol are more than ten feet in thickness. According to the legend, it was built by " Saucy Mary," the daughter of a Scandinavian king. By the maintenance of a barrier in the form of a great chain that stretched across the kyles from a point below the Castle, she is recorded to have prevented all foreign vessels from passing through, until they had paid the necessary toll.

For centuries Castle Maol was occupied by the MacKinnons of Strath. The older part of it is thought to date back to the tenth century ; while the newer portion is possibly early fifteenth. In old documents Castle Maol is referred to as Duna-kyne or Dunakin (Dewnakin) ; but it was commonly designated Caisteal nam Faochag, the Castle of the Whelks. Strath was often alluded to derisively as Strath of the Whelks (*Srath nam Faochag*) ; and the MacKinnons of Strath were familiarly called Clan Fingon of the Whelks. Sometimes the folks of Strath went by the name of *Na Faochagan*—" the Whelks." It has been suggested that these nick-names originated from the fact that whelks were particularly plentiful around the MacKinnons' earlier residence in Mull. Be it noted in passing that the folks of Sleat, who till within recent years were a community *per se*, were called *Na Faoileagan* —" the Seagulls."

Castle Ringill.

In Strathaird, and hard by the south-western shore of Loch Slapin, are the venerant ruins of Castle Ringill, where the first chiefs of Clan Fingon

ruled in state as long ago as the ninth or tenth
century. Castle Ringill breathes a whiff of romance,
as indeed does all Strathaird. Can you not imagine
when sailing down Loch Slapin that from the
harper's window (*uinneag a' chlarsair*) in old Dun
Ringill a twanging of strings is wafted across the
deep, still waters?

Lovely is this spot in the sunshine and peace of
summer: lovelier still is it when Autumn has been
extravagant with his purple and gold. But you
should pass by Castle Ringill when, except for the
timid deer that in search of food come down from
the mountains, and for the grouse and snowy
ptarmigan that speed lowly and shyly across the
moors, every creature seems to be in hiding, when
the nival precipices of Blaven soar mysteriously into
the clouds, and Loch Slapin lies below, shadowy
and cold and still—when, in short, Old King
Autumn has been deposed and in his stead King
Winter reigns Monarch Supreme.

XXXV

AT A BROADFORD CEILIDH

YARNS OF AN OLD SEA CAPTAIN

THE POETRY OF THE SAILING SHIP

" Within the sober realm of leafless trees,
    The russet year inhaled the dreamy air ;
Like some tanned reaper, in his hour of ease,
    When all the fields are lying brown and bare."

I CAN remember that October afternoon in Broadford as distinctly as though it had been yesterday afternoon. We were engaged in examining the exterior of Liveras Cairn—that turf and broom-clad mound situated within a yard or two of the southern gable of our house, and regarded as being the earliest evidence of human existence in the Parish of Strath—when, somehow or other, I was reminded that we might be having an interesting visitor in the person of Captain MacKinnon, whose schooner, awaiting the incoming of the tide that was necessary to float her to her wonted berth at the quay, rode at anchor in the bay.

It was, moreover, an afternoon with a wintry semblance : out of doors it was clear but very cold ; and the finches' toes seemed to be nearly frozen to the leafless twigs of the mountain ash that distinguishes our garden from all its neighbours.

You should have seen the autumn tints on our tree before the sparrows robbed it of its rich clusters

Kyleakin from Kyle of Lochalsh.

"The grey gulls wheeling ever, and the wide arch of the sky."

of rowans, and the previous nights' frost nipped off the last of its searing foliage.

To appreciate the rest of the setting in which our seafaring friend entertained us that afternoon, you must be told that our house within was (as, indeed, it is at all times) warm and cosy and inviting : the sudden spell of cold weather had prompted us to pile the logs on the fire at a rate that, in normal circumstances, one justifiably might have thought extravagant in an Island possessing so little natural wood.   Still, to any one passing by our window in the gloaming, and seeing on the window-panes and ceiling the reflection of our ruddy fire, there was an unmistakable sign of welcome about our *ceilidh*.

If you are acquainted with Highlanders, particularly with those who have had some experience of life in many lands, you will endorse my averment when I say that they are peculiarly shy and reserved : as a rule, the surest way of getting no enlightenment from a sea captain, whom you may never have met before, is by pointedly asking him for information.   To throw a string of direct interrogations at him, however well meaning you may be, is the very way to drive a reticent Highlander into his shell.   But, after all, most people, who speak to some purpose and have had any real acquaintance with life, are extremely shy about communicating their knowledge, unless they should happen to do so of their own accord, or are more than ordinarily friendly with their audience.

So, you will understand it was with no small fear of creating suspicion that gradually we humoured our seafaring friend to tell us some yarns.   And is it not extraordinary how, when once begun, one yarn leads to another, and the story of a wreck suggests the story of a hairbreadth escape from disaster at sea—and so on ?

By the merest accident and at the psychological moment our hostess went ben to the other end of the house in order to infuse a stroup of tea ; and during her few moments' absence we succeeded in rekindling in our story-teller memories of wild, wild days at sea.

A Leith Puffer the Topic of Conversation.

As it so happened, that afternoon the *Oberon*, a 120-ton puffer registered at Leith, had steamed into the harbour, after having battled for the best part of the day against a steady head-wind in the Sound of Sleat. In fact, we had been down at the shore watching her making the quay ; and long will I remember the grim, stern, unshaven face of the sooty-black skipper, as he stood at his wheel, peeping inquisitively above the shaking canvas that surrounded him on three sides, and shouting directions that at the time were as inaudible as they were incomprehensible to the casual onlooker.

Thus it was that our conversation veered round to a discussion on the general suitability of the *Oberon* type of boat. And it was agreed by all present that a small, flat-bottomed boat had certain real advantages, especially when it was employed in the transport of coal and such-like merchandise between places that could boast no proper harbour or quay, and whose accessibility, therefore, very largely depended on the state of the tide.

To commence with, such a boat draws less water, and floats comfortably when a vessel of a greater draught and with a more pronounced keel would ground ; and, owing to its shape, it does not require to be propped to keep it upright when the tide recedes, leaving it high and dry by a quay or on a beach.   In addition, it obviously has a relatively greater tonnage capacity because of its bulging sides ; and, as one may readily imagine, it has the advantage of being able to pass with comparative ease through canals and locks, meeting no obstacle and experiencing no delay except the loss of a few minutes in the opening and closing of the latter. Of course, the most patent handicap placed on such a vessel is its water resistance and the consequent reduction in speed.

And it was by preliminary remarks such as the foregoing that we were able to inveigle Captain MacKinnon into telling us tales of tropical surfs, of New Caledonian typhoons, of Magellan storms, of weird and supernatural happenings at sea, and even of the mariner beguiled by the Corrievreckan, our Highland maelström, wherein many a skilfully handled ship has been disembowelled and dismasted.

By the bye, I should have informed you ere this that our friend is not only celebrated for his seamanship (a tradition that he has inherited from his father who sailed for more than half a century before him), but also for his " second-sight," a faculty which he possesses in a remarkable degree, as you will be prepared to confess presently.

The Poetry of the Sailing Ship.

Had I known more of nautical phraseology, I would have gleaned from his conversation much that since I have forgotten, and much that at the time I only vaguely understood.   I was just beginning to recall the distinguishing characteristics of the ketch, sloop, smack, sailing yacht, schooner, brigantine, and a score of other kindred names, when our *ceilidh* was terminated by the advancing hour ; and to this day I only remember in a hazy way the location and names of the multifarious ropes and tacks and sheets and sails that made sailing in the olden days an art only to be undertaken by the most intelligent, by the strongest, by the most fearless. Reflect for a moment on the times when even the least qualified seaman would think shame of himself were he in the dark of the darkest night unable to place his hands on a single namable object of the ship's equipment ! And can you not picture a large sailing-vessel at sea in a tempest or engirdled by fog in pre-lighthouse days, when all night long a watchman kept vigil in the crow's nest in case the ship collided with another, or ran aground on treacherous rocks ?

Surely those were the days when almost every voyage was a drama in poetry !

"THE GOOD SEA CAPTAIN."

And I have just finished reading that delightful essayette by Thomas Fuller (1608-1661) on the ideal, seventeenth-century sea captain who has his letters of mart, who is well armed, victualled, appointed, and acquits himself with distinction, and who " daily sees and duly considers God's wonders in the deep."

That was the era when a sea captain was a monarch in the island of a ship, and in all causes a judge supreme, and above appeal : that was the era when, after a storm, a sea captain was pious and thankful (as, doubtless, captains still are) and careful in observing the Lord's Day, for " he hath a watch in his heart, though no bells in the steeple to proclaim that day by ringing to prayers."   And his voyages were not only for profit, but also for honour and knowledge and discoveries, because he counted it a disgrace that those who dwelt in the parlour (Europe) should be ignorant of the outlodgings of the same dwelling-place.

Here is a pithy paragraph : " In dividing the gains he wrongs none who took pains to get them. Not shifting off his poor mariners with nothing, or giving them only the garbage of the prize, and keeping all the flesh to himself.   In time of peace he quietly returns home, and turns not to the trade of pirates, who are the worst sea vermin, and the devil's water-rats."

A model captain, indeed ; and a model essayette !

STORNOWAY'S NAUTICAL SCHOOL.

And often has my father (who, by the way, travelled a hundred thousand miles on land and sea) spoken of the times when, on entering Stornoway harbour, one scarcely could discern the town for the fleets of sailing ships that besieged the foreground in the days when Stornoway was a port of call for all vessels passing by the Northern Hebrides. Those of you who have read *Behold the Hebrides !* will be reminded that I dilated at length on the port of Stornoway in olden days, when it could muster as fine a sailing fleet as any town in the United Kingdom, and had a harbour recognised by the mariners of all maritime nations to be " abundantly safe in all weathers."

Even to-day Stornoway produces sea captains of the first order, though what is required of them in this golden age of mechanism is very different from what was expected of those lads who in Stornoway, nearly a century ago, gathered round John MacKay, a teacher in what was then the Free Church School, and learned from him the way of a ship in the sea. Nothing of sail navigation was unknown to MacKay: it was a subject which he had taken up as a hobby, and which he taught unofficially and in his spare time. Yet, indeed, in after days his pupils gained proficiency and distinction, both in theoretical and in practical sailing, for his teachings were not merely of a rudimentary nature. And many of those pupils were granted certificates, and occupied, as do their successors at the present time, important positions on the great trading vessels and passenger liners of the world.

Nowadays, apart from economic considerations, it would be extremely difficult to enlist a crew which had any knowledge of sail-adjustment or of Windward Great Circle Sailing, because wind-sailing is old-time, and a lost art forby. And, in any case, the inducements are few : small wages, long voyages, inferior accommodation, salten foods, the risk of scarcity of the necessaries of life, the ever-present element of danger, the uncertainty as to atmospheric conditions, whether for good or for evil, largely have been superseded in the irresistible march of what we vaguely call progress.

As a result of the increase in costs of steam navigation due mainly to causes traceable to the recent war, there was a slight revival of the sailing vessel in non-coal-producing maritime countries like Norway, Sweden, and Denmark. These vessels were employed chiefly in the transit of cargoes such as timber and tar and commodities that, in common with them, were unlikely to deteriorate during delayed voyages.   As one might have expected, such a revival could be only of a temporary nature ; and so to-day, except for the faithful remainder of our Scottish Herring Fleet that gradually is being ousted by steam-drifters and trawlers, the sailing ship has vanished.

And, alas, its poetry has gone with it !

Still, occasionally we do see a full-rigged schooner ; and we welcome her as a stray visitor from another era.

Every sailing vessel is a poem—a poem whose stanzas are of wind and tide, a poem whose lines are rhythmic and graceful, a poem whose language is understood at the uttermost ends of the earth, a poem whose similes are coincident with, and invariable as, the natural laws of the Universe, a poem whose metaphors are its voyagings with sun and moon and stars as pilots.

Only the other day at Granton I saw such a poem ; and I committed it to memory in going over it again and again.

OF HERRING AND THEIR WAYS.

Nothing is more fascinating than a chat with an intelligent seaman.   One should go down to Kyleakin when the local fishermen are not absent at the Loch Fyne fishings to hear some plausible and unique reasons for the migration of herring shoals— reasons which to me appear to be very acceptable, and probably just as accurate as the scientific explanations put forward by the Fishery Board. At Kyleakin you will be told that the paucity of shoals is no indication that herrings are scarce in that particular part of the sea, and that conditions of density of atmosphere and intensity of light have an influence on the locality of fish even greater than at first seems credible.

In this connection it is recognised that, when the temperature of the sea is warm and the atmosphere is wet and dull, fish is more likely to be caught at the surface by the ordinary drift-net than when the atmospheric conditions are cold and bright. And, conversely, unrecorded statistical evidence ascertained from Breton fishing crews, whose equipment, by the bye, lends itself to ready adjustment, proves that nets which may be lowered and raised relatively to the floats, in order to suit varying temperature and barometric conditions, produce better results than do the nets where, as in the case of the gear commonly used in the west of Scotland, the depth-line automatically is fixed.

Were the Kyleakin fishermen less conservative in their methods, they would adopt the Breton system. In the same way, line-fishermen are grumbling continually about the scarcity of bait, and will spend days in digging for shell-fish, etc., when they might be at sea using artificial bait of almost any kind, and probably with more remunerative results.

LACK OF CO-OPERATION.

The Hebridean fishermen should co-operate more. It would be greatly to their advantage if, instead of each family possessing a small boat, they put their capital together and purchased a boat of the Loch Fyne type with a reliable outfit—a boat that even in fairly boisterous weather could go to sea in comparative safety. Again, they would be well advised to own a swift motor-boat for the ready

Photo. by R. C. MacLeod of MacLeod.

Broadford Bay and the Red Hills.

transport of fish from the several boats operating
on the fishing-grounds to the early morning fish
markets, such as are held at Mallaig and Kyle.
It is because the Skye fishermen have been slow
to appreciate the importance of rapid transport that
frequently they find themselves in the unenviable
position of being unable to dispose of their catches.
I have even witnessed fishermen from Broadford
rowing several cran of fish all the way over to Kyle
of Lochalsh, a distance of nearly nine miles, in an
endeavour to be in time for the passenger train
travelling south some hours later than the regular fish
train. On comparing the methods still employed
in some localities with those which obtained at the
time that Murdoch MacKenzie (*circa* 1750) prepared the nautical maps to which he appended a
hydrographical account of the tides, rocks, channels,
anchorages, and shoals of the Orcades and the
most northerly of the Outer Hebrides, it seems
obvious that, in some respects at any rate, little
has been done by way of improving either the
methods of catching fish, or of marketing it when
it is caught.

By analogy, the crofters ought to co-operate and
remove the wasteful and extravagant boundaries
that render their strips and patches suitable only
for the use of the cumbersome *cas-chrann*, and too
small to permit of tillage by a plough. Then, in
some areas almost every crofter has a horse, which
nearly all the year round is roaming the hills and
doing no work.

In my humble judgment there is nothing (except
the ever-present personal element) to prevent the
crofters from combining with one another to buy a
plough, reaper, binder, and other useful agricultural

implements, and to work the land of their own respective townships as club farms, and in a manner similar to that in which many of them presently work their sheep stock. It should be noted, however, that the opinions expressed above are entirely personal, and, no doubt, are open to dispute.

ILLEGAL TRAWLING.

And, while we are concerned with the vexed subject of fishing, some pertinent remarks might be made with regard to an evil that during recent years has been having a very adverse effect on the material prosperity of the West Highland fishermen. The super-abundant supplies of fish, that in the reigns of the Jameses attracted to the west of Scotland speculative and klondyking adventurers from all parts, have diminished to a mere tittle in comparison with what they used to be even within living memory. There are many who remember when fishing in the Hebrides and along the shores of North-Western Scotland was so prosperous that the communities, which since have been reduced to a state of want and discontent, were supported entirely and amply by the harvest of the sea, and often had no need to devote more than casual attention to their unremunerative crofts.

To-day, however, conditions are changed.

While not herein entering scientifically into the migratory movements of herring and the numerous accessory causes that render once-productive areas devoid of fish, it may be fitting to add a word or two in connection with an evil that more than any other is responsible for the regrettable decline in fishing, particularly in West Highland waters. I refer to illegal trawling. The wholesale trawling of prohibited areas has been a long-standing grievance in Scotland. And little wonder ! What has it resulted in ? It has destroyed trillions of immature fish : it has ruined the most prolific spawning-grounds : it has damaged irreparably the gear of poor fishermen who have no means of replacing that gear : it has reduced several fishing communities to poverty, having almost obliterated the livelihood of the line-fisherman : it has added, and, in truth, continues to add, its merciless quota to the extinction of one of the hardiest and most law-abiding sections of the country.

And, without meantime going into the Acts dealing with domestic trawling, and the delicate position presently recognised by International Law, it must be obvious to all who are *au fait* with the existing state of affairs that matters are very unsatisfactory.

Illegal trawling should be considered an offence more serious than at present it is deemed ; and the penalty should be made to fit the offence. Most of the harm is done at night-time, although I have witnessed in broad daylight trawling within the statutory limit and within sealochs that are less than six miles in width at their entrances.

There is a strong case for increased vigilance on the part of the Fishery Board cruisers ; but there is an even stronger case for the revision of territorial limits, and for the closure of certain sheets of water to home and to foreign trawlers alike. The present position certainly merits our closest attention from an economic as well as from a political point of view.

A Pigmy Crew.

But I hasten to resume our chat about Captain MacKinnon, and to tell you some of the weird things I heard from him round that glowing hearth in Broadford lately. One evening, while he was waiting near by the shore at Connel Ferry for a companion, he perceived a large vessel out at sea ; and coming towards him was what he took to be the vessel's boat, manned by four bluejackets, and carrying a passenger who was seated on the stern sheets, and appeared to be a naval officer. As the small boat drew nearer, it seemed to diminish in size, till at length it ran aground, whereupon, to his intense astonishment, he found that its occupants were only eighteen inches in stature—he actually demonstrated their height while telling his story by raising his hand the equivalent distance from the floor. The boat, be it observed, was correspondingly small.

Although not in any way afraid, Captain Mac-Kinnon turned away for a second to look for his belated companion ; but in the interval the small boat and the pigmy crew and the vessel, from which they had come, had vanished. He affirms that to his knowledge this strange apparition had no sequel.

An Extraordinary Premonition at Sea.

While on duty at the steering-wheel in his capacity as mate on a vessel that during the recent war sailed between Glasgow and various Irish ports, he noticed that on the bridge-deck there lay a tiny piece of paper which repeatedly rose up to the level of the wheel, and then fluttered again to its original position. To begin with, he thought that its conduct was being caused by a slight eddy of wind ;

but a little later on it rose to the height of the mast-head, and returned to the deck the size of a sheet of notepaper.   Having picked it up and found it to be in actuality a sheet of notepaper, he promptly folded it, and put it into one of his pockets.   When he was being relieved by the next watch (who, incidentally, was the quartermaster), he told him of the strange things that had been happening during his vigil ;   but they agreed to keep the matter to themselves and await results.

Now, while the quartermaster was at the wheel—and by this time the ship was well out to sea—an unusually large gull continued to circle around his head, uttering eerie cries :   strangely enough, on the morrow every member of the crew independently insisted that during the previous night's voyage he had been prevented from sleeping by the clanking of chains in the fo'c'sle.   By this time Captain MacKinnon felt certain that something untoward was to befall the vessel ;   and so he resolved to leave her at the first port of call, and join another ship.   This he did ;   and it is an absolute fact that, two days afterwards, the former vessel was lost at sea with all hands, presumably owing to enemy action.

Captain MacKinnon told us that on two occasions he had a presentiment in dreams that he should not rejoin the ship on which he had engaged to sail :   on both occasions he obeyed the warning by having stayed ashore ;   and both vessels foundered with most of their crews.

THREE MYSTERIOUS BLACK CATS.

There was a time when Captain MacKinnon and his father each owned a schooner.   When not at

sea, they were in the habit of anchoring their boats
in a sheltered bay about five miles away from their
home in Lismore. One midnight, while they were
ashore, there arose a great storm ; and our seannachie, who was fidgety about the safety of the
schooners, got out of bed and set off with his dog
for the bay, having taken with him a substantial
cudgel with which to feel his way in the dark.

When he had reached about two miles from his
home, suddenly he became conscious that something was following him ; and, on turning round,
he discovered to his amazement that it was his
own shadow. The point to be noted here is that
the night was particularly black, and that there
was no light anywhere to throw such a shadow.
Naturally, he felt uneasy ; but it was not until the
same shadow appeared to be walking in front of
him that the fear was actually on him.

At last the situation got on his nerves ; and
in his exasperation he raised his stick and struck
at the shadow. Thereupon he heard a sound that
led him to suppose that he had struck a tall column
of water, a supposition strengthened by the fact
that several drops of water spluttered in his face.

Savagely all this time had his dog been growling ;
but now the creature commenced to bark excitedly.

MacKinnon pursued his journey ; and, when
nearing the bay where the schooners were moored,
he noticed on the roadway what in the darkness he
took to be three large stones. He could not
imagine for what purpose they had been placed
there. Having drawn nearer, he found that in
reality they were not stones at all, but were three
black cats sitting on the road, and facing the direction in which he was proceeding. Firmly he

clutched his stick, and passed between the first two cats, which, as it were, formed the base of an equilateral triangle of cats. Without further hesitation he passed the third cat at the apex of the triangle ; but nothing happened, for the cats remained motionless. Now he quickened his pace ; and, on arriving at a point on the shore close to where the schooners lay, he quickly realised that his dog was absent. It was fully an hour later that the dog, dripping with water and peaty mud, and apparently very much terrified, turned up on the beach.

That night Captain MacKinnon was too alarmed to return to his home. Having kindled a fire in the cabin of his schooner, he remained there until after daybreak.

Our Ceilidh Ends.

No doubt, those of you who are endowed with the " second-sight " and who possibly have had uncanny experiences of this nature, will find explanations for some of the foregoing tales. But be it remembered by those who are blessed in having no such faculty (for in some ways these are blessed !), that these stories are not mere yarns. Need I say more ?

That evening's recital has left on my mind an indelible impression : it is curious how some incidents, though seemingly paltry and of trifling significance at the moment, tend to recur again and again to the mind in their full and complete setting.

*   *   *   *   *   *

Happy reflection creates a scene, and gives it that atmosphere, that environment, that pleasing comprehensiveness, which frequently we fail to appreciate during the original enactment of the scene. Looking back, it so often occurs to us how little we gleaned from, or gave to, what was then the present, for many of us find it difficult to live each day as it comes along. Disappointments and disillusionments and unrealised dreams at one end of the arc described by life's pendulum are counter-balanced at the other by the designing of gigantic and far-off projects, and the building of many flimsy *châteaux en Espagne* ; and, since we are human and not infrequently err, the resultant as a rule is a desire, a yearning, an anxiety to be in the *other* place, and to be doing everything but the thing that is to hand. Admittedly, such tendencies have their drawbacks ; but surely they have their virtues too.

And thus, like old wine that mellows in the passing of years, the tenderest of our memories become sweeter and more sacred as they recede into the dim cloisters of time, where they take their meet place somewhere during the complexity of our sojourn here on earth.

And so the memories of that wintry garden with its leafless rowan tree, of that bright hearth with its note of welcome and of cheer, of that protracted tea-party in the gloaming, of the soft, subdued voice of our story-teller and the gist of his tales, of his strong profile, that at one moment was silhouetted against the glow of the fire and at another was chiselled out on the wall of our shadowy room, are bottled up within me, and are mellowing as the wine of an old and precious remembrance such as is wont to fill our hearts at vesper-time.

Photo. by A. D. Young.

Over the Sea to Skye—at Isle Oronsay.

328

XXXVI

RUSSET SLEAT

GOOD-NIGHT TO SKYE

" 'Twas then that warlike signals wake
Dunscaith's dark towers and Eishort's lake."

It is at bramble-time that one should visit " Russet Sleat of the beautiful women," for I cannot conceive of a surfeit of delight more satisfying, more delectable, more engaging than a day's tramp, let us say, from Kinloch or Isle Oronsay to Land's End at the rugged Aird of Sleat, when the leaves are rusting and the rowans are red. Talking of brambles, one seldom sees larger and more luscious berries than are to be plucked along the sides of the way that, winding behind Ostaig, leads past a moorland sheepfold at the other end of Glen Meadhonach, and terminates on the western seaboard of Sleat at Dalavil.

To Sleat has been given the appropriate name of the garden of Skye ; and many historical accounts of that Island testify to its productiveness and to the relative succulence of its pastures. Chiefly in virtue of its agricultural value, there was a tendency for Sleat to be retained and governed to a large extent by a number of prosperous tacksmen who personally supervised the cultivation of their own particular farms, and who themselves may have been proprietors in a small way. By no means the least interesting of such accounts of Sleat is the following : " Slait is occupiet for the maist pairt be gentlemen, thairfor it payis but the auld deuteis, that is, of victuall, buttir, cheis, wyne, aill, and aquavite, samekle as thair maister may be able to spend being ane nicht (albeit he were 600 men in companie) on ilk merkland. There is twa strenthie castells in Slait, the ane callit Castell Chammes, the uther Dunskeith. Trouternes will raise 500 men, and Slait 700 men."

A NIGHT'S PORTION.

The statement just quoted contains an allusion to the custom anciently recognised among Celtic communities, whereby a chief or a superior, from whom lands were held on the fulfilment of certain specified conditions, was entitled to so many nights' hospitality. In the Highlands and Islands this exaction was known as the *cuid-oidhche* (corrupted to cuidichie and cuddiche). It strictly referred to a night's entertainment or a night's lodgings. In degree and in duration the " cuddiche " varied in accordance with the economic prosperity of those upon whose tenure of land this and other servitudes, such as stenting, were placed. From the *Chamberlain Rolls* we learn that in the reign of Alexander the Third this burden on land held in thanage prevailed in Forfar and Glamis under the name of *waytinga*. At that time the *waytinga* of Fettercairn amounted to one night in the year. The *waytingas* of Kinross were computed at four nights. In ancient Welsh law the custom by which the head of a tribe received from his tenants, when passing through his territory, a night's feasting was known as the *dovraeth* ; while the equivalent in Ireland was the *coinmhedha* or coigny (cf. *coneveth*). The word, *conyow* (coigny), appears in a contract between the Bishop of the Isles and Lauchlan MacLean of Duart in 1580, wherein the latter binds himself not to oppress, trouble, or molest the lands of Iona by insisting on his title to this old-time exaction.

Since Sleat usually enjoyed an appreciable degree of rural prosperity, we may be assured that its lairds were not slow to avail themselves of such extravagances as in the southern peninsula of Skye were in keeping with the statutory night's portion.

At Isle Oronsay.

Some little distance south of Kinloch and the birchen steeps of Beinn na Seamraig the road leading to within a couple of miles to our Land's End, at the Point of Sleat, travels through Duisdalemore, keeping close to the seashore until the picturesque, land-locked harbour of Isle Oronsay is reached. Isle Oronsay, with its pretty little Mission Church dedicated to Saint Columba, is a poem. On the tiny Isle of the Fox (Eilean Sionnach), which is situated very close to, and at the south-eastern corner of, Isle Oronsay, is an imposing lighthouse whose flash under favourable conditions can be seen as far distant as Mallaig. As does the secluded waterway of Loch an Dail, the bay of Oronsay at all times affords a safe retreat to coasting vessels and fishing-boats that are haven-seeking from the squalls which so frequently ruffle the Sound of Sleat. Loch an Dail, in fact, signifies the loch of waiting for storm-stayed ships.

Beyond Isle Oronsay the road, passing through

Duisdalebeg, ascends to Loch nan Dubhrachan (Uirichean) of water-horse notoriety, and is deprived of its maritime companion until it again descends to the shore at Knock Bay, where stands the castle of An Cnoc or Knock.

THROUGH GLEN MEODAL TO ORD.

The township of Duisdale, as elsewhere I have mentioned, was bestowed on a family of the name of MacKinnon by the MacDonalds of Sleat, to whom the former acted as standard-bearers. Just at Loch nan Dubhrachan a road of inferior classification strikes westwards into Glen Meodal and, crossing the head-waters of the Ord, follows the course of that pearly river to within a few yards of Loch Eishort.

Ord, indeed, is a bonnie place. The view around it is superb. Little wonder that in his *Summer in Skye* Smith was moved to sing of Blaven, that prince among mountains, as seen from his windows overlooking Loch Eishort, Loch Slapin, and Strath-aird. In zig-zag fashion this road of doubtful category threads southwards from Ord and, never losing sight of Loch Eishort, meanders through Tokavaig and hazelled Tarskavaig to Achnacloich. There it turns inland, skirts Loch Dughaill, the haunt of the peregrine falcon, and conveys one back to the eastern seaboard of Sleat at Ostaig. Near Tokavaig are the eloquent ruins of Dunscaith Castle of which I will speak with you in a moment ; while a little to the north is Inver Aulavaig, in the vicinity of which have been unearthed some remarkable stone barrows or graves supposed to be connected with the early occupation of Dunscaith.

MARY OF THE CASTLE.

In order to complete the survey of our journey to the Aird of Sleat, we must return to the Sound and retrace our steps to the ruins of Knock. This is a castle of many names and many legends. Often it is referred to as Castle Camus. Long, long ago this Castle of the Bay was known as Caisteal I Chamuis. In the seventeenth century it received the name of Knock; while in more recent times it has been styled Caisteal Uaine— Green Castle—possibly in consequence of the ivy that now smothers part of it.

The structure itself is perched on a rock that to-day is comparatively accessible from all sides at low tide. In architecture it is partly modern (1792) and partly ancient. It was long a stronghold of the MacDonalds of Sleat. Tradition has it that during the reign of James IV. it was besieged by the MacLeods, and that ultimately the siege was raised through the daring efforts of one, Mary of the Castle, who was numbered among its defenders. I seem to have read somewhere that in the early seventeenth century Donald Gorm retained Sleat on the understanding that at all times he was prepared to receive at Knock either the king himself, or his representatives. With Castle Camus are linked a score of eldritch superstitions.

THROUGH KILMORE AND OSTAIG TO ARMADALE.

At Kilmore, the Great Church (a' Chill Mhor), is the site of the place of worship that is said to have been erected by a divine named Crotach Mac Gille Gorm, who came to Skye from Lovat at the beginning of the thirteenth century. Historians tell us that, like the Church at Trumpan, it was fired, not by the MacDonalds but by the MacLeods, in an endeavour to smoke out a band of MacIntyres who at the time occupied this bit of Sleat and had taken refuge within it. The Lochaber Bard, Iain Lom, informs us that the more recent church was built in Sleat-of-the-Waves by Sir Donald MacDonald of Sleat, who died in 1695. It was here that Dr. Johnson read the inscription to Sir James MacDonald, the Marcellus of the Isles, that he regretted had not been written in Latin, since, he declared, that language was more universally understood by scholars.

The hagiology of the district round Kilmore is very extensive ; but I fear that requirements of space will not permit of our entering into it here.

Within a mile or so of the Mill Bridge at Ostaig and encircled by rooky trees is the modern castle of Armadale, the most recent seat of the once-great MacDonalds. It was built about 1815, and is therefore too new to have suffered sieges or to have witnessed such regal scenes as took place in the earlier strongholds of the Lords of the Isles. Perhaps the chief object of interest in Armadale Castle is the stained-glass window above the staircase representing the mighty Somerled, *Rex Insularum*. The Castle is full of relics, and can boast some excellent pictures.

Half as Old as Time.

I have deemed it fitting that our sojourn in this wonderful Isle should terminate at Ardvasar, the tiny seaport of Sleat that is distant from Armadale about a mile ; but, before bearing you there, I feel that we ought to sally over to Loch Eishort again and tarry at old Dunscaith, if only for a moment or two. Dunscaith one associates with everything Ossianic—it was here that Cuchullin had his headquarters : hither he sent the fair-bosomed Bragéla that she might be in safe custody during his campaignings in Erin : it was here that the Fingalian warriors gathered together to be instructed in the use of arms. Nearby one may still see the stone (*Clach Luath*) to which Cuchullin chained Luath, his favourite hound, after the chase. And even to this day, when the storm is swelling among the Coolian and the winds are whistling in its glens, the old people of Skye will tell you that Cuchullin is ahunting with Luath.

Dunscaith draws one through the hazy morning-light of history into the dim mists of antiquity. Personally, I find satisfaction in accepting that as a fortress its earliest foundations at least are half as old as Time. And why dispute its age in any case ? The whole poetry of a place so old is lost when men attempt to assign a date to its origin, and argue about it in quasi-scientific terms.

GOOD-NIGHT TO SKYE !

Now let us return to Ardvasar where at nightfall one may feel the everlastingness of the hills and the boundless strength of the sea. Here, on the beach and just below high-water mark, you will find an overturned boat with a rusty keel and a rusty anchor, and groups of mews and sea-swallows settling in rows for the night by the water's edge, and maybe the fragments of a tide-borne crate or two left among the dried dulse and clusters of sea-pinks.

The tide is at the flowing ; and across the Sound of Sleat the flickering lights of Mallaig wax in effulgence with the waning of the day. The gleaming gold of Morar's sands has gone with the deep dipping of the sun ; and on every side the mountains raise their darkened heads to a windless heaven.

Twilight it is ; and the day is done. And into the rest-seeking soul steal the peace that is begotten of eventide and a sense of the omnipresence and omnipotence of the Supreme Artist who designed this magic scene, and whose wondrous works we can never fathom : into the open heart creeps the essence of a divine mystery, leaving an aching void the world can never fill.

It is memory-time—and our dearest memories are as keepsakes that long have lain in the sweet lavender of devotion and of love, and are unfolded only at the silent meditation of eventide. Like the mollient influence of an ineffable sacrifice, like the echo of a broken melody, like the sweet, mellowing remembrance of a first and last love, like the recollection of something vague and almost forgotten, their fragrance lingers with us when the petals have fallen and the flower of love is withered and gone.

Nightfall it is ; and the seabirds call by the shore at Ardvasar. And there remains but a silvern afterglow among the westward hills—and by the margin of the sea a shadowed bird.

And it's " Good-night ! " to Skye.

Photo. by R. C. MacLeod of MacLeod.

Twilight at Knock Castle (Castle Camus), in the Sound of Sleat.

Y

GLOSSARY

Airidh, a shieling.

Airt, direction, way.

Alltan, a little brook.

Anait, a chapel or cell; the site of such.

Anent, concerning, about, with reference to.

Auld, old.

Auld Reekie, Edinburgh.

Banshee, a faery.

Bicker, to move quickly and noisily.

Bided, awaited, abided. *Bided his time*, waited his opportunity.

Bieldless, shelterless, unshaded, unprotected.

Biggit, built.

Birlinn, the barge or galley of a Hebridean chieftain.

Bodach, an old man. *Bodachan*, a little old man.

Bordar, a villein retaining his hut at his superior's pleasure.

Bothy, a shack or hut.

Brag, boast, exaggeration.

Bratach, a flag or banner.

Briar, the wild rose.

Brieve, a judge or law-giver; a brehon.

Brochan, water-gruel, thin porridge.

Bruikis, possesses, owns, enjoys.

Bucht, a pen in which sheep are impounded; a fank.

Bynamed, nicknamed.

Caileag, a girl, a lassie.

Cailleach, an old woman.

Cairidh, an enclosure frequently consisting of a low wall of stones placed in shallow water at the head of a bay or inlet, in which fish were left when the tide receded.

Caller, fresh, bracing.

Canach, mountain-down, cotton-grass.

Canty, cheerful, lively, pleasant.

Caoran, a little peat, a *peatag*.

Y

Cas-Chrann (*cas-chrom*), a foot-plough.

Cateran, a robber, freebooter (*vide* ceatharnach).

Ceatharnach, one capable of bearing arms; a kern or soldier. Since a freebooter, when outlawed, frequently concealed himself in the woods, he became known as a *ceatharnach-coille*, or " cateran."

Ceilidh, a social gathering, usually round the peat-fire, for the telling of tales and the singing of songs.

Ceol-mara, sea-music.

Ceol-mor, literally " big music."

Chuckie-stanes, small pebbles.

Clachan, a village or hamlet.

Clach-neart, a putting-stone.

Clarsach, a harp.

Clarsar, a harper.

Claymore, a big sword formerly used by Highlanders; the old Celtic one-handed, two-edged longsword; now applied inaccurately to the basket-hilted sword of the officers of Highland regiments.

Cliaranaich, bards and poets, minstrels, men of renown.

Clype, to gossip, to tell tales.

Coomb, a hollow in the mountain-side.

Coorie, to crouch timidly, cower.

Corrie, a cirque or semi-circular hollow in mountains.

Coulterneb, the puffin.

Cratur, creature.

Creach, *creagh*, booty, plunder, foray, spreagh.

Cromag, a shepherd's crook.

Cronan, a croon, lullaby.

Cronie, a good old friend.

Cruisie, a small crucible-like lamp burning oil.

Cuddiche, *Cuid-oidhche*, a night's portion, which was a burden on land. A sixteenth-century account of the Isle of Lewis defines it as " feisting thair maister quhen he pleases to cum in the cuntrie, ilk ane thair nicht or twa nichtis about, according to thair land and labouring."

Cuddy, young coal-fish, saith.

Curach, a coracle, canoe.

Davoch, an ancient measure of land, averaging 416 acres.

Dearg, red.

Deisul, motion according to the apparent course of the sun; a sun-wise turn; opp. to *Withershins*.

Delve, dig.

Dene, a dell.

Divot, a thin, flat sod.

Dool, grief, sorrow.

Dour, sulky, sullen, obstinate.

Dovering, slumbering lightly.

Dreich, dreary, dull, monotonous.

Drochaid, a bridge.

Drouthy, droughty, thirsty, dry.

Dun, a fort or castle, a stronghold.

Dyke, a wall of stone or turf.

Each-Uisge, a water-horse. The Highland water-horse is akin to Vikhor, the Whirlwind of Russian folklore.

Eirde, earth.

Eldritch, weird, eerie, gruesome.

Eothen (ἑως), eastern, from the dawn.

Eric, the blood-fine which the old Brehon Laws required a murderer to pay to the relatives of his victim. *Vide* Wergild.

Erst, in the first place, formerly.

Fank, an enclosure for cattle and sheep; a sheep-cote.

Feadan, a chanter.

Forby, besides, in addition.

Fornent, opposite to; in front of.

Furth, forth, distant, removed.

Gist, the main point or theme.

Glaisrig, a gorgon, an ugly monster.

Gowk, a fool or blockhead.

Grieve, the foreman on a farm.

Gusted, tasted.

Haft, a handle.

Heich, high, tall.

Hirsel, the feeding-place of a flock of sheep; sometimes the flock itself.

Hurling, wheeling, trundling.

Ilk, the same name, place, etc. "Of that Ilk," said of a person who has the same name as his property or title.

Ilka, each, every.

Knowe, a knoll or hillock.
Kyles, narrows, straits.

Lair, a resting-place ; a family grave.
Lang syne, long since ; long ago.
Lere, learn.
Linn, a pool.
Lochan, a little loch, a pond.
Lochlannaich, *Lochlanners*, terms applied generally to the North-men ; Scandinavians.
Luath, swift, fleet.
Luinneag, a lyric, sonnet.

Machar, a sandy tract near the sea.
Maisloch, mixed peas and oats ; a coarse kind of bread.
Merk, a silver coin, worth 13½d. stg. ; a measure of land.
Mools, a grave or the earth of a grave ; dust.
Mutch, a woman's cap.

Odhar, sallow, dun.
Outwith, without or beyond the scope or bounds.

Partan, the common crab.
Pickle, a small quantity ; a few ; same as puckle.
Piobar, *Piobaire*, a piper.
Policies, the private grounds attached to a mansion or country-house.
Pother, bustle, confusion, turmoil.
Pottering, fiddling about ; loitering.
Press, a cupboard with shelves.
Put to the Horn, in Scots Law to denounce as a rebel ; to outlaw a person for failing to appear at the court to which he had been summoned. This was done when a messenger-at-arms proceeded to the Mercat Cross at Edinburgh, and, amongst other formalities, gave three blasts with a horn, proclaiming the person cited to be a rebel because of his contempt for the king's authority.

Reeky, smoky.
Riever, a robber or pirate.
Roving, thieving, plundering, rieving.

Sassenach, a term applied by Highlanders to Lowlanders; Englishmen.

Scaith, harm, hurt, injury, scathe.

Scart, Scarf, cormorant.

Seannachie, a story-teller, a historian.

Sgeir, a rock surrounded by the sea.

Sgeulachd, story-telling, traditionary lore.

Sgian-dubh, a small, black knife formerly carried in the hose.

Sheltie, a pony.

Shilpit, pale, pinched, sickly.

Sib, a kinsman or relation.

Skailing, scattering, dispersing.

Skalk, a morning drink.

Skeely, skilful, dexterous.

Skerry, a rocky islet.

Skirl, a shrill sound.

Snecked, fastened by the latch.

Sorn, to exercise the ancient right by which a chief was entitled to obtrude himself on others as their uninvited guest.

Spaewife, a female fortune-teller.

Spree, drunken jollification.

Spulzing, spoiling, plundering.

Stenting, the alloting of a limited amount of work or the prescribing of a fixed task; taxing; assessing.

Stook, a full shock of sheaves as erected in a harvest-field.

Stroup, the spout of a teapot or kettle.

Syne, since, ago.

Tacksman, a leaseholder or tenant farmer.

Taibhsear, a visionary, one gifted with the " second-sight."

Talla, a hall (*Ossian*).

Thegn, a nobleman who, according to ancient Saxon Law, was " worthy of his boc-right."

Thoft, a rower's seat in a boat.

Threep, to insist or assert pertinaciously.

Threttein, thirteen.

Tine, to forfeit; to lose.

Tirling at the Pin, making a rattling with the latch as a polite warning prior to entering.

Tonnag, a tartan shawl.

Tumbler, a large drinking-glass, so called because formerly, having had a pointed base, it could not be set down without its tumbling.

Uamh, a cave.
Uinneag, a window.

Vylt, a vault, arch.

Weaned, accustomed to nourishment other than the mother's
milk; ablactated.
Wergild, the payment made in Anglo-Saxon times by the kindred
of a murderer to the relatives of the person whom he murdered;
"blood-money." There was a fixed scale, ranging from more
than 1200 shillings (about £24) in the case of an archbishop
or a freeman to 200 shillings for a villein. A serf's wergild
was about 40 pence.
Whaup, the curlew.
Withal, moreover, likewise.

Yonter, more distant, further.

GENERAL INDEX

Photo by A. D. Young.   "Good-night" to Skye—at Ardvasar, on the Sound of Sleat

Printed in Great Britain by
W. & R. CHAMBERS LTD., Edinburgh.

BEHOLD THE HEBRIDES!

OR, WAYFARING IN THE WESTERN ISLES

AN APPEALING AND HEART-STIRRING SERIES
OF HEBRIDEAN SKETCHES

By ALASDAIR ALPIN MACGREGOR

WITH FOREWORD BY LORD ALNESS

(THE RIGHT HONOURABLE ROBERT MUNRO, LL.D.)

"Into his book Alasdair Alpin MacGregor has put all his love for the land of his fathers, and makes its bravely borne hardships, its great natural beauties into a tale well worth the telling and reading."—*Queen.*

"The book is redolent of the tang of the sea, or the crisp champagne air from the fens."—*Sheffield Daily Telegraph.*

"Mr. MacGregor has in fact written a chapter of social history, the value of which will increase as the years go by."—*Birmingham Post.*

"Mr. MacGregor will write much more and still better. Already his young life has come close to the fragrant earth, to the hearts, to the passions and dreams of men."—*Rand Mail.*

"To the exile in particular this little volume cannot fail to recall early and sacred memories of the homeland, and will make them live again."
Belfast News Letter.

"To any one who loves the Hebrides this little volume is a treasure-trove for its excellent illustrations."—*Glasgow Herald.*

"No part of the British Isles has a richer store of picturesque legend ; nowhere is it less difficult for an imaginative mind attuned to the surroundings to transfer itself from the prosaic present to a past peopled with the heroes, bards and sages of old."—*Northern Whig.*

W. & R. CHAMBERS, Ltd., 38 Soho Sq., London, W.1; and Edinburgh.

TRADITIONS OF EDINBURGH
By ROBERT CHAMBERS, LL.D. 21s. net.

ILLUSTRATED BY J. RIDDEL, A.R.S.A.

WITH 30 CHARACTERISTIC DRAWINGS IN COLOUR AND 60 CHARMING PEN-AND-INK SKETCHES

THE SPEAKING HOUSE

"When I forget thee, Auld Reekie, may my right hand forget its cunning."
—*R. L. Stevenson.*

"A beautiful edition of a book which can never grow old."—*Evening Standard.*

W. & R. CHAMBERS, Ltd., 38 Soho Sq., London, W.1; and Edinburgh

TRADITIONS OF EDINBURGH
By ROBERT CHAMBERS, LL.D.
POPULAR EDITION, 5s. net.
WITH PEN-AND-INK SKETCHES BY J. RIDDEL, A.R.S.A.

MYLNE'S COURT

W. & R. CHAMBERS, Ltd., 38 Soho Sq., London, W.1; and Edinburgh.

THE STANDARD EDITION OF BURNS

Dr ROBERT CHAMBERS'S
Life and Works of
ROBERT BURNS

REVISED AND PARTIALLY REWRITTEN BY

WILLIAM WALLACE, M.A., LL.D.

In Four Volumes, Crown 8vo, cloth, £2

Illustrated from Original Drawings by

C. MARTIN HARDIE, R.S.A.   R. B. NISBET, R.S.A.
W. D. MACKAY, R.S.A.   G. O. REID, R.S.A.
and GEORGE PIRIE, A.R.S.A.

In this Edition Dr Wallace has spared no trouble to secure and present the true reading of all the poems; to elucidate difficulties by notes and explanations; to give a full marginal glossary of Scots words likely to puzzle the reader; to make the Edition more complete, by the addition of poems, versicles, and songs not included by Dr Chambers; and to incorporate all new biographical and historical facts.

The poems, the biography, and the letters are so combined and arranged as to show their relation to one another, to present a view of contemporary social life in Scotland, and to illustrate the circumstances in which Burns lived his life and wrote his immortal poems.

Respecting such an arrangement, it is interesting to read that Lord Rosebery, in the course of the Address which he delivered at St Andrew's Hall, Glasgow, on the occasion of the Centenary Celebrations, and in which he described Dr Wallace as that "high and excellent authority," expressed himself in the following terms :—

"I must confess myself, then, one of those who think that the life of Burns doubles the interest of his poems. . . . *The life of Burns I love to read with his poems.* . . . It is a life of worth, and truth, and tenderness."

Sir J. M. BARRIE writes—"I have read your estimate of Burns's character and genius with uncommon pleasure. As for the genius, that he is the great poetic glory of Scotland, none, I suppose, would now seek to deny; but as for his character, you seem to me to offer the truest conception of it I have ever read. He was a great soul who had to fight a grim fight with himself all through, and to half win the battle, as you show so elaborately he did, was a great achievement. I remember Stevenson writing to me about some other writer: 'The author may not be like his books—he *is* his books.' And Burns *is* his poems."

W. & R. CHAMBERS, Ltd., 38 Soho Sq., London, W.1; and Edinburgh

741 pages, price 7/6 net

A SCOTS DIALECT DICTIONARY

COMPRISING THE WORDS IN USE FROM
THE LATTER PART OF THE SEVENTEENTH
CENTURY TO THE PRESENT DAY

Compiled by ALEXANDER WARRACK, M.A.

Minister Emeritus of the United Free Church of Scotland at Leswalt

WITH AN INTRODUCTION AND A DIALECT MAP BY

WILLIAM GRANT, M.A.

Lecturer in Phonetics to the Aberdeen Provincial Committee for the Training
of Teachers, and Convener of the Scottish Branch of the English Association

---

All Readers of R. L. Stevenson, J. M. Barrie, J. Laing Waugh,
O. Douglas, Captain Campbell, and other Scottish Writers,
should have this volume at their elbow.

W. & R. CHAMBERS, LIMITED

38 SOHO SQUARE, LONDON, W.1; AND EDINBURGH

HISTORY OF THE REBELLION OF 1745-6

3/6 net] [3/6 net

By ROBERT CHAMBERS, LL.D.

HISTORY THAT IS AS FASCINATING AS FICTION

Extract from the Author's Preface:

"Knowing how these men did all in honour, I deem it but just that their adventures should be detailed with impartiality, and their unavoidable misfortunes . . ."

W. & R. CHAMBERS, LTD., 38 Soho Sq., London, W.1; and Edinburgh